THE **H.I.P.** WAY
TO BUY AND SELL
YOUR HOUSE

STOP PRESS!

Amendments

Since publication of this book, and following an emergency announcement in the House of Commons on 22 May 2007 by Ruth Kelly, the Secretary for Communities and Local Government, the following amendments have been made to the HIP legislation:

◆ Introduction of the HIP legislation has been delayed from 1 June 2007 until 1 August 2007. This means that home owners may place their property on the market before 1 August 2007 without a valid HIP. Properties that are placed on the market prior to 1 August 2007 will not need to supply a HIP provided the property is sold by 31 December 2007.

◆ The announcement confirmed suspicions that there were insufficient numbers of accredited Energy Assessors to complete the Energy Performance Certificates that will be needed once the HIP legislation comes in. The implementation of the HIP will therefore be phased in to allow sufficient numbers of Energy Assessors to qualify. Initially, only home owners of homes with four or more bedrooms will be required to have a HIP in place when they put the property on the market. Owners of smaller properties need not have a HIP in place before marketing their property for the time being. The government will phase in HIPs for smaller properties as more qualified Energy Assessors become available.

◆ Until the end of 2007 all home owners will be allowed to market their property without a HIP provided they can prove that they have ordered one.

◆ As a temporary measure homes may be marketed with an Energy Performance Certificate (EPC) that is up to 12 months old at the First Point of Marketing. The previous requirement was for the EPC to be no more than three months old at the First Point of Marketing.

The government have announced that a further review of the HIP legislation, and how it is working in practice, will be made at the end of 2007.

Sharon Buthlay

Further amendments will be kept up to date at the following web page: http://www.howtobooks.co.uk/hip/update.htm

THE **H.I.P.** WAY TO BUY AND SELL YOUR HOUSE

How to use the *Home Information Pack* to improve your move...

S H A R O N   B U T H L A Y

howtobooks

Published by How To Books Ltd,
Spring Hill House, Spring Hill Road,
Begbroke, Oxford OX5 1RX, United Kingdom
Tel: (01865) 375794. Fax: (01865) 379162.
info@howtobooks.co.uk
www.howtobooks.co.uk

ISBN: 978-1-84528-152-6

British Library Cataloguing in Publication Data
A catalogue record for this book is available from the British Library

Cover design by Baseline Arts Ltd, Oxford
Produced for How To Books by Deer Park Productions, Tavistock, Devon
Typeset by PDQ Typesetting, Newcastle-under-Lyme, Staffs.
Printed and bound by Bell & Bain Ltd, Glasgow

NOTE: The material contained in this book is set out in good faith for general guidance and no liability
can be accepted for loss or expense incurred as a result of relying in particular circumstances on
statements made in this book. The laws and regulations are complex and liable to change, and readers
should check the current position with the relevant authorities before making personal arrangements.

Contents

Introduction

From 1 June 2007 the new Home Information Pack (HIP) legislation will come into force. This book sets out to explain in plain English how the new Home Information Pack Regulations 2007 (the Regulations) will affect homeowners, buyers, property professionals and lenders.

In Chapter 1 we look in detail at the HIP, its contents, how much it will cost and how long it will take to prepare. The duty of the seller, and their estate agent, to provide the HIP is explained, as are the conditions that may be imposed upon the buyer. Some types of property will be exempt from the Regulations and a comprehensive guide to those exemptions is included here.

It was originally intended that the Home Condition Report, a type of mid-range survey, would be a compulsory inclusion in the HIP. This requirement was dropped in July 2006 and currently the inclusion of the Home Condition Report is voluntary. The Energy Performance Certificate Interim Energy Assessment or Predicted Energy Assessment (whichever applies) is a compulsory HIP requirement and is an added expense in the home selling process. Chapter 2 explains what these two reports entail. The reader is guided through each type of inspection, and a helpful pre-inspection check list is included.

One of the aims of the HIP is to improve the quality of the housing stock by encouraging property owners to put their homes into good repair before marketing. The Home Condition Report will expose any defects in the condition of a property and this information will be passed on to potential buyers free of charge. Buyers will often overestimate the cost of repairs, in order to beat the sale price down, and it makes sense for sellers to be forearmed with reliable estimates that potential buyers will accept. Chapter 5 explains how to obtain competitive estimates and find reliable tradesmen to carry out any necessary work. By doing some simple ground work you can avoid the pitfalls that so many homeowners encounter when having work done to a property.

The HIP will be sold by many different agencies within the property industry. Lenders, estate agents, conveyancers, surveyors and search companies are setting up their own HIP companies. Competition to supply the HIP will be fierce and it is vital that sellers choose to buy their HIP from a reliable source. Chapter 5 guides the seller through the pros and cons of the various HIP offerings and HIP suppliers.

I make no apology for dedicating the remaining chapters of this book to the intricacies of successfully buying and selling a house. Yes, I know it has been done before, but it hasn't been done by someone who has worked as a property lawyer for over twenty years. My long background and experience in property law, estate agency and as a director of a legal marketing company has given me a unique insight into every aspect of property from choosing the right estate agent, the secrets of a successful sale, how to get a really good conveyancer on your side, understanding the legal process, how to find the best property your money can buy and then how to get a superb mortgage deal on it. All of this and more is shared with you, including my Move Master Plan, and a useful chapter on troubleshooting just in case you do hit problems.

If you are thinking of selling a property in 2007 my advice is to do it before 1 June 2007. It is likely that the property industry will initially struggle to comply with the HIP legislation, particularly as it comes into force during the peak conveyancing period. Major changes will be required across every profession which will include the introduction of new technology and systems and the training of staff.

Every summer the legal profession creaks and groans with the increased workload as buyers and sellers scrabble frantically to complete their transactions during the summer holiday period. The sheer volume of new surveys, searches and documents that will be needed to prepare a HIP for every new property coming onto the market, could overwhelm the various agencies responsible for providing them. Some property professionals are predicting a general 'meltdown' of the conveyancing systems. There is a good time to move and a bad time to move, as explained in the Move Master Plan, and summer, particularly the summer of 2007, is not a good time to move.

It is vital that homeowners, buyers and property professionals are aware of their new legal requirements. Failure to comply with the rules could result in legal action and on-the-spot fines. Estate agents who flout the law are subject not only to fines but may lose their licence to trade.

'The HIP way to Buy and Sell your House' is crammed full of easy to understand, common sense advice that will enable buyers, sellers and property professionals to understand the new legal system and how to use it to their best advantage. My goal when writing this book was not just to explain the new HIP Regulations, but to help my readers to feel confident in all areas of buying and selling property.

By reading through the book, using the check lists and HIP Tips, I hope that you will be delighted with the way you are able to keep ahead of the game, to take control of your property transaction and to achieve the outcome you desire.

Finally, I have referred throughout the book to the HIP changes taking place in the United Kingdom. At present the new legislation relating to the HIP affects only England and Wales. Scotland is considering a form of the HIP but this is not dealt with in this book.

Wishing you the very best of luck with your property transaction in the new HIP era.

Sharon Buthlay

(1)

The Home Information Pack Explained

AN OVERVIEW OF THE HOME INFORMATION PACK

How the Home Information Pack (HIP) became law

The Home Information Pack (HIP), formerly known as the Sellers' Pack, was first introduced by the Labour Party in its Manifesto in 1997. The HIP Legislation is contained in Part 5 of the Housing Act 2004 and the Home Information Pack Regulations 2007.

As from 1 June 2007 the HIP is a legal requirement throughout England and Wales. From that date the responsible person, i.e. the seller or a person acting as their estate agent, must by law have a HIP in their possession or control before marketing a residential property and must provide a copy, on request, to potential buyers.

HIP TIP

From 1 June 2007 all sellers of residential property in England and Wales, unless exempt, *must* by law provide a HIP to potential buyers on request. When a seller instructs an estate agent to sell the property the legal duty to provide the HIP passes to the estate agent.

PREPARING THE PROPERTY INDUSTRY AND THE PUBLIC FOR THE INTRODUCTION OF THE HIP

How the dry run will operate

To ensure a smooth transition to the new HIP regime on 1 June 2007 a national, voluntary dry run of the HIP procedures has been carried out to test the HIP and the full Home Condition Report.

The purpose of the dry run is to test the practicalities of producing the HIP, to explore methods that ensure that consumers receive the best possible benefit from the HIP and to test consumer reaction to the Energy Performance Certificate.

The dry run has been managed by the Government in partnership with industry. In September 2006 the Department for Communities and Local Government (now known as the CLG) pledged £4 million to support six area trials for the HIP in Bath, Newcastle, Southampton, Northampton, Huddersfield and Cambridge. In January 2007 the Government announced that two further areas would be included in the HIP trials, namely Gwynedd, Conwy and the Isle of Anglesey in North West Wales and in the London Borough of Southwark.

The £4 million investment is being used to publicise the trials, to explain the benefits of the HIP, to subsidise the production of the HIP (many sellers will be provided with a free or subsidised HIP and many buyers will benefit from free searches and survey during this period) and to fund the independent research required to monitor the trials.

Participants in the trials include estate agents, property lawyers, mortgage lenders, HIP providers, certified Home Inspectors, homeowners and buyers. Participants in the dry run will report their findings back to the Government, explaining how the new measures work in practice and what effect they have on the home buying and selling procedures. This information has been independently monitored and used to make any necessary amendments to the HIP Regulations 2007 prior to their final implementation.

The initial findings reveal that it is taking on average 10 days to produce a HIP but this varies according to area. The production of packs is being slowed by local authorities, some of whom are taking up to four weeks to produce the local search. There have also been problems obtaining the required leasehold documents. It is taking on average an additional seven days to produce a HIP for a leasehold property.

The Government stipulated that during the dry run the following provisions should apply:

◆ The scheme is open to anyone who wishes to put together the documents required for the HIP, including specialist HIP providers.

◆ The Government has provided some sample forms for the Index, Sale Statement, Property Use form and Home Contents form. These forms are currently available to view and download on the CLG website at www.communities.gov.uk. The HIP regulations 2007 do not currently provide that these forms must be used as standard because they are subject to further testing.

♦ The energy efficiency report must comply with the EU Directive 2002/91/EC.

♦ The certification scheme for Home Inspectors and the electronic databank for Home Condition Reports and Home Inspectors should be fully operational to ensure that:
  – only Home Inspectors who have qualified under an approved certification scheme are able to provide the Home Condition Reports;
  – Home Inspectors and their reports are adequately insured so that sellers, buyers and lenders will have the right in law to rely upon the Energy Performance Certificate and the Home Condition Report and to claim redress for negligence or error;
  – Home Inspectors are 'fit and proper' persons.

♦ Lenders will, with the seller's permission, have access to the databank to obtain information about the property condition for the purposes of mortgage applications.

Despite calls for a compulsory element to the dry run it remains voluntary and there is no obligation for sellers, buyers or estate agents to participate.

Note: The Government has the power under Section 162 of the Housing Act 2004 to suspend the duties to supply a HIP even after the HIP Regulations 2007 come into force on 1 June 2007.

WHY DO WE NEED THE HIP?

Consumers have complained for years that the English conveyancing system is inefficient and slow. The high rate of transactions that begin, but do not proceed to completion, leads to frustration, heartache and financial loss. Research carried out by the Government into the home buying and selling process found that fewer than half of buyers and sellers were satisfied with the current legal process and that about 28% of all the property transactions that begin do not complete. The cost of these failed transactions to consumers and to the property industry is estimated to be in the region of £1 million per day.

The principle behind the HIP is to provide, at the outset of the transaction, relevant information that will inform the potential buyer about the property. This information is currently unavailable until after the buyer has made a formal offer to purchase and has instructed a conveyancer. The aim of the HIP is to reduce the time taken between the initial offer and exchange of contracts and to reduce the number of property transactions that fall apart because of adverse information being discovered after the initial offer has been made.

OPPOSITION TO THE HIP

Some of the key organisations in the property industry, such as the Law Society, the National Association of Estate Agents and the Council of Mortgage Lenders have expressed grave concerns about the HIP. Those against the HIP argue that it is an unnecessary and costly intervention that will lead to higher moving costs for consumers. While it is true that our conveyancing system is slow, by international standards, it is currently one of the cheapest in the world.

Arguments against the HIP

Those against the HIP maintain that the conveyancing system is gradually improving, without Government intervention, through competition and technology. The Land Registry, for instance, continues to progress with the implementation of 'e conveyancing', a system that has been designed specifically to improve conveyancing procedures. Local authorities, which used to take from two to six weeks to provide a local authority search result, are becoming automated and many can turn searches around in days or hours rather than weeks.

Following a recent ruling by the Office of Fair Trading, local authority search information is being made more readily available to the public and personal search providers. This ruling will enable personal search companies to produce searches far more quickly and cheaply than ever before. The majority of property professionals are now connected to the internet, enabling fast communication via email, and sophisticated case management systems produce lengthy legal documents at the click of a mouse.

Omissions from the HIP

Regrettably, the HIP does not address the major delay in property transactions, which is the phenomenon of the 'chain' where several parties are all trying to move toward one completion date. Nor does it resolve the problem of sellers or buyers who simply change their mind mid-transaction and decide not to proceed.

Pros and cons in moving towards the HIP

The introduction of the HIP remains controversial. There has been fierce opposition from several major players in the property industry.

The Law Society has expressed concerns that buyers may be pressurised into proceeding without proper legal advice; they have also warned that the HIP will increase costs for consumers. WHICH, the consumer advice agency withdrew support for the

HIP when the Government announced that the Home Condition Report would not be included as a compulsory document. WHICH argue that the consumer remains at a disadvantage because, without a Home Condition Report, they will not have the information relating to the physical condition of the property before they make their offer to purchase.

The National Association of Estate Agents (NAEA) is worried that the HIP will cause delays to sellers who need to market their property quickly, and that the cost of the HIP will deter some sellers from marketing their property at all. The NAEA is also concerned for their members as the HIP imposes the greatest burden upon estate agents, who become legally responsible for the provision of the HIP when instructed by a seller. Also, for the first time, estate agents will be subject to a compulsory redress scheme.

The Council of Mortgage Lenders (CML) has voiced its opposition to the HIP on the grounds of the cost and the potential adverse effect on the property market. The CML has also resisted pressure to accept the Home Condition Report for mortgage valuation purposes, and remains adamant that they will still require their own independent mortgage valuation to be carried out.

The supporters of the HIP mainly consist of companies who are involved in the certification schemes, the training and regulation of Home Inspectors and the supply of the HIP.

The Government has insisted, despite the opposition, that when the HIP is introduced it will be on a mandatory basis, and that a property may not be marketed until the HIP is in place. They argue that, in addition to reducing the number of transactions that do not proceed, the cost of the HIP will keep sellers who are not serious about selling their property out of the market.

HIP TIP

Approximately 28% of all property transactions fall through before legal completion. Post-HIP, buyers will be given a copy of the HIP and it is hoped that the provision of this information early on will lead to a reduction in abortive transactions.

WHO IS RESPONSIBLE FOR SUPPLYING THE HIP?

The Home Information Pack Regulations 2007 state that the duty to supply the HIP applies to the *responsible person*. The definition of the responsible person is contained within Part 5 of the Housing Act 2004 and includes any person who is responsible for marketing the property.

The regulations stipulate that the property owner (i.e. the seller) is the responsible person, unless they appoint someone to market the property for them. A marketing agent would usually be an estate agent, but could also include any solicitor, conveyancer or other type of firm that markets property. Once a seller instructs an estate agent, who has a place of business in England and Wales, to put their property on the market, the estate agent and not the seller is considered the responsible person. Under the Regulations, only the seller or a person acting as an estate agent for the seller may be responsible for marketing the property.

Responsibility of the seller to provide a HIP

For the purposes of the regulations the seller is defined as the owner of the freehold, commonhold, or long leasehold interest in the property (i.e. only the seller can be the property owner). The seller of the property becomes a 'responsible person' when they take one of the following actions:

- they put the property on the market;
- they make public the fact that the property is on the market.

The seller's responsibility ceases when they satisfy one of the following conditions:

- They employ someone to act as their estate agent who is responsible for marketing the property.
- They cease to market the property publicly.
- They arrange for any marketing activity by any person, other than their estate agent, being undertaken on their behalf to cease.
- They take the property off the market.
- The property is sold.

Responsibility of the estate agent to provide a HIP
A person is classed as an estate agent under Part 5 of the Housing Act 2004 if their business is based in England or Wales and they accept instructions from a seller to sell their property. There are further obligations placed on the estate agent where the property is not publicly marketed or the estate agent is not yet instructed.

For the purposes of the 2004 Act marketing means to carry out the seller's instructions with a view to:

- Introducing to the seller a purchaser who wishes to buy the property.
- Selling the property by auction or tender.

For the purposes of the Regulations it is immaterial whether or not the person accepting marketing instructions describe themselves as an estate agent.

The estate agent becomes the responsible person when they:

- put the property on the market;
- make it publicly known that the property is on the market.

The estate agent's responsibility ends when:

- their contract with the seller is terminated;
- they cease to take any action to make known publicly that the property is for sale;
- they arrange for any action being taken on their behalf to market the property to cease;
- the property is taken off the market;
- the property is sold.

The 2004 Act stipulates that the agent must have a HIP in their possession, or under their control, if they communicate, by any means, to a third party that the property is for sale. This applies whether they are formally instructed or not, and even if the property is not yet on the market. Thus the selling agent cannot side-step the regulations by selling a property to a third party known to them, even where the agent has not formally placed the property on the market, or put it into the public domain that the property is for sale.

THE DUTY TO HAVE A HIP

It is the duty of the responsible person to have in their possession, or under their control, a HIP that complies with the HIP Regulations before the property can be marketed. The duty does not apply where the responsible person is the seller and has either instructed an estate agent to sell the property, in which case the estate agent becomes the responsible person, or has reasonable grounds to believe that the estate agent has a qualifying HIP in their possession or under their control.

The duty to provide a copy of the HIP on request

The responsible person has a duty to provide an *authentic* copy of the HIP or any document included in the HIP when requested to do so by a potential buyer. The copy must be supplied within the 'permitted period' of 14 days, beginning with the day the request is made, or within 14 days of the potential buyer complying with the permitted conditions (see below). For the purposes of the regulations 'authentic' is defined as:

◆ A copy of the HIP, or any document which is included in the HIP, as it stands at the time when the document is provided.

◆ A copy of a document (or part of a document) that complies with the HIP Regulations.

The duty to supply a HIP does not apply, if during the permitted period of 14 days, the responsible person has reasonable grounds to believe that the person making the request:

◆ Is unlikely to have sufficient means to purchase the property.

◆ Is not genuinely interested in buying a property of the general description that applies to that particular property.

♦ Is not a person to whom the seller would be prepared to sell the property (this section does not authorise anything which would be considered an unlawful act of discrimination and does not apply if the responsible person knows or suspects that the person making the request is an officer of an enforcement authority).

♦ The duty does not apply to a seller who is marketing the property via an estate agent. If the seller is approached directly for a copy of the HIP then the seller must take reasonable measures to inform the potential buyer or law enforcement officer that the request should be made to the marketing agent.

The duty does not apply where the responsible person ceases to be responsible for marketing the property before or during the permitted 14 day period, whether it has been withdrawn from the market, sold or for any other reason.

Note: the responsible person does not comply with the duty to provide a HIP if they do so in electronic form, unless the potential buyer has consented to receiving it in that form. It is estimated that in the region of 40% of the UK population do not have any form of home computer and the demand for a paper copy of the HIP must therefore be complied with.

Imposition of conditions upon a potential buyer
The HIP Regulations provide that a potential buyer, who has requested a copy of the HIP, may be required to comply with either or both of the following conditions before any copy is provided:

♦ They may be required to pay a reasonable charge for the supply of a paper copy of the HIP and the cost of sending the document. The regulations stipulate that the charge must not exceed the cost of making and sending the document.

- The potential buyer may be required to accept any terms specified in writing which:
  - are proposed by the seller;
  - relate to the use or disclosure of the copy document or any information contained in or derived from it.

Any conditions must be notified to the potential buyer before the end of the permitted 14 day period. The potential buyer must then comply with the condition by making the payment demanded or accepting the terms proposed.

If either or both of the conditions referred to above are imposed on the potential buyer, the duty to supply the HIP commences on the day that the last condition was complied with, e.g. the day that the potential buyer pays the charge and/or accepts the imposed terms.

ENFORCEMENT OF THE HIP REGULATIONS

The HIP Regulations will be enforced by the local weights and measures authority. A trading standards officer can request the responsible person, who appears to have been subject to the duty to provide a HIP, to produce for inspection a copy of the HIP or of any document that should be contained within it. The power conferred upon the enforcement authority includes:

- Power to require production in a visible and legible documentary form (i.e. a paper copy) any document contained in the HIP which is held in electronic form.

- Power to take copies of any document for inspection.

The responsible person has seven days to comply with the above requirements. The seven day period commences on the day following the request. The responsible person is not obliged to comply with the requirements to provide a copy of the HIP if they have a reasonable excuse for not complying.

The requirement to produce the HIP to a law enforcement officer may not be imposed more than six months after the last day the responsible person was subject to the duty to provide a HIP. This provision means that sellers or their estate agents will have to retain a copy of the HIP for at least six months after:

◆ The property sale has been completed.
◆ The property has been withdrawn from the market and all marketing has ceased.
◆ The estate agent has been disinstructed by the seller.

Should the responsible person be found to be in breach of the HIP Regulations within the six month period allowed, the enforcement officer may serve a penalty charge notice on the responsible person. The current penalty charge is £200 and the regulations provide that the charge is subject to a maximum fine of £500.

Any person who obstructs an officer of an enforcement authority in pursuance of their duties, or who impersonates an enforcement officer, is guilty of an offence and if found guilty is subject to a summary conviction and a fine.

If the responsible person is an estate agent the law enforcement officer may also report the breach to the Office of Fair Trading, which could result in the estate agent being banned from trading.

The responsible person will not be held liable for any breach of the Regulations in relation to the accuracy or compliance of the HIP documents, other than the HIP index and Sale Statement, provided that the responsible person believes on reasonable grounds that the document(s) complies with the regulations.

Note: Payment of the penalty fine does not entitle the responsible person to continue to market the property without a HIP that complies with the regulations. Should the responsible person continue to market the property without a qualifying HIP they would be liable to further penalty charges. If the responsible person were an estate agent, the continued breach could be considered an 'undesirable practice' for the purposes of the Estate Agents Act 1979 and could therefore result in action being taken by the Office of Fair Trading to ban the estate agent from trading.

Right to take private legal action to enforce the HIP Regulations

If a responsible person is in breach of the HIP Regulations then a potential buyer will have the right to take action against them. Where the potential buyer has to obtain and pay for a document or report that should have been included in the HIP, they are entitled to recover from the responsible person any reasonable fee paid by them in order to obtain the document provided that:

- The property is on the market.

- The potential buyer and the seller are attempting to reach an agreement for the sale of the property.

- The potential buyer has not been provided with an authentic copy of the document.

The definition of 'property interest'

The term 'property interest' is used in the HIP Regulations to describe the 'legal' interest that the seller is proposing to sell, rather than a reference to the property itself. The legal interest would be either a freehold, leasehold or commonhold interest in land.

The definition of a 'residential property'

The term 'residential property' is used in the HIP Regulations to mean any premises in England and Wales consisting of a single dwelling house together with any ancillary land. Therefore a HIP will be required for each dwelling that is on the market unless exempt (see below).

The definition of a 'dwellinghouse'

The term 'dwellinghouse' means a building or part of a building (such as a flat or granny annexe) occupied or intended to be occupied as a separate dwelling and includes a newly built, part constructed or to be constructed property. Therefore the term dwellinghouse would extend to a flat, maisonette or any other type of property intended as living accommodation.

Definition of 'on the market'

The term 'on the market' means the residential property market in England and Wales. A residential property is considered to be on the market when the fact that it is, or may become, available for sale is made known to the public either by or on behalf of the seller.

For the purposes of the Regulations the property is considered as being publicly marketed when it is advertised or communicated in any other way to the public (i.e. by means of telephone, email, text alert, post etc.). The expression 'on the market' extends to any communication to a third party other than the seller or their estate agent that the property is for sale. Therefore the property need not be publicly advertised or promoted to be considered as on the market, and one telephone call or email to a potential buyer is enough to trigger the duty to provide a HIP. The property is regarded as being on the market until it is formally taken off the market or sold.

EXEMPTIONS FROM THE HIP REGULATIONS

A HIP is only required when a responsible person places a residential property on the market in England and Wales. There are exemptions from the duty to supply a HIP which are as follows.

Exemptions for 'business use' and 'non-residential' premises

The duty to supply a HIP only extends to a residential property that will or could be used as a permanent residential dwelling. Therefore an office or factory that is being sold as a business is a straightforward exception from the HIP regulations as it is exempt by virtue of being a business.

Definition of 'non-residential' premises

Many residential properties are used for home working or running a business from home. Whether premises are classed as residential or non-residential for the purposes of the regulations will be determined by their 'primary' use. The criteria used to judge the primary use will be one or more of the following:

for the purposes of the Regulations 'non-residential' premises include:

◆ premises where the most recent use of the premises is or was primarily non-residential; and

◆ any dwelling-house where:
   − it is clear from the manner in which it is marketed that it is due to be converted for primarily non-residential use by the time its sale is completed; and
   − all the relevant planning permissions and listed building consents exist in relation to the conversion.

Definition of business use

There is no duty to provide a HIP when marketing a business or non-residential premises for sale. The definition of business use for the purposes of the regulations is a non-residential property whose current or last formal planning use is, or was, primarily business. For instance, if a factory or office with the appropriate commercial planning permission is placed on the market, a HIP would not be required.

For the purposes of the regulations the use of a vacant property is determined by its last formal planning use. Therefore, if the last formal use of a vacant property was a business use, a HIP would not be required.

Note: This exception does not apply where the property or part of the property will have been converted for primarily residential use by the time the sale of the property is completed. For instance where a public house is to be converted to a residential dwelling by legal completion and the necessary planning permissions and any listed building consents are in place, a HIP would be required.

Residential property converted to business use

This exemption includes residential property that will be converted for primarily business use by the date of completion. For instance if a property with residential planning permission was to be converted to offices by completion it would be exempt, provided that both of the following conditions apply:

♦ It is clear from the marketing literature that the property is to be converted from residential to business use by the time the sale is complete.

♦ That all the necessary planning permissions and any listed buildings consents are in place.

Note: The term 'business use' *does not* include buildings which are residential but are used for the following.

Rental purposes

For the purposes of the regulations if a residential property is vacant and is being marketed as suitable for rental purposes it would not be classed as a business use and a HIP would be required.

Note: The duty to supply a HIP does not apply under Section 160 of the Housing Act 2004 if the entire property being sold is subject to a tenancy. However, if the property comprises a dwelling-house which is divided into two or more dwellings and the whole dwelling-house is being sold subject to a tenancy or part of that dwelling then a HIP will be required and a copy of the appropriate lease or licence must be included within the HIP.

Holiday accommodation

For the purposes of the regulations a residential property that is being marketed as suitable to let out as a holiday cottage would not be classed as a business and a HIP would be required.

Some hotels, guesthouses and bed and breakfast dwellings would be classed as a business in the following circumstances:

◆ They must have all the necessary planning/ building regulations consents for the use of the property as a hotel, guesthouse or B&B.

◆ A guesthouse/B&B which does not provide any living accommodation for its owner would be considered as a business premises and a HIP would not be required.

◆ A guesthouse/B&B which provides living accommodation for its owner, within the same building, would be classed as having dual use i.e. both residential and non-residential use and a HIP would not be required (see Dual Use properties below).

◆ A guesthouse, which is sold together with a separate building that provides accommodation for its owner, would be considered as being a mixed commercial/non-residential sale and a HIP would not be required (see Mixed Use Property below).

Note: to be considered as a guesthouse or B&B the property must have been adapted to provide guest accommodation. Residential properties that simply let one or two rooms to guests would be classed as residential and a HIP would be required. The key point is whether a guesthouse or B&B has been adapted to provide extra guest accommodation. For instance, the installation of additional bathrooms would count as an adaptation to provide guest accommodation.

Home working

Many people now use part of their homes for home working or run their business from home. If the primary use of the property remains residential a HIP would be required. For instance, converting a room to an office or using a garage or outbuilding for commercial purposes would not mean that the property could be classed as business premises because the primary use of the property remains residential.

Mixed commercial/residential sales

The duty to supply a HIP does not apply to sales where one residential property is being marketed for sale with a building or land ancillary to it that is used for commercial purposes. For instance a shop with a flat above would be exempt from supplying a HIP provided both of the following apply:

◆ At the First Point of Marketing the seller intends to accept only an offer for the properties together (i.e. the non-residential premises/land together with the residential dwelling).

◆ The marketing makes clear to potential buyers that offers will only be accepted for the non-residential and residential properties together (i.e. offers will not be accepted for the residential dwelling alone).

Note: If during marketing the seller decides to market the residential dwelling as for sale, independently of the non-residential land or building, a HIP would then be required in respect of the residential dwelling.

Should an offer be received for the residential dwelling only, while the property is marketed as a mixed use dwelling, the responsible person is not required to supply a HIP, provided the residential dwelling had never been marketed separately from the non-residential property. Under these circumstances the sale would be treated as a private sale (see Private Sales below).

Note: If more than one residential property is being marketed with ancillary land/non-residential premises then the exemption for portfolios of properties may apply (see Portfolio of Properties below).

Seasonal and holiday accommodation

The duty to provide a HIP does not apply to a residential property that has a planning restriction which limits one or both of the following:

◆ The occupancy of the property to 11 months or less in any 12-month period.
◆ The use of the property for holiday accommodation only.
◆ That regulation of the use of the dwelling-house is clear from the manner in which the property is marketed.

Dual use

Where a property is, or if vacant has been, used simultaneously for both residential and business use a HIP will not be required. The property must have the appropriate planning use. The question of whether the property has dual use, as opposed to a residential property used for home working, will be determined by the area of property given over to the business and the circumstances of the use.

For instance, where part of the property or land has been converted from residential use to commercial premises which has then been leased to a third party, or where a large house is sub-divided in two to provide a doctor's surgery in one half and a residential dwelling in the other, these would be classed as dual use properties.

A dual use property will be exempt from the HIP requirements only if both of the following provisions apply:

- It is currently dual use or, if vacant, its last use was dual use.
- It is being marketed as having:
  – business use; or
  – both residential and business use.

Note: This exemption would apply only to a property with current planning permission for business and residential use. A seller could not avoid the HIP Regulations by advertising the property as having potential for business use where it does not have current planning permission for that use.

Residential property with ancillary land

In this regulation where residential property is being sold with ancillary land it may be considered as non-residential if all of the following provisions apply:

- The total area of the land covers five hectares or more. The land in question need not be immediately adjacent to the property and does not have to comprise one parcel of land.

- The most recent use of the land is or was primarily for one or more of the following purposes:
  - Horticulture or cultivation. A residential property with an allotment or smallholding used to provide food for the

property owners and their non-paying guests would not be classed as having business use.

– The breeding or keeping of animals or livestock. A residential property with a kennels or cattery with business use would come under the heading 'mixed business and residential use' and would be exempt. A residential property that kept goats, pigs, chickens etc. for the use of its owners and their non-paying guests would not be exempt.

– Grazing or woodland. A residential property that used its gardens, fields or woodlands for the purposes of grazing, hunting etc. for the purposes of its owners and their non-paying guests would not be exempt.

Note: The key point is that if a residential property is using its land for the sole or primary benefit of the occupant, potential occupant or their non-paying guests it would not be classed as a business use.

Portfolios of properties

The duty to supply a HIP does not apply where more than one residential property is to be sold and the seller does not intend to accept an offer for one property in isolation from the others. Therefore, no HIP would be required for the sale of a residential property that comprised several flats or a number of different properties held in a portfolio for investment purposes provided that:

◆ The residential properties are not ancillary to each other (i.e. you could not claim that a house with a granny flat or a property with separate guest accommodation in an outbuilding represented a portfolio as they effectively form part of the main property).

- At the First Point of Marketing it must be clear from the marketing that the properties are being sold as a portfolio and that the seller does not intend to sell any one property in isolation from another.

- The dwelling-houses are available fro sale with vacant possession.

- The dwelling-house does not form part of a sub-divided building, in which part(s) of the property is being sold with vacant possession and the other part(s) is being sold subject to a tenancy.

Note: Should the seller subsequently decide to market the properties separately, or indicate that they would be prepared to sell one property in isolation from the other(s), the exemption would no long apply in relation to the property being sold individually and a HIP would be required. The date of the decision to sell one property in isolation from the other(s) becomes the First Point of Marketing.

Should an offer be received for one of the properties in a portfolio, provided that property had never been marketed in isolation from the portfolio, a HIP would not be required. In these circumstances the sale would be deemed as a private sale.

Unsafe properties

The duty to supply a HIP does not apply where the property being marketed is considered as unsafe. For the purposes of this regulation, unsafe would mean a residential property that poses a serious risk to the health or safety of its occupants, potential occupants or visitors. The property remains exempt, *provided that* the unsafe condition of the property does not cease to pose such a risk by the time the sale of the property is complete. For instance, a developer could not market a derelict property without a HIP where that property would be made safe, renovated and suitable for occupation by legal completion. This exemption applies only where the following provisions are met:

◆ The property is vacant.

◆ The condition of the property renders it unsuitable for occupation because it poses a serious risk to the health and safety of potential occupants and visitors.

◆ The property is marketed as unsuitable for occupation in its present condition.

Demolition properties

There is no duty to provide a HIP for a residential property that is being marketed as suitable for demolition and redevelopment as other premises, *provided that* if the property ceases to be marketed in that fashion it will no longer be exempt. The date that the seller or their agent ceases to market the property for demolition shall be the First Point of Marketing date and the seller will be required to provide a HIP. This exemption applies only where all of the following provisions are met:

◆ The marketing of the property must make clear that the residential dwelling is only suitable for demolition and that it is being sold as a site suitable for redevelopment.

◆ All the necessary planning permissions, listed building and conservation area consents have been obtained for the demolition of the existing dwelling.

◆ That outline planning permission or planning permission (or both) together with any listed building or conservation area consents have been obtained for the redevelopment of the site.

Private sales – properties not sold on the open market

Properties which have never been placed on the market but have been sold privately to friends, relatives or neighbours are exempt. Properties sold by landlords to tenants who are already living in the property are also exempt. This includes sales by local authorities or housing associations to tenants *in situ* under the Right to Buy legislation. It does not include sales of vacant dwellings by Local Authorities or Housing Associations.

Note: Where the property comprises two or more dwellings in a sub-divided building and the whole of the building is being sold, subject to a tenancy in one part of the property, a HIP must be provided. The HIP must include a copy of the tenancy agreement or lease of the occupied part of the building.

For example, if a residential house with a basement flat is being sold with vacant possession of the house but subject to an existing tenancy of the flat (or vice versa) then a HIP would be required.

Transitional exemption from 1 June 2007 – 31 December 2007

The regulations include an exemption for properties which are already on the market before 1 June 2007.

Where a property is placed on the market prior to 1 June 2007 the duty to supply a HIP will not apply until 31 December 2007. This exemption applies only where both of the following provisions are met:

- The property was put on the market by or on behalf of the seller before 1 June 2007.

- The property was actively marketed at any time during the period 1 June 2006 to 31 May 2007 by or on behalf of the seller and the responsible person made public the fact that the property was for sale.

- Marketing action was taken with the intention of selling the property before 1 June 2007.

- Marketing action was sustained to a reasonable extent after it was put on the market, during the period 1 June 2006 to 31 May 2007.

Should the property be placed on the market prior to 1 June 2007 and an offer be made and accepted for the property which does not proceed, either because it has been withdrawn by the potential buyer or repudiated by the seller, the duty to supply a HIP will not apply until 31 December 2007 provided that:

- The property was on the market prior to 1 June 2007.

- The property was taken off the market because the seller had accepted an offer to buy the property (before, on or after 1 June 2007).

- The property was then returned to the market within 28 days of the offer being withdrawn or repudiated.

Note: From 1 January 2008 the responsible person is required to provide a HIP for a property whether or not it was placed on the market prior to 1 June 2007, unless it is exempt under the Regulations.

HIP TIP

Most but *not all* property owners have to provide a HIP. There are exemptions for businesses, private sales and run-down properties. There is also a transitional exemption for properties placed on the market prior to 1 June 2007 until 31 December 2007. Ask your conveyancer to check whether your property is exempt.

SOME HIP DETAILS

When must the HIP be in place?
The seller, or their selling agent, must have the original documents that comprise the HIP in their possession or control at the First Point of Marketing. To satisfy the regulations the responsible person must either:

◆ Hold an original copy of the HIP in paper format or, if it is in the possession of a third party, they must have the right to take immediate possession of the documents on demand and without payment; or

◆ If the HIP is in an electronic format the HIP is only considered as being in the control of the responsible person if they are readily able to view the document in a form that is visible and legible, and can produce copies in a visible and documentary form.

Definition of First Point of Marketing
The First Point of Marketing is the date the property is offered for sale by the seller, or their agent, on the open market. The property must not be advertised for sale, nor be marketed to prospective purchasers, even on the telephone, before the HIP is in place.

The First Point of Marketing also has relevance to certain of the required pack documents which must not be more than three months old at the First Point of Marketing. These include the Energy Performance Certificate and recommendation report, the interim energy assessment, the predicted energy assessment and official entries and the searches.

It is also relevant to certain required commonhold and leasehold documents which must be the most recent communications and which must relate to the 12-month period immediately preceding the First Point of Marketing; these would include demands for service charge and ground rent payments (see below).

The date at which a document is included in the HIP becomes the First Point of Marketing for that particular document and, as the various pack documents are likely to be included at different times, documents included in the HIP may have a different First Point of Marketing date. The responsible person must record the First Point of Marketing date for each document in the index and is responsible for updating that document, where necessary, at the appropriate time.

The First Point of Marketing can begin again if the seller removes the property from the market for more than one year after the original First Point of Marketing date (see below).

Charge for supplying a copy of the HIP

Subject to the conditions outlined above, an authentic copy of the HIP must be made available to potential buyers upon request. A reasonable charge, which should not exceed the cost of making a paper copy of the HIP and the cost of any postage and packing, may be levied by the responsible person for producing and sending a paper copy of the HIP if requested to do so.

The HIP will include a number of lengthy documents and is likely to run to hundreds of pages. It is estimated that a reasonable charge for providing a paper copy of the HIP will be in the region of £25.

HIP TIP

A buyer is entitled to demand a paper copy of the HIP, but the seller or their agent is entitled to make a 'reasonable' charge for the copy.

What will be included in the HIP?

The HIP Regulations 2007 stipulate which documents are *required* to be included in the HIP, which are *authorised* and may be included in the HIP and documents that are prohibited from being included in the HIP.

The documents that comprise the HIP are divided into two categories:

* **A. Required documents** (i.e. those that *must* be included by law – see below);
* **B. Authorised documents** (i.e. those that *may* be included – see below).

The regulations categorically state that the HIP must not contain any documents that are not included in the list of required and authorised documents. Unauthorised documents, such as marketing, advertising and promotional material, must be kept entirely separate from the HIP. The reason for this is to differentiate official HIP documents from unauthorised marketing or promotional material, to ensure that consumers can distinguish between the two and are not pressurised into accepting additional products or services from the HIP provider.

The regulations require that all of the documents in the HIP must be the original documents, official copies from the Land Registry or true copies. The meaning of a true copy is not defined by the regulations. The guidance notes provided by the Government state that it should be taken to mean that a true copy does not have to be an exact copy but the original should be reproduced with sufficient accuracy to enable the copy to be clearly understood.

The documents contained in the HIP must be clear and legible (save where the original is not). Plans must be coloured with sufficient accuracy to enable them to be identified from the documents which refer to them (e.g. if a document refers to a plan describing the boundaries as edged red, it does not matter what shade of red is used but they must not be coloured green).

The HIP must be written in English where the property is in England and in English, Welsh or a combination of English and Welsh where the property is in Wales.

The HIP is likely to be produced in a variety of formats which could include an original paper copy, a CD, a memory stick and a web-based version that can be accessed by authorised persons using a secure login and password.

HOW LONG DOES THE HIP TAKE TO PREPARE?

It is estimated that the HIP will take up to two weeks to prepare. Much will depend upon the supplier as some will be more efficient than others. The launch of the HIP Regulations will involve the whole property industry working together as an efficient unit to provide the end result. The timing will also depend on whether the property to be marketed is registered with the Land Registry and whether it is freehold/leasehold or commonhold.

HIP REGULATIONS

Will the HIP need to be updated?

The regulations stipulate that the documents listed below must not be more than three months old at the First Point of Marketing.

Documents that must not be more than three months old at the First Point of Marketing

- The required searches (see below for a full list).
- The required official copies as stipulated in the regulations (see below for a full list).
- The required certificate of an official search of the Index Map (if the property has not been registered at the Land Registry).
- Energy Performance certificate and recommendation report, the interim energy assessment and the predicted energy assessment (whichever applies).

Leasehold and commonhold documents that are time sensitive

The leasehold and commonhold documents listed below are also deemed by the regulations to be time sensitive:

- Leasehold statements or summaries of service charges must relate to the 36 month period preceding the First Point of Marketing.

- Demands for financial contributions in respect of leasehold property must be the most recent communications and relate to the 12 month period preceding the First Point of Marketing including:
  – Service charges.

– Ground rent.

– Buildings insurance (if separate to the service charge).

– Public liability insurance (if separate to the service charge).

♦ Where the property is commonhold, the most recent demands for payment or financial contribution which relate to the 12 month period preceding the First Point of Marketing including, where applicable:

– Commonhold assessment.

– Reserve funds.

– Insurance against damage for the common parts (if made separate from the commonhold assessment).

– Public liability insurance (if made separate from the commonhold assessment).

ASSEMBLY OF HOME INFORMATION PACKS

The Regulations stipulate that the HIP must be assembled in the following order:

1. HIP Index.
2. Energy Performance Certificate and the recommendation report or the interim energy assessment or predicted energy assessment (whichever applies).
3. The remaining pack documents which may be included in any order.

TIME AT WHICH HIP DOCUMENTS ARE TO BE INCLUDED

The Regulations stipulate that the following documents must be included *before* the First Point of Marketing.

♦ The HIP Index.

♦ The EPC and recommendation report, or the interim energy

assessment or predicted energy assessment (whichever applies) see below for information on energy documents that are not available at the First Point of Marketing.
* Sale Statement.
* Evidence of title for registered property, i.e. the official entries of the individual register and the official copy of the filed plan (for property which has been registered at the Land Registry).
* A certificate of an official search of the index map (for property which has not been registered at the Land Registry).

The remaining 'required' documents as listed below must be included within the HIP within 28 days of the First Point of Marketing:

* Documents required to deduce title to an unregistered property (see below for information on documents which are completely unobtainable).
* Required commonhold documents (see below for list).
* Required leasehold documents (see below for list).
* Any leases or licences to which the property is or may become subject.
* Local authority search and local enquiries.
* Drainage and water enquiries search.

Updating the HIP

There is no requirement under the 2004 Act or the HIP Regulations to update the HIP while the property remains on the market. However, if the HIP is prepared but there are delays in getting the property to market, or if the seller takes the property off the market and puts it back on again 12 months after the original First Point of Marketing, the seller may have to pay for some or all of the HIP documents to be updated.

If the seller or estate agent voluntarily updates a required document the old document must be removed and the new document inserted. The HIP index must be updated to show the date the new document was included, and any additional versions or summaries of the HIP must be amended or updated accordingly.

The date of the document was amended or updated becomes the new First Point of Marketing for that document.

UPDATING OF ENERGY PERFORMANCE INFORMATION

If the property is not physically complete before or at the First Point of Marketing and is completed after that time but before legal completion of the sale takes place, the responsible person update the HIP where the property is physically completed and must include in the HIP:

a) The Energy Performance Certificate and recommendation report; or
b) The interim energy assessment where a property was constructed at a time when regulation 17C of the Building Regulations 2000 applied to the work, and where the property is physically complete at or before the First Point of Marketing, and the First Point of Marketing falls between 1 June 2007 and 16 September 2007, the responsible person must include in the HIP an Energy Performance Certificate and recommendation report no later than 1 October 2007.

The documents referred to a (a) and (b) above must be included in the HIP:

- within 14 days of the property becoming physically complete; and
- must replace any predicted or interim energy assessment already included in the HIP.

The date of the EPC and recommendation report are added to the HIP becomes the First Point of Marketing for those documents.

Sellers must be aware of the critical timing when deciding to remove a property from the market for more than 12 months after the date of the original First Point of Marketing otherwise they could end up paying for the HIP twice.

Re-marketing after a property has been withdrawn from the market

If a property is withdrawn from the market after a HIP has been prepared, provided that the original seller puts the property back on the market within one year of the original First Point of Marketing date, they will not be required to update the time sensitive required documents.

A seller who withdraws a property from the market for more than a year may have to pay to renew those required documents that are time sensitive (see above), if they no longer comply with the regulations at the time when the property is put back on the market.

Many of the required documents will be out of date if the HIP is more than three months old at the time the property is returned to the market. The Government has decided to allow the market to decide whether any documents in the HIP require updating. If the time sensitive HIP documents are out of date the seller may choose to update them but is not obliged to.

The seller's duty to check the HIP

The regulations provide that the seller must be provided with a copy of the HIP documents by the HIP provider in order to check their accuracy. This regulation also ensures that the seller is able to retain a copy of the HIP documents that relate to their property.

The difference between required and authorised documents

The HIP *must* include the *required* documents listed below. *Authorised* documents as listed below may be included when the HIP is prepared or at any time afterwards. It is not obligatory to include authorised documents, although the Government is strongly encouraging sellers to include a Home Regulation Report and a summary.

THE REQUIRED DOCUMENTS

A. Standard forms and documents

An index of the HIP contents

Although the Government has not prescribed the form of index in the regulations they have supplied a sample index on their website www.homeinformationpacks.gov.uk/hipbenefits.aspx. The index may be set out in another format provided it complies with the regulations.

The index must prominently display the title 'Home Information Pack Index' and must also contain the address or proposed address of the property. The index lists all the documents that are required or authorised to be included in the HIP and it must include a checklist to ensure that no required documents are missing. Any authorised documents which are not included in the HIP may be deleted from the index.

Part 2 of the index relates to commonhold information and Part 3 relates to leasehold information, these parts may be deleted if not applicable.

Note: The Index must be updated whenever a document is included or removed and must indicate if a required document:

- is missing;
- the reason why it is missing;
- the steps that are being taken to obtain the document;
- the date the responsible person expects to obtain the document;
- the reason for the delay in obtaining the document
- if the missing document is not included in the HIP by the predicted date a further predicted date must be entered on the index and the reason for the further delay must be given by the responsible person.

The index may indicate where a particular document can be found in the HIP.

A sale statement
This describes the property being sold. The regulations do not provide a prescribed sale statement. A sample statement is

available on the CLG website (address above). A sale statement
must:

- prominently display the title 'Home Information Pack Sale
  Statement';
- contain the address or proposed address of the property;
- state the property interest (i.e. freehold, commonhold, leasehold)
  and a brief description of the property;
- state whether the property is registered at the Land Registry at
  the First Point of Marketing;
- contain the name of the seller and the capacity they sell in (i.e.
  beneficial owner, trustee or personal representative);
- state whether the property is vacant or subject to a tenancy and
  the nature of that tenancy.

Creation of an interest in land

Where the sale of the property involves the creation of a new
interest in land, i.e. the whole of part of a commonhold unit
which, at the First Point of Marketing, has not been registered at
the Land Registry, or a leasehold property interest which at the
date of the First Point of Marketing has not yet been created, the
sale statement must:

- Be completed as though the freehold estate had been registered
  at the Land Registry.

- The HIP is not required to include the required official entries
  for the new commonhold or leasehold interest (as they do not
  yet exist).

- For a commonhold interest the HIP must include the proposed
  commonhold community statement and estimates or the
  payments that are likely to be required of the unit-holder within

12 months of the completion of the sale, including commonhold assessment, reserve funds, insurance against damage for the common parts, and public liability insurance.

♦ For a leasehold property the HIP must include the terms of the proposed lease and estimates of the payments that are likely to be required of the lessee within 12 months of completing the sale, including services charges, ground rent, insurance against damage for the building and common parts, public liability insurance.

Where the sale of the property involves the creation of a new freehold interest which forms part of a registered or unregistered freehold property, then the sale statement must be completed to show the actual interest being sold. The HIP must include official copy entries and filed plan of the individual register out of which the interest is being created or documents required to deduce title to the unregistered estate.

B. The legal information

Freehold – details of the title (evidence of legal ownership)
With *registered title,* i.e. a property that has been registered with the Land Registry, the HIP must include official copies of the individual register from the Land Registry. This would usually include the Property Register which gives the property description, the Proprietorship Register which gives details of the property owners and the Charges Register which gives details of any mortgages, charges or loans secured on the property. The HIP must also include an official copy of the filed plan. The required official copies must not be more than three months old at the First Point of Marketing.

The Land Registration Act 2002 gives a purchaser or a mortgagee the right to rely on the official copies, and entitles such persons to be indemnified by the Chief Land Registrar if they suffer loss resulting from a mistake in an official copy.

The official copies may refer to other documents that contain details of rights of way, restrictive covenants etc. The details of such rights and restrictions may be set out in the official copies in full, if not the HIP may include a 'filed copy' of the document as an authorised document. The buyer's conveyancer will require a copy of any such document and it will save time later in the transaction if any such copies are included in the HIP.

With *unregistered title*, the HIP must include a certificate of an Official Search of the Land Registry Index map and evidence of the seller's title (ownership) to the property. This would usually consist of an original document, such as a conveyance or lease, which provides a good root of title. The root of title document must be at least 15 years old. In addition to the root of title document the HIP must include either an Abstract of Title which is a certified record of every transaction since the root document, or an Epitome of Title which is a schedule of all the documents since the root of title, with the original or certified copies of those documents attached.

Where part of the property in a sub-divided building is not sold with vacant possession
All leases, tenancies or licences that relate to the property must be included.

Commonhold – additional documents required
Unregistered commonhold land does not exist. A freehold estate in commonhold land must be registered at the Land Registry.

Commonhold was created by the Commonhold and Leasehold Reform Act 2002. It relates to a freehold ownership or part of a multi-occupied development, e.g. a flat in a block of flats. The title to the flat is held by the individual property owner and title to the common parts of the development – which usually consists of external areas such as gardens and car parks, walkways, entrance halls and stairs etc. – belongs to a commonhold association, which is a company formed specifically for the purpose and which is limited by guarantee.

Additional documents to be included in the HIP if the property is commonhold:

◆ A completed commonhold part of the HIP index. All entries for the required HIP documents must be listed in the index. Authorised documents that are not included in the HIP may be deleted from the index.

◆ An official copy of the individual register and title plan for the common parts. This is in addition to the official copy of the register and the filed plan for the individual unit.

◆ An official copy of Commonhold Community Statement as referred to in the individual register for the common parts – this can be obtained from the Land Registry. This document sets out the rights and obligations of the unit (individual property) owners and the commonhold association. The Commonhold Regulations 2004 stipulate that a model commonhold community statement must be used.

Except where they are included in the Commonhold Community statement, the documents listed below are also required to be included in the HIP where:

— they are in the seller's possession or under his control;

— the seller can reasonably be expected to have access to them;

— the seller is able to obtain them by making reasonable enquiries of the individual unit holder (if this is not the seller), the commonhold association or any other person or company responsible for managing the building.

♦ Copies of any rules and regulations that have been made by the commonhold association or managing agents or their predecessors.

♦ Copies of any requests for payments made relating to the 12-month period preceding the First Point of Marketing in respect of commonhold assessment, reserve fund levy and insurance (if not covered by a request for commonhold assessment).

The documents listed below are also required to be included in the HIP where:

— the seller can reasonably be expected to be aware of such matters;

— the seller could obtain the documents by making reasonable enquiries of the individual unit holder (if this is not the seller), the commonhold association and any managing agents.

♦ The name and address of any managing agents or other person appointed by the commonhold association to manage the commonhold.

♦ Amendments proposed to the Commonhold Community Statement and other rules which are not included in the Commonhold Community Statement.

♦ Summary of works affecting the commonhold (current or proposed).

- New commonhold properties only – Proposed Commonhold Community Statement.

- New commonhold properties only – an estimate of commonhold assessment, reserve fund and insurance payments expected during the 12 months following completion (e.g. all the costs expected of the unit holder in the first 12 months of new ownership).

Leasehold – additional documents required

- A completed version of the leasehold part of the HIP index. All entries for required leasehold documents must be listed. If authorised documents are included these must be listed also. Authorised documents referred to but not included in the HIP may be deleted from the index.

- A copy of the lease. This may be an official copy obtained from the Land Registry or any other copy of the lease. If the original lease is unavailable and cannot be obtained, despite all reasonable efforts, then an edited form of the lease from the Land Registry may be included. The buyer's conveyancer will insist upon seeing a full copy of the lease if a sale proceeds.

The documents listed below are also required to be included in the HIP where:
   – they are in the seller's possession or under his control;
   – the seller has access to them;
   – the seller can obtain them by making reasonable enquiries of the leaseholder (if this is not the seller), the lessee and any managing agents.

- Rules and regulations outside the lease.

- Written summaries or statements of service charge for the 36-month period preceding the First Point of Marketing.

- The most recent requests for payment of service charges, ground rent and insurance for the 12-month period immediately preceding the First Point of Marketing.

The information and documents listed below are also required to be included in the HIP where:
  - the seller can reasonably be expected to have the information;
  - the seller can obtain it by making reasonable enquiries of the leaseholder (if this is not the seller), the lessee or the managing agents.

- The name and address of the current or proposed landlord.

- The name and address of the current or proposed managing agents.

- The name of any other person or company responsible for managing the property.

- Details of any proposed amendments to the lease, or the rules and regulations relating to the management of the company.

- Where S.20 of the Landlord and Tenant Act 1985 applies to any qualifying works or long-term agreement that relate to the property, a summary of:
  - any contribution which is required by such qualifying works or agreement and which has not been paid by the First Point of Marketing;
  - the total or estimated total cost of any such works or agreements;
  - the expected remaining relevant contribution of a lessee of the property;
  - the date or estimated date that the works or agreement will be concluded;
  - the date or estimated date that the remaining relevant

contribution will be required of the lessee of the property.

◆ New leasehold properties only – the proposed lease.

◆ New leasehold properties only – estimate of service charges, ground rent and insurance payments expected during the 12 months following completion.

C. Condition documents

◆ An Energy Performance Certificate accompanied by the recommendation report for the property
The regulations stipulate that the HIP is required to contain a stand alone Energy Performance Certificate as the first document in the pack. If the HIP contains a Home Condition Report this will automatically include an Energy Performance Certificate but, if a Home Condition Report is not included, then a separate Energy Performance Certificate must be obtained.

An Interim Energy Assessment

Homes that are sold 'off plan' and are incomplete at the time of marketing will require an Interim Energy Assessment. This report will include similar information to that contained in the Energy Performance Certificate.

The Interim Energy Assessment must:

◆ display prominently the title 'Interim Energy Assessment';
◆ contain the following statement: 'This document is an Interim Energy Assessment required to be included in a HIP during an interim period for recently built properties. By 1 October 2007, a full Energy Performance Certificate and recommendation report will be required for the sale of the property';

- contain the address or proposed address of the property;

- be compiled otherwise than by a visual inspection of the property;

- express the asset rating of the building in a way approved by the Secretary of State under regulation 17A of the Building Regulations 2000; and

- contain an explanation of that asset rating.

The Interim Energy Assessment will only relate to a property:

- which is physically complete before the First Point of Marketing;

- where the First Point of Marketing falls during the period 1 June 2007 to 16 September 2007; and

- which was constructed at a time when regulation 17C of the Building Regulations 2000 applied to the work.

Predicted Energy Assessment
If a property is not physically complete before The First Point of Marketing but is physically completed before the sale of the property legally completes the HIP must include Predicted Energy Assessment which must:

- display prominently the title 'Predicted Energy Assessment';

- contain the following statement: 'This document is a Predicted Energy Assessment required to be included in a HIP for properties marketed when they are incomplete. It includes a predicted energy rating which might not represent the final energy rating of the property on completion. Once the property is completed, the HIP should be updated to include information about the energy performance of the completed property;

♦ contain the address or proposed address of the property;

♦ be compiled otherwise than by a visual inspection of the property;

♦ contain the predicted asset rating of the building:
  – based on its plans and specifications; and
  – expressed in a way approved by the Secretary of State under regulation 17A of the Building Regulations 2000; and
  – contain an explanation of that predicted asset rating.

Note: The definition of a completed property is one which is constructed, or converted and fit for residential purposes. Where there is doubt a property is deemed physically complete if:

♦ it is wind and weather proof;
♦ it is safe and sanitary;
♦ it has the facilities for the supply of heating, hot and cold water and electricity;
♦ it has washing and drainage facilities.

D. The required searches

Local authority search
A search report which relates to the property and which records the results of a search of all parts of the appropriate local land charges register:

♦ in the form of an official search certificate, in the case of an official search made pursuant to section 9 of the Local Land

Charges Act 1975; or

♦ in any other form that accords with Parts 1 and 2 of Schedule 7 to the HIP Regulations 2007 (see below) and in the case of a personal search made pursuant to Section 8 of the Local Land Charges Act 1975.

Local enquiries
A search report that:

♦ complies with Parts 1 and 2 of Schedule 7 of the HIP Regulations 2007 (see below); and

♦ records the results of a search of records held by or derived from a local authority.

Drainage and water search
A search report which complies with Parts 1 and 2 of Schedule 7 with the Schedule of the HIP Regulations 2007 (see below).

In order to ensure that buyers and lenders will feel confident to rely upon the searches provided in the HIP the regulations stipulate that the required searches must be provided as follows:

Terms for the preparation of required searches
♦ The search report must be prepared with reasonable skill and care.

♦ The search may be copied for the purposes of the HIP notwithstanding any copyright claimed by the search provider.

♦ The seller, buyer and mortgage lender will have direct legal rights to rely upon the results of the search.

♦ The search provider will hold professional indemnity insurance that is placed with an insurer authorised by the Financial Services and Markets Act 2000, for the minimum sum required by the regulations, and that third parties such as sellers, buyers and mortgage lenders will be entitled to claim financial compensation for any liability arising as a result of negligence of defects in the search.

The above provisions do not apply to the 'authorised' searches.

General provisions for required searches as contained in Schedule 7 to the HIP Regulations 2007
The regulations provide that the following information must be contained in the required search reports included in the HIP:

◆ The address of the property which is the subject of the search.

◆ A statement as to whether there is any professional or personal connection between the search provider and any other person involved in the sale of the property, including the seller, estate agent or conveyancer.

◆ The form of the questions that were asked to obtain the search information.

◆ The results of the search.

◆ The date upon which the search was completed.

◆ Details of the records, and where they are held, that were examined to obtain the information in the search report.

◆ Details of any other records searched to obtain the results, and where they are held.

◆ The name and address of the person who carried out the search.

- The name and address of the person responsible for preparing the report (if different from the person who carried out the search).

- The name and address of the person who is responsible for dealing with any errors in the search report.

- Details of the search provider's complaints and redress scheme.

- The contractual terms on which the search is provided (which should follow the minimum terms laid down by the regulations).

- The name and address of the person liable to pay financial compensation as a result of defects or errors in the search.

Additional search information

The regulations provide that the search reports may include additional information which assists in the explanation of the search results or the identification of the property but prohibits the inclusion of marketing or advertising material on behalf of the search companies.

Unavailable search results

The regulations provide that the search report must include all the information sought except where the said information cannot be obtained under any circumstances from the relevant authority or person. The fact that the relevant authority makes a charge for the information does not absolve the search provider from the obligation to provide the information. If required information is missing from the search, the report must contain a statement explaining what information is missing and why.

The Local Authority Search and enquiries

Local authority searches can be carried out in two ways.

1. The conveyancer or the HIP provider will send a search request directly to the local authority by post, or they may order the search online or by fax via a search provider such as the National Land & Property Information Service (NLIS). If the search is ordered directly from the local authority by post it is usually made by sending standard forms called CON 29 Part I and LLC1, together with a plan of the property and the required fee. If the search is ordered via a search provider the provider requests the search electronically from the relevant authority. In either case, the local authority then reply to the questions raised and send the search result back with a search certificate. The certificate provided by the local authority is a guarantee that the search results were accurate at the time the search was made. If the search result later proves to have been negligent, or inaccurate, the buyer or the lender has a right of redress under the Land Charges Act 1975 against the local authority. For this reason local authority search results are only valid for three months from the date of the search certificate.

2. The conveyancer or the HIP provider will instruct one of the many companies that provide 'personal searches'. Most of these companies visit the local authority in person to obtain answers to the questions contained on the CON 29 Part I. However, some companies obtain the information electronically from a database. The search result is then returned to the conveyancer or HIP provider. Personal search companies cannot provide the local authority certificate of guarantee and therefore provide indemnity insurance. Should the search later turn out to be negligent or inaccurate then the buyer or their lender have redress against the search company and will claim against the search company's professional indemnity insurance.

The regulations provide that the search must relate to the property being sold and be in the form of an 'official search' or a 'personal search' under the Local Land Charges Act 1975. Whether the search is an 'official search' or a 'personal search' it must comply with the following conditions:

♦ It must include the address of the property which is the subject of the search.

♦ It must include a statement advising whether there is any personal or financial connection between the provider of the search report and anyone involved in the sale of the property, i.e. the seller, their estate agent or conveyancer. The statement must include details of any business referral arrangements.

♦ It must include a copy of the questions asked to provide the search report. This would usually be a copy of the Law Society form CON 29 Part I (standard enquiries of a local authority).

♦ The results of the search.

♦ The date the search was completed.

♦ A description of the records that were examined to obtain the search information.

♦ The name and contact details of the person who carried out the search report and the name and contact details of the person responsible for preparing the search report.

♦ The name of the person who is responsible should any errors be found in the report.

♦ Details of the procedures for consumer complaints and redress and of any indemnity insurance provided.

♦ The terms on which the search report is provided (which should include the minimum terms laid down by the regulations).

♦ Specify the results of any records found in the departments listed below and if such records are found the search must specify whether they are available to a potential buyer and where they can be obtained. Alternatively, the search may include copies of any records found such as planning permissions, building regulations consents etc. The search must also indicate whether any charge is made for any such copy documents.

Matters that must be covered by a Local Authority search
Planning decisions and pending applications
The search must stipulate what applications for any of the following have been approved or rejected or whether there is a decision pending by the relevant local authority:

♦ Planning permissions.
♦ Listed building consents.
♦ Conservation areas.
♦ Certificates of lawful use of existing use or proposed use or development.
♦ Building regulations approvals.
♦ Building regulations completion certificates.
♦ Planning designations, plans and proposals.
♦ Highways.
♦ Land required for public purposes.
♦ Land to be acquired for road works.
♦ Drainage agreements and consents.
♦ Nearby road schemes.
♦ Nearby railway schemes.
♦ Traffic schemes.
♦ Outstanding notices in relation to building works, the environment, health and safety, housing, highways or public health.

◆ Contravention of building regulations.

◆ Planning enforcement. Notices, orders directions and proceedings under planning acts.

◆ Compulsory purchase.

◆ Conservation areas.

◆ Contaminated land.

◆ Radon gas.

Additional local enquiries

The local authority may also answer specific additional enquiries. These additional enquiries are not required under the HIP Regulations but may be included in the HIP as authorised information. The CON 29 has an additional question section CON 29 Part II from which the conveyancer or HIP provider can select additional enquiries. A typical enquiry would be whether the property is affected by a public footpath or by-way. The local authority charges an additional fee per enquiry. The conveyancer or HIP provider can also raise additional enquiries of the local authority in a separate written enquiry. The local authority charges an additional fee for this service.

Access to local authority records – interim measure

Some local authorities do not currently allow personal search companies access to all their records and as a consequence a personal search may not contain answers to all the required enquiries which are set out in Part 2 of Schedule 8 of the HIP regulations relating to:

◆ Planning and building decisions and pending applications.

◆ Planning designations and proposals.

◆ Roads.

◆ Land required for public purposes.

- Land to be acquired for road works.
- Drainage agreements and consents.
- Nearby road schemes.
- Nearby railway schemes.
- Traffic schemes.
- Outstanding notices.
- Contravention of building regulations.
- Notices, orders, directions and Proceedings under Planning Acts.
- Conservation areas.
- Compulsory purchase.
- Contaminated land.
- Radon gas.

The interim measure applies where:

- The First Point of Marketing falls before 1 April 2008.

- The local authority holds the records required to deduce the answer or result.

- The local authority has a policy that does not allow other persons to inspect the necessary records.

- The local authority has not been asked to provide the search report (i.e. it is a personal search).

- Any enquiries not answered are the subject of a contract of insurance against the liabilities that if they had been answered they would have affected an actual buyer's decision to buy the property or the price an actual or potential buyer would be prepared to pay for it, and results in financial loss.

In the above circumstances the search will comply with the HIP Regulations provided that the personal search company hold a contract of insturance to protect the potential or actual buyer and their mortgage lender from financial loss. The insurance contract must:

♦ be a contract authorised by the Financial Services and Markets Act 2000;

♦ cover any liability for financial loss arising as a result of the circumstances described above such financial loss to be met by compensation paid by the personal search company or if they cease to exist by their governing body;

♦ the search report must contain a description of the terms and effect of the insurance described above and must identify which enquiries have not been answered and in respect of which insurance has been obtained.

Water and drainage enquiries CON29DW
The terms and requirements laid down for the water and drainage search are the same as set out above for the local authority search. The search must specify the results of a search of the records set out below and, where the search finds any entries in the records, it must provide a description of them. If entries are revealed the search must indicate whether copies are available to a potential purchaser, where they are obtainable and whether any copying fee will be charged. Alternatively the search may attach any such copies.

Matters that must be covered by a Water and Drainage search:

♦ Public sewer maps.
♦ Foul drainage and surface water.

- Public adoption of sewers and lateral drains.
- Public sewers within the boundary of the property.
- Public sewers near to the property.
- Building over a public sewer, disposal main or drain.
- Map of the waterworks.
- Adoption of water mains and service pipes.
- Sewerage and water undertakers.
- Connection to mains water supply.
- Water mains, resource mains or discharge pipes.
- Current basis for sewerage and water charges.
- Charges following change of occupation.
- Surface water drainage charges.
- Water meters.
- Sewerage bills.
- Water bills.
- Risk of flooding due to overloaded public sewers.
- Risk of low water pressure or flow.
- Water quality analysis.
- Water quality standards.
- Sewage treatment works.

The required searches must not be more than three months old at the First Point of Marketing.

Documents that are unobtainable at the First Point of Marketing

The Regulations provide that in certain circumstances the property may be marketed without certain required documents if:

- the required documents is completely unavailable (see below); or
- the responsible person reasonably believes that the required document will become available within 28 days of the First Point of Marketing; or

♦ the document is an energy performance certificate, recommendation report, interim energy assessment or predicted energy assessment and the First Point of Marketing does not take place until 14 days have elapsed from the date that the document was ordered.

Energy information available before the First Point of Marketing
If, despite all reasonable efforts and enquiries by the responsible person, the required Energy Information document is not available at the First Point of Marketing the property may be marketed, provided:

♦ 14 days have elapsed since the document was applied for in accordance with the regulations;

♦ the responsible person continues to use all reasonable efforts to obtain the document before 28 days from the First Point of Marketing has elapsed;

♦ the missing document is included in the HIP as soon as is practicable;

♦ proof of the request for the missing document is included in the HIP at the First Point of Marketing.

The time at which the missing document is added to the HIP becomes the First Point of Marketing for that document.

Documents required within 28 days of the First Point of Marketing
The Regulations provide that where the following documents are not available at the First Point of Marketing but the responsible person reasonably believes that they will become available within 28 days of the First Point of Marketing the property may be marketed without them provided:

- the date the missing document is ordered falls before the First Point of Marketing;

- the responsible person continues to use all reasonable efforts to obtain the document(s) within 28 days from the First Point of Marketing;

- the responsible person records details of the missing document, what steps are being taken to obtain it, the date the responsible person expects to obtain the document, the reason for any delay which has occurred and if the document is not obtain by the original date predicted such further date as the responsible person believes the document will be available by;

- the document is included in the HIP as soon as the responsible person obtains it; and

- proof of the request for the document is included in the HIP at the First Point of Marketing.

The time at which the missing document is added to the HIP becomes the First Point of Marketing for that document.

List of documents to be included with 28 days of the First Point of Marketing
1. Documents required to deduce title to property that has not been registered at the Land Registry.

2. Required commonhold documents (see below for full list) expect for the official entries and filed plan.

3. Required leasehold documents (see below for full list).

4. Leases or licences that affect the property.

5. The Local Authority Search and Enquiries.

6. Water and Drainage Search.

Required documents which are unobtainable at the First Point of Marketing and are unlikely to become obtainable

If the documents listed below are unobtainable before the First Point of Marketing, and the responsible person reasonably believes that they are unlikely to become obtainable at a later date, provided the regulations have been complied with, the property may be marketed without them:

◆ The required documents that deduce title to an unregistered property (for full list see above).
◆ Interim Energy Assessment.
◆ Predicted Energy Assessment.
◆ Required commonhold information (for full list see above).
◆ Documents required to deduce title to an unregistered property.
◆ Required leasehold information (for full list see above).
◆ Leases or licences for dwelling-houses.

Where a required document is missing or unobtainable in order to comply with the regulations the responsible person must state in the index:

◆ that the document cannot be obtained from any person;
◆ that it cannot be created by any person; or
◆ that it no longer exists in any form.

Definition of a proper request for a required document

A proper request for a required document must:

◆ be in the form required;
◆ be properly addressed to a person who usually provides or is likely to provide the type of document requested;
◆ contain all necessary information;

- include such payment as is required, or an undertaking to make payment.

Proof of a request for a document means a written statement of the following matters:

- which of the required documents has been requested;
- the date that a request for the document is delivered (see below);
- the name of the person to whom the request has been addressed;
- the date the responsible person believes the document is likely to become available; and
- confirmation that the request was properly made in accordance with the regulations (see above).

To constitute proper delivery the request must be:

Delivery of documents
A. The day a document is deemed to be delivered under the Regulations is:

- The day the request is served personally upon the intended recipient.
- The day the request would be delivered in the ordinary course of the post of (if sooner) the day it is proved to be delivered to the intended recipient.
- The day that it is left at the intended recipient's address.
- The second day after it is left at the document exchange of the person making the request or, if sooner, the day on which it is proved to have been delivered to the intended recipient.
- The day the request is sent by fax or electronic communication to the intended recipient's address or, if later, the day upon which it is proved to be delivered.

B. Where a request for a document is delivered to the Chief Land Registrar the day the request is delivered shall be taken to be as set out above but may also be delivered:

- orally;
- by telephone, fax or other electronic method.

HIP TIP

A seller should be able to market their property after 14 days without certain required HIP documents *provided* they have complied with the HIP Regulations.

Required documents which must be included in the HIP at the First Point of Marketing

The regulations stipulate that the documents listed below must always be included in the HIP before the property is placed on the market because they should always be available:

- The sale statement.
- The Index.
- The official entries and filed plan (for registered property).
- Official certificate of search of the Index Map (for registered property)

Quick reference to required documents

- HIP Index – must be included at First Point of Marketing.

- Energy Performance Certificate and recommendation report – must be applied for before First Point of Marketing and included within 14 days.

- Interim Energy Assessment or predicted energy assessment – Must be applied for before First Point of Marketing and included within 14 days. The property may be marketed without them if they are completely unobtainable.

- Sale Statement – must be included at the First Point of Marketing.

- Official copies and filed plan (for property that has been registered at the Land Registry).

- A certificate of an official search of the Index Map (for property that has not been registered at the Land Registry) – must be included at the First Point of Marketing.

- Documents required to deduce title to an unregistered property – must be applied for before the First Point of Marketing and include within 28 days. The property may be marketed without them if they are unavailable.

- Commonhold property required commonhold documents (see list) – must be applied for before the First Point of Marketing and included within 28 days. The property may be marketed without them if they are completely unavailable.

- Leasehold property required leasehold documents (see list) – must be applied for before the First Point of Marketing and included within 28 days. The property may be marketed without them if they are completely unavailable.

- Leases or licences that affect the property – must be applied for before the First Point of Marketing and included within 28 days. The property may be marketed without them if they are completely unavailable.

- Local Authority Search and enquiries – must be applied for before the First Point of Marketing and included within 28 days. Personal searches may exclude some answers to enquiries subject to providing adequate indemnity insurance.

* Drainage and Water Authority Search – must be applied for before the First Point of Marketing and included within 28 days.

THE AUTHORISED DOCUMENTS

The regulations provide that the authorised documents do not need to be included in the HIP before the property is marketed. They may be included at that time or at any time thereafter. If an authorised document is added to the HIP, the HIP index must be updated.

Listed below are the authorised documents which *may* be included in the HIP, but are not required by law to be included:

* An accurate translation of the HIP into any language.

* An additional version (in Braille or large print).

* A summary or explanation including legal advice on the content of the HIP or any HIP document.

* A description, photograph, plan, map or drawing which is intended to identify the property.

* Information concerning the source or supply of any document contained in the HIP, and complaints and redress procedures relating to the documents and information contained in the HIP.

* Official copies of documents referred to in the individual register (e.g. filed copies).

* Additional commonhold documents that supplement the information contained in the required documents and which provide similar or related information.

- Additional leasehold documents that supplement the information contained in the required documents and which provide similar or related information.

- A Home Condition Report which complies with the Regulations.

- Reports of work carried out since the Home Condition Report together with any relating guarantees or warranties.

- Guarantees, policies and warranties that relate to the property or its contents.

- Details of the property's contents, fixtures and fittings. The regulations do not prescribe a standard form but the CLG have provided a sample form on their website (details given above) and recommend the use of that form.

- Information about the design or standards to which a property has been or will be built.

- Any documents referred to in the Local Authority Search and enquiries or the Drainage and Water Search.

- Details that would be revealed in the standard form of pre-contract enquiries, the Law Society's Property Information Form or on the CLG sample form known as the Property Use Form, a copy of which is available from their website (see below).

- Information held by or communications with the Land Registry that relate to the property.

- Other searches. The regulations provide that additional searches may be included in the HIP as follows:
  - mining search;
  - additional enquiries of the local authority;

- a local authority search on adjoining or adjacent land;
- a commons registration search;
- a tin mining search;
- a brine search;
- a limestone search;
- a china clay search;
- a natural subsidence search;
- an environmental search;
- a telecommunications search;
- searches relating to utility services;
- searches relating to the potential or actual effects of transport services, including roads, waterways, trams and railways;
- a chancel repair search or other search relating to the liability to maintain buildings or land outside the property interest;
- other searches not detailed but relating to information about matters connected with the property that would be of interest to a potential buyer.
- Rights of access to, over or affecting the property.
- Additional relevant information relating to:
  - energy performance, environmental impact or sustainability;
  - potential or actual environmental hazards that might affect the property or its occupants;
  - the price at which the property is for sale;
  - the price at which the property was previously sold;
  - the length of time the property has been for sale;
  - the property location or address;
  - the aspect, view, outlook or environment;
  - proximity and identity of local services, facilities and amenities;
  - Welsh-speaking communities in the local area;
  - the use of the Welsh language;
  - history of the property including its age, ownership or use

of the property or the land upon which it is or will be situated;

- the tenure or estate;
- details of any statutory provision which restricts the use of land or requires it to be preserved or maintained in a specified manner;
- existence or nature of any covenants or restrictions on resale, restrictions on use or pre-emption rights;
- existence of any easement, servitudes or wayleaves;
- equitable interests in the property;
- rights of way or access or over:
  - the property (not including ancillary land); or
  - land outside the property.
- Rights of way or access to or over any ancillary land to the property including:
  - obligations to maintain such land; or
  - whether any payments for maintaining such land are outstanding
- Obligations to maintain the boundaries.
- Communications from any public authority or statutory body or person that affects or may affect the property including whether any request made by them has been complied with.
- Acquisition of land by a public authority or statutory body or person which affects or might affect the property.
- Standards of safety, building, repair or maintenance to which the property, its contents or the building ought to comply and whether such standards have been complied with.
- The property's suitability or potential suitability for occupation by a disabled person.
- Alterations or works relating to the property and the date/ approximate date they occurred and whether any necessary permissions for any such alterations or works have been obtained; or whether relevant consultations have been

conducted.

♦ The identity of the person who designed, constructed, built, produced, treated, processed, repaired, reconditioned or tests the property or its contents.

♦ Measurements of the property.

♦ Use or occupation of the property or of other premises which affect or may affect it.

♦ Utility services connected.

♦ Similar information as authorised that relates to neighbouring adjoining, or nearby land or premises.

HIP providers

The HIP may be provided by a number of organisations such as:

♦ estate agents;

♦ solicitors and licensed conveyancers;

♦ lenders;

♦ commercial HIP providers.

HIP TIP

A list of current HIP providers is provided in the directory at the end of the book and Chapter 3 gives more detailed advice on HIP providers.

HIP QUESTIONS

Who pays for the HIP and when?

The seller of the property is liable to pay for the cost of the HIP. The seller will be obliged to order the HIP and must ensure it is in place before marketing their property. Some suppliers may offer a deferred payment scheme whereby the property owner will be asked to sign an agreement to pay for the HIP at a later date.

How much will the HIP cost?

It is currently estimated that the average HIP will cost in the region of £300–£400 without a Home Condition Report and £650–£800 with a Home Condition Report. The cost will vary according to the tenure of the property, e.g. whether it is freehold, leasehold or commonhold, and the location and the size of the property. There are many more documents to obtain on leasehold and commonhold properties and the cost of obtaining these documents will be added to the cost of the HIP.

The typical costs of the separate components of the HIP are estimated to be:

Example of the cost of a HIP		
The HCR (Including an Energy Performance Certificate)	£300	– £500
A stand-alone Energy Performance Certificate	£100	– £200
The required searches	£150	– £250
The legal content	£100	– £150
Copy documents	£ 20	– £ 40
Leasehold information	£ 75	– £150
Additional authorised searches	£75	– £150

The cost of the HIP will vary from provider to provider and the seller should shop around, considering cost, speed and quality, before proceeding to order the HIP.

HIP TIP

It is estimated that the average cost of a HIP for a freehold property, with a Home Condition Report, will be £600 rising to £1,000 or more for a leasehold or more complicated property.

Will the HIP law be retrospective?

The regulations provide that if a property is placed on the market prior to 1 June 2007 the responsible person will be exempt from the requirement to provide a HIP until 31 December 2007. This is to allow sellers, whose property is already on the market when the HIP comes into being, time to sell their property and complete on the sale. If the property is on the market prior to 1 June 2007, and the seller or their agent continues to actively market the property this exemption will apply.

If the property is placed on the market prior to 1 June 2007 but is taken off the market during the transitional period because a sale is proceeding, should that sale fall through then provided the property is placed back on the market within 28 days of the offer falling through this exemption will continue to apply.

From 1 January 2008 all property that is on the market must have a qualifying HIP in place.

2

Understanding the Home Condition Report and the Energy Performance Certificate

The HIP Regulations 2006 stipulated that the Home Condition Report would be a required document and must by law be included in the HIP. Several weeks later the Government announced that the status of the Home Condition Report would be changed from a required document to an authorised document. The HIP Regulations 2007 revoiced the HIP Regulations 2006.

The HIP Regulations 2007 stipulate that homeowners will not be obliged to include a Home Condition Report in the HIP when the legislation comes into force on 1 June 2007.

A stand-alone Energy Performance Certificate and recommendation report, or an Interim Energy Assessment or a Predicted Energy Assessment remains a required document and must be included in the HIP by law.

The Government has strongly advised the property industry to encourage sellers to voluntarily include a Home Condition Report in their HIP for the following reasons:

◆ It will not cost significantly more to have a full Home Condition Report than a stand-alone Energy Performance Certificate – the difference is likely be in the region of an additional £200–£400.

◆ Buyers will prefer properties that have a Home Condition Report.

◆ The Home Condition Report will add transparency to the transaction from day one, meaning that there will be fewer reasons for the buyer to withdraw later on in the transaction.

◆ Sellers will be alerted to any problems with the property that can be rectified before a sale commences, or can be reflected in the asking price.

THE ENERGY PERFORMANCE CERTIFICATE

The Energy Performance Certificate and the recommendation report will become a mandatory part of the HIP from 1 June 2007. The report must be prepared and the certificate issued by a properly qualified Home Inspector or Domestic Energy Assessor. The current accepted levels of qualification are the ABBE level 4 Diploma in Home Inspection or the ABBE level 3 Diploma in Domestic Energy Assessment.

Inspectors must also be certified by one of the approved certification schemes before they will be allowed to carry out the Energy Performance Certificate inspection on behalf of members of the public. This will ensure that energy assessment inspectors will be subject to the same strict training, regulation, compliance and background checks as fully qualified Home Inspectors.

The Government estimates that 2,500–4,500 qualified inspectors will be required to carry out the energy assessment inspections.

The Energy Performance Certificate will give the property an A–G rating dependent upon how energy efficient the property is. The report will also contain practical advice for consumers on how to cut their fuel bills and carbon emissions. A sample energy performance assessment and Energy Performance Certificate is set out below:

SAMPLE ENERGY PERFORMANCE CERTIFICATE

Energy Performance Certificate

Property address and postcode:

Report reference number (RRN):

Inspection date:

Report date:

Dwelling type:

Home Inspector's name:

Certificate number:

Floor area:

The home's performance ratings

This home has been assessed using the UK's Standard Assessment Procedure (SAP) for dwellings. Its performance is rated in terms of the energy use per square meter of floor area, energy efficiency based on fuel costs and environmental impact based on Carbon Dioxide (CO_2) emissions.

Energy Efficiency Rating
Energy efficient = lower running costs
Not energy efficient = higher running costs

Sample energy efficiency rating table *

Energy Efficiency rating	Current	Potential
(92–100) A		
(81–91) B		
(69–80) C		77
(55–68) D	60	
(39–54) E		
(21–38) F		
(1–20)		
UK 2007 Directive 2002/91/EC		

The energy efficiency rating is a measure of the overall energy efficiency of a home. The higher the rating the more energy efficient the home is and the lower the fuel bills will be.

*Sample environmental impact rating table**

Environmental (CO2) Impact rating Very environmentally friendly = lower CO2 emissions Not environmentally friendly = higher CO2 emissions		
	Current	Potential
(92-100) A		
(81-91) B		
(69-80) C		
(55-68) D		67
(39-54) E	49	
(21-38) F		
(1-20) G		
UK 2007 Directive 2002/91/EC		

The environmental impact rating is a measure of a home's impact on the environment in terms of Carbon Dioxide emissions. The higher the rating, the less impact it has on the environment.

The Energy Performance Certificate will also include a table showing the estimated energy use for the property. The table will give an indication of the typical cost to heat and light the property. It is important to check the date of the certificate as fuel prices are liable to increase and an old certificate may underestimate the true amount of fuel costs for the property.

Sample Energy use table *

	Current	Potential
Energy use	249 KWh/m2 per year	200 KWh/m2 per year
CO_2 emissions	3.40 tonnes per year	2.38 tonnes per year
Lighting	£30 per year	£27 per year
Heating	£220 per year	£180 per year
Hot Water	£45 per year	£42 per year

The Energy Performance Certificate includes a summary of the property's energy performance related features and gives an assessment of the key elements, showing how they impact on the performance rating. Each element is given a rating as follows: Very Poor/Poor/Average/Good/Very good.

Sample Energy Performance Certificate summary form *

Element	Description	Current performance
Main walls	Cavity	Good
Main roof	Pitched, no loft insulation	Poor
Main floor	Wooden floorboards/insulated	Good
Windows	Part double glazed	Average
Main heating	Mains gas boiler	Average
Main heating controls	Programmer	n/a
Secondary heating	None	n/a
Hot water	From main	n/a
Lighting	No low energy lighting	Poor
Current energy efficiency rating		D55
Current environmental impact rating		D57

The report will include a table of recommended measures to improve the property's performance ratings. The most cost-effective measures are highlighted in the report and they appear in the table in order of importance.

Sample recommended measures table *

Lower cost measures (up to £500)	Performance ratings after improvement		
	Typical savings	Energy efficiency	Environmental impact
1. Put 150mm jacket on hot water cylinder	£25 per year	D:60	D:58
2. Install loft insulation to 250mm	£10 per year	D:62	D:60
Higher cost measures over £500			
3. Double glaze single glazed windows	£25 per year	C:70	C:70
Potential energy efficient rating			C70
Potential environmental impact rating			C71

*The figures given in the tables are for illustration purposes only.

Further measures section
This section discusses measures which could further improve the energy efficiency of the property such as solar water heating.

About the measures to improve this home's performance ratings
This section includes an explanation of the measures recommended together with estimated costs and advice upon installation.

About this energy inspection
This section of the report provides details of the Home Inspector who has carried out the inspection and an explanation of the training, regulations and legal requirements for the report.

About this home's performance ratings
This section explains the calculations used to obtain the performance ratings so that one property can be fairly compared with another.

This home's impact on the environment
This section explains the impact on the environment of Carbon dioxide and how domestic fuel use contributes towards the distribution of CO_2 into the atmosphere.

What can I do today?
This section advises the property owner what immediate measures can be taken to save energy and reduce carbon emissions e.g.:

◆ Reduce the central heating thermostat to 21 degrees centigrade in living areas.

◆ Use the timer programme to ensure that the property is heated only when necessary.

- Check the thermostat on the hot water cylinder to ensure it is not too high. The suggested temperature is no higher than 60 degrees centigrade/140 Fahrenheit.

- Turn off lights when not in use and don't leave appliances on standby.

When the report is complete

This final section explains what happens to the report when it is complete. Details are given of the central register where the report will be stored and the property owner is advised of the URL and the unique reference number (URN) needed to access the report.

The Home Inspector's contact details, licence number and qualifications are given at the end of the report.

THE HOME CONDITION REPORT (HCR)

The Home Condition Report is an objective report by a qualified Home Inspector on the physical condition of a property and includes an energy efficiency report and Energy Performance Certificate (see above). The purpose of the report is to provide reliable information about the condition of the property and its energy efficiency to the seller, the buyer and the mortgage lender.

The provisions contained in the HIP Regulations guarantee direct legal rights for sellers, buyers and lenders to rely upon the Home Condition Report. This provision means that even where a report has not been prepared or paid for by such persons they will still be able to claim legal redress and financial compensation against the Home Inspector if the report is later found to be negligent.

In order to justify its claims that the HIP will reduce the number of wasted surveys carried out, thus saving consumers money, the Government needs lenders to rely upon the Home Condition Report when considering a property for a mortgage. Currently a mortgage valuation costs on average £250. If lenders were prepared to rely upon the Home Condition Report for the physical inspection of the property and seek only an automated valuation, which costs on average £50, this would lead to savings for their borrowers and mean that only one physical inspection of the property is carried out.

Although some lenders are already using Automated Valuation Models (AVMs) many are not geared up to use this technology as yet. The fact that not all lenders are ready to use AVMs and their general lack of enthusiasm towards the Home Condition Report is one of the reasons that the status of the Home Condition Report was changed from mandatory to voluntary.

A Home Condition Report must not be included in the HIP if it was not completed for the purposes of the sale of the property interest by the seller.

No document may be described as a Home Condition Report unless it complies with the regulations.

The format of the Home Condition Report

The detailed format of the Home Condition Report will not be predetermined in the regulations because the content of the Home Condition Report is expected to vary over time as Home Inspectors gain more knowledge about the processes and as building construction methods change.

The certification schemes (see below) will be responsible for devising an industry standard format for the Home Condition Report. They will be required to provide the Home Condition Report in a common format so that it can be easily understood by the buyer, the seller and the mortgage lender.

Every Home Condition Report will be given a unique reference or code so that it can be easily identified. The report must include the name of the Home Inspector and their office address.

The Home Inspector must state on the report whether they have any personal or business relationship with anyone involved in the sale to avoid the possibility of a conflict of interest.

The regulations prohibit the inclusion of personal data in the report to protect the privacy of individuals. The report is also prohibited from including information that relates to the security of the property that could be misused.

The Home Condition Report register

A Home Condition Report is valid only once it is entered onto a central register. Consumers, using the unique reference number, will be able to check the register to ensure that the Home Condition Report is authentic.

Once registered the Home Condition Report must not be altered. Should an error be found in a Home Condition Report it must be cancelled from the register by the relevant certification scheme.

A Home Condition Report entered on the register must be kept on the register for a period of 15 years.

There is a fee for entering a Home Condition Report on the register which is currently £1.15.

Disclosure of the Home Condition Report

As the Home Condition Report is not a required document the seller may choose not to disclose it to third parties. This regulation applies to any other archive of Home Condition Reports, or information contained from a Home Condition Report whether or not obtained directly from the keeper of the register.

Upon the seller's instructions a Home Inspector may inform the keeper of the register, in writing, that the seller does not wish to disclose the Home Condition Report to:

i)   All persons; or
ii) All mortgage lenders or automated valuation suppliers.

If the seller has authorised that the Home Condition Report may be disclosed to third parties the keeper of the register may require from the person or company seeking disclosure of the Home Condition Report:

◆ Proof of identity.

◆ Details of the report reference number.

◆ Proof of their status as agent, lender, valuer, conveyancer, seller, buyer, certification scheme or company dealing with complaints against Home Inspectors, enforcement officers, Office of Fair Trading.

◆ Proof that disclosure is required for the purposes of the sale of
the property, for mortgage valuation purposes, to deal with a
Home Inspector complaint or to check the authenticity of a
Home Condition Report.

The keeper of the register may disclose the Home Condition
Report to the seller and, with the seller's permission, their agent.
Once the report has been disclosed to the seller they may disclose
it to third parties but the seller's agent may only do so with the
seller's consent.

If the Home Condition Report disclosure is required for the
purposes of prevention of crime or to facilitate legal proceedings
and court orders the keeper of the register or any person may
make a disclosure of the Home Condition Report.

A person who discloses a Home Condition Report in
contravention of the regulations is guilty of an offence and liable
on summary conviction to a fine not exceeding level 5 on the
standard scale (which is currently the sum of £5,000).

THE CERTIFICATION SCHEME

The role of the certification scheme is to set up and manage
proper regulation, training and redress schemes for the Home
Inspector industry. The certification scheme is also responsible for
setting the industry standards and format of the Home Condition
Report and for the central register.

The aim of the scheme must be compatible with protecting the
interests of potential home buyers, sellers and lenders of
residential properties and to promote the reliability and
trustworthiness of its members and the HCR

The standards for the certification scheme have been set by the DCLG, and the Secretary of State is responsible for approving the certification scheme members. There are currently three organisations running approved certification schemes, the Surveyors and Valuers Accreditation body (SAVA), The Building Research Establishment (BRE) and the Royal Institute for Chartered Surveyors (RICS).

The purpose of the certification scheme is to ensure that:

◆ They must ensure that members of the scheme are fit and proper persons who are qualified to produce Home Condition Reports. This process is expected to take approximately six weeks and will involve a rigorous check into the training and background of the Home Inspector, including a criminal records check.

◆ They must ensure that their members have in place suitable indemnity insurance at all times. This is to ensure that consumers are protected and can claim under the insurance where they suffer a loss owing to the Home Inspector's negligence.

◆ They must provide a complaints and redress scheme to resolve complaints against their members.

◆ Their members are qualified by their education, training and experience to produce Home Condition Reports.

◆ For requiring Home Condition Reports made by their members to be entered onto a register kept pursuant to the regulations contained in Section 165 of the Housing Act 2004.

◆ A public register of its members is kept.

- Their members produce a Home Condition Report using a standard form for the type of dwelling-house which is or forms part of the property.

- The standard form used by its members contains a statement regarding the complaints procedure for the resolution of complaints against its members, a statement of the procedures to be followed for the rectifying of any inaccuracies in a particular Home Condition Report, and a numerical scale for rating the conditions within the property.

- For publishing a çode of conduct required of its members.

The schemes will be required to continually monitor and assess their Home Inspector members and to publish a Home Inspector code of conduct to ensure that consumers may safely rely upon the information provided by the Home Inspector in the Home Condition Report. The scheme will also be responsible for ensuring that the content and quality of the Home Condition Reports, prepared by their members, meet the prescribed industry standards.

All Home Inspectors must become a member of such a certification scheme before they are allowed to prepare Home Condition Reports for the public.

THE HOME CONDITION INSPECTION

The Home Condition Inspection is carried out by a Home Inspector in order to produce the Home Condition Report. The inspection will be similar to a mid-range survey such as the current Home Buyers Survey and Valuation. It will not be as detailed as a full structural survey, or a building survey, but will be much more detailed than the current mortgage valuation.

The inspection will be a 'non invasive' inspection. The Home Inspector is not required to lift flooring, move heavy furniture or remove panels or fitted furniture. The inspection will include all areas that can be seen without causing damage and the report will detail any areas it has not been possible to inspect. If further investigation is deemed necessary the Home Inspector will mention this in the report. The inspection will include an investigation for damp.

What the Home Condition Report covers

The Home Condition Report will encompass the exterior and interior of the property including any cellar or attic. The Home Inspector is not required to stand on walls or to enter neighbouring property to carry out the exterior inspection and, where possible, the inspection will be carried out from public areas such as footpaths and open spaces. The examination of the roofs and external walls will be from ground level, using binoculars if appropriate. A ladder, not exceeding 3 metres in height, may be used to inspect flat roofs to single storey buildings. The Home Inspector will assess gutters and down pipes only if there is heavy rain at the time of the inspection.

The inspection of a flat in a block of flats is limited to a non-invasive inspection of the flat and its immediate surrounding area only. It will not include a *detailed* inspection of the rest of the block, but will include a *general* inspection from which the Home Inspector will form an opinion of the condition of the block as a whole.

The Home Inspector will provide information to the conveyancer about the outside and shared parts so that the conveyancer can check that the lease contains adequate repair and maintenance clauses. The inspection will include any shared access/ entrances to the flat and any shared car parking or garage area, but will not include all shared areas to the block.

The Home Inspector will require access to the attic and any cellars and the inspection will include the exterior of the property and the grounds.

What to expect

During the inspection do not be surprised to find the Home Inspector climbing ladders, taking photographs, preparing sketches, lying on the ground to check the damp proof course, turning on taps, flushing the toilet, asking for the heating to be turned on and lifting manhole covers and inspection chambers.

The Home Inspector may ask a lot of questions about the property. Don't be concerned, it is all part of the requirements of the report. At the end of the inspection the Home Inspector must give an objective, unbiased view on the condition of the property.

The Home Inspector may have copies of the results of the legal searches made against the property and, if so, will be able review the results of those searches against the actual physical position on the ground.

The Home Inspector will also note additions, alterations and work to the property and may be able to check the searches for any required planning, building and listed building consents. Any omissions or queries may be referred back to the conveyancer for further investigation.

HIP TIP

The Home Inspector may have the Land Registry plan of the property and the results of the searches. From these the Home Inspector should be able to spot any unauthorised additions or alterations to the property or any discrepancies in the boundaries of the property.

THE HOME INSPECTOR QUALIFICATIONS
The inspection must be carried out by a Home Inspector who has qualified under an approved Certification Scheme and holds an ABBE (the Awarding Body for the Built Environment) Diploma in Home Inspection. All Home Inspectors must carry suitable indemnity insurance and the certification scheme must also carry back-up insurance to protect consumers against uninsured Home Inspectors.

CONDITION RATINGS
If the Home Inspector find any defects or concerns with the property these will be noted in the Home Condition Report and rated according to how serious they are. The condition ratings, known in the industry as 'the good, the bad and the ugly' are:

1. No repair is currently needed. Normal maintenance must be carried out.
2. Repairs or replacements are needed but the Home Inspector does not consider these to be serious or urgent.

3. There are defects which are either serious and/or require urgent repair or replacement.

HIP TIP

All areas inspected will be given a condition rating from 1–3. A condition rating of 3 would indicate a relatively serious or ongoing problem.

Dealing with defects found by the Home Inspection

If defects are found in the property the seller has three options:

◆ **Remedy the defects** – the Home Inspector will call again to inspect the remedy and to document the changes. Any subsequent repairs and guarantees will then be included in the HIP as authorised documents. There may be an additional fee if the Home Inspector has to revisit the property.

◆ **Obtain estimates** – these may be included in the HIP as authorised documents. Potential buyers can then assess this information when putting forward an offer to purchase.

◆ **Ignore it** – the seller can simply ignore the results of the Home Condition Report and market the property 'warts and all'.

THE ENERGY EFFICIENCY REPORT

The Energy Performance Certificate is a required document and from 1 June 2007 must be included in the HIP by law. If the seller is not having a full Home Condition Report then they must obtain a stand-alone Energy Performance Certificate or an Interim Energy Assessment or Predicted Energy Assessment. Climate change is currently at the top of the political agenda and Britain has a duty to comply with EU directive 2002/91/EC (Energy Performance of Buildings Directive) by January 2009. The directive requires all sellers to provide potential buyers with a report revealing how energy efficient their property is.

You can obtain a free energy efficiency check online at *www.est.org.uk*. The Energy Savings Trust is a non-profit organisation funded by the Government and private industry. Their website provides free advice on energy efficiency and enables you to arrange a physical inspection of the property if required. Full contact details are given in the directory at the back of this book.

HIP TIP

The EU directive is designed to make homeowners more responsible for the energy efficiency of their property. Government grants may be available towards the cost of improving the energy efficiency of your home.

THE HOME CONDITION REPORT FORMAT

The Home Condition Report will be read by many people, including first time buyers, who will have no previous experience of buying a property. The aim is to ensure that the Home Condition Report is written in plain English to a standard format so that it is easy to understand and compare (see pages 96–111).

HIP TIP

Details of the methods used to prepare the Energy Efficiency Report can be viewed at www.projects.bre.co.uk/sap2005 (Reduced Data Standard Assessment Procedure: RDSAP) and www.ncm.bre.co.uk (Simplified Building Energy Model: SBEM).

At the end of the report are the following details:

◆ Confirmation that the report will be held on an electronic register and who the register is run by.

◆ Details of where to view the report.

Example format of the Home Condition Report

Section A:

General information

This section includes the standard contract terms of the Home Inspector and describes the Home Inspection. It sets out the role of the Home Inspector and the extent of the Home Condition Report. It explains the areas of the property that the Home Inspector will be reporting on and what the condition ratings mean. This section will also include the name of the certification scheme that has licensed the Home Inspector and will include details of the complaints procedure. Details will include:

◆ address of property inspected;
◆ Home Inspector's name;
◆ Home Inspector's licence number;
◆ company name (if any);
◆ company contact details.

Section B:

Note: this section will be used by mortgage lenders when considering the property for mortgage purposes.

This section includes a summary of information relating to the property, a description of the accommodation, the reinstatement costs for insurance purposes, a summary of the condition ratings and an overview of any defects highlighted in the report including:

◆ date of inspection;
◆ report reference number;
◆ disclosure of conflict of interest;
◆ weather conditions at the time of the inspection;
◆ property furnished/unfurnished;
◆ year of property construction;
◆ year of property extension (if any);
◆ year of property conversion (if any);
◆ type of property;
◆ occupants/tenants living at the property;
◆ area property situated in;
◆ listed/conservation area and listed grade if known.

Flats/maisonettes:
◆ position of flat in the block (i.e. which floor it is on and how many floors in the block);
◆ number of flats in the block;
◆ purpose built flat or converted;
◆ whether there is a lift;
◆ whether any property in the block is being used for commercial use;
◆ if commercial use in the block what percentage and where situated in the block.

Accommodation:
- lists rooms in building and where situated, e.g. first floor;
- gives gross external/internal floor area;
- reinstatement cost.

Construction:
A description of the construction of the building.

Services:
- lists mains services connected to the property;
- states whether there is full or partial central heating and what type.

Outside:
- states whether there is a garage on or off site/integral to the building. Gives details of whether single or double garage;
- states whether there is a carport;
- gives number of allocated parking spaces and whether on or off site;
- states whether there is a garden to the front, side and back;
- states whether there are any outbuildings and if so how many and how they are used;
- states whether the roads and footpaths are made up.

Summary of ratings and condition:
The summary lists each section of the report, identifies the area inspected and gives the condition rating for each area. At the foot of the summary details are given of any widespread problems that affect the property, a summary of structural movement and recommendations for further investigations required.

Section C:
This section includes information collected by the Home Inspector for use by the conveyancer and others. This section also documents health and safety points that need to be brought to the attention of the property owner. These would include:

- roads and footpaths;
- drainage and water;
- planning/other permissions needed;
- covenant consents needed;
- flying freeholds;
- mining;
- rights of way and easements;
- boundaries and party walls;
- liability for repairs to shared areas;
- previous structural repairs;
- new building warranties;
- buildings insurance/ongoing claims;
- tree preservation orders;
- whether the property is let;
- dangerous materials/contaminated land;
- subsidence and flooding;
- health and safety risks.

Section D:

This section lists the parts of the property that the Home Inspector has inspected from the outside and gives a condition rating, justification for the rating and comments. (See checklist below.)

Section E:

This section lists the parts of the property that the Home Inspector has inspected inside the property. Each area will be given a condition rating, a justification for the rating and any comments.

Section F:

This section deals with the services to the property such as gas, electricity, oil, water, heating and drainage. Only those services that are visible will be inspected. Specialist tests will not be carried out and the visual inspection does not include testing to see whether the services work or not. If any services are turned off and cannot be inspected this will be stated in the report. Only the services detailed above will be inspected and any other services including domestic appliances are not tested, e.g. smoke alarms, security equipment, cookers, hobs, washing machines, etc. General safety warnings are given. Each service is given a condition rating, justification for the rating and any comments.

Section G:

In this section the Home Inspector reports on the grounds of the property including any garages and permanent outbuildings, walls, paved areas, shared facilities, detached conservatories and other structures. No inspection is made of any leisure facilities such as tennis courts, swimming pools or non-permanent outbuildings.

Where the property has common or communal facilities these are also reported on here. There are no condition ratings in this section.

Section H:

This section includes the energy report. The Home Inspector will set out how energy efficient the property is and give advice on what measures can be taken to improve energy efficiency. The Home Inspector will take into account levels of thermal insulation, types and efficiency of the heating system including its controls and ventilation of the property. The report will include an energy performance certificate that complies with EU legislation. The certificate will be prepared using a government approved methodology known as Reduced Data Standard Assessment Procedure (RDSAP) for standard homes and Simplified Building Energy Model (SBEM) for larger or more unusual homes.

Signature and Date:

The final report is then signed off by the Home Inspector who undertook the inspection.
The sign off includes the Inspector's licence number, name, qualifications, address and contact details and confirms the report date again.

The Home Condition Report Checklist

Exterior	Common problems to check for	DIY job	Professional job estimate needed
Chimney stacks	Inferior pointing, worn or missing lead flashing, inadequate support.		
Roof coverings	Worn, slipped, missing or damaged slates or tiles and cracks in the roofing felt. Flat roofs have a limited life span and should be replaced every ten to 15 years.		
Roof drainage	Check for worn or blocked gutters. Leaky old cast iron gutters should be replaced with a modern alternative.		
Eaves, fascias and soffits	Wood rot, dilapidated paintwork, bird and wasp nests.		
Main walls	Deterioration in the pointing, cracks in the brickwork or mortar, spalling, cracked or blown plaster. Severe cracks in the brickwork that could indicate structural damage or subsidence.		
Sub-floor ventilation	Check for air bricks which have become blocked over time by soil or vegetation, and ground levels that have risen above the damp-proof course or ventilation bricks.		
Windows	Wood rot, dilapidated paintwork, badly fitting frames and condensation between double glazed panes. Ensure that windows open and shut properly and that window locks and handles are in good working condition.		

Exterior doors	As for windows, plus glazed doors must be of toughened glass as required by current building regulations.
Exterior decoration	Check that exterior paintwork and rendering are in good repair. If exterior windows and doors are stained ensure that they have been recently treated with a wood preservative.
Special features	This will cover any areas that are unique to the property, for instance a balcony.
Interior	
Roof construction	Check for wood rot and timber infestation in the roof beams, inadequate roof felt and lack of insulation.
Ceilings	Check for cracked plaster which may indicate structural movement. Polystyrene tiles are a fire hazard and breach current building regulations.
Walls, partitions and plasterwork	Check for cracked plaster which may indicate structural movement. Check for dampness in walls. More serious problems include the removal of internal walls without sufficient support being installed.
Fireplaces, flues and chimney breasts	Where chimney breasts have been removed or blocked up ensure adequate structural support has been installed. Check for sufficient ventilation, blocked chimneys and lack of flue lining.

Floors	Creaky floorboards can indicate structural movement. Wooden floors can suffer from dry rot, damp and timber infestation.
Basements, cellars and lofts	Check for damp and also for safe access. More serious problems include conversion to dwelling space without planning or building regulations consent.
Windows	As for exterior windows.
Interior doors	As for exterior doors. Current building regulations require that some doors are self-closing or fireproof.
Staircases	Safety issues, e.g. lack of stair rail or banisters, badly maintained stairways, narrow stairways or insufficient ceiling height, open stair treads, poor lighting.
Kitchen	Poor condition, old or broken appliances and badly planned layout.
Sanitary fittings	Leaking pipes, faulty toilet, blockages in sinks or baths, dripping or broken taps, electric installations, such as showers and heaters that do not comply with safety regulations.
Interior décor	Old, dirty or peeling paintwork and wallpaper.

Services

Drainage: the drainage and water search will reveal whether the foul and surface water drain to a public sewer. The Home Inspector will inspect the drainage system, lifting manholes and inspection chambers to inspect any underground system. The report will state whether there is evidence of overflow or blockage by debris or tree roots.

Check for leaks, blocked drains caused by debris or tree roots.

Private drainage

Septic tanks and cesspools will be inspected where access is available. Check for faulty systems that require emptying often, blocked pipes and weeper drains.

Cold water: The drainage and water search will reveal whether the property is connected to the mains water supply and whether there is a water meter. The location of the stopcock will be noted. Any visible storage tanks will be inspected. The pressure flow of the water will be tested, the Home Inspector will check the pipes in the loft to see whether they are correctly installed, supported and insulated. The Home Inspector will check for suitable overflows.

Common problems:
Leaks, poor water pressure, lack of insulation. If the property is not connected to the mains water supply, the water supply must be regularly inspected and certificates of water purity must be provided.

Gas/oil: the Home Inspector will report whether the property is connected to mains gas, liquid petroleum gas or oil. The whereabouts of any meters will be noted. The visible pipe work including its protection and support will be inspected and the Home Inspector will look for signs of DIY installations. The Home Inspector will check for adequate permanent ventilation in rooms with gas fires and open flue boilers.

Common problems: check for insufficient ventilation for gas and water heaters, unsafe appliances. Gas systems and appliances must have been installed or inspected by a CORGI registered engineer. Oil installations should be inspected regularly to protect your home from risk of fire, carbon monoxide poisoning and pollution from leaks. Further information can be obtained from OFTEC (Oil Firing Technical Association). All installation works undertaken after 1 April 2005 should be identified by an OFTEC Certificate or Building Control completion certificate.

Electricity: the Home Inspector will report whether the property is connected to mains electricity and the whereabouts of any meters, the type of fuse board, whether it is old or modern, has rewireable fuses, miniature circuit breakers, whether the electricity cabling is old or modern. If the property has been rewired or had electrical work carried out the Home Inspector will recommend that a NICEIC certificate of completion be provided.

Common problems: old systems can be unsafe, check for two pin plugs, lack of modern circuit breakers, damaged cables, or cables coated in black rubber or lead, lack of earth bonding to the fuse board, gas and water mains.

Hot water/heating: the Home Inspector will advise how the hot water/heating is supplied, including the type and condition of the boiler, whether it is insulated and whether the water is heated via immersion heater or via the central heating system. The Home Inspector will report on whether the visible parts of the system appear in satisfactory condition and whether there is evidence of regular servicing.

Common problems: faulty or leaking boiler and/or hot water tank, faulty immersion heater or thermostat, insufficient lagging, inadequate tank size, system not working effectively and efficiently, faulty or missing room and radiator thermostats, leaky or insufficient number of radiators.

Thermal insulation: the type of insulation will be reported.

Common problems: lack of or inadequate insulation.

Grounds

The site: the Home Inspector will report on the shape and location of the site and whether it is level or sloping. A general overview of the condition of the garden will be given.

Garages: The construction of the garage will be reported upon. The Home Inspector will check whether there is suitable vehicular access to the garage. The overall condition of the garage will be reported on.

Common problems: Faulty garage doors, lack of legal or physical access, poor condition.

Permanent outbuildings: These include conservatories, summerhouses, barns, etc. Where there are permanent outbuildings the fabric and condition will be reported upon.

Common problems: Dilapidated condition, rainwater goods ineffective, lack of planning consent.

External areas/patios/paths: the Home Inspector will report on the construction material of drives, access ways, patios and external areas and give an opinion on condition.

Common problems: Cracked and ruptured drives which can indicate structural problems caused by tree roots. Slippery paths and moss growth can present safety issues.

Retaining walls/earth retaining structures: the Home Inspector will report on the construction material of any retaining walls or structures and provide an opinion on their current condition.

Common problems: bulging walls can suggest structural problems.

Boundaries and fences: The Home Inspector will give an opinion on the boundary demarcation lines, will report on the construction of the boundaries (e.g. fences, hedges, walls) and will give an opinion on their current condition. The Home Inspector will have a Land Registry plan of the property and will be able to report on whether the boundaries are clearly defined on the site and whether there are any anomalies in the plans that need to be referred back to the conveyancer.

Common problems: check for walls/fences in poor condition, inadequate legal definition of boundaries.

Structural risks

Environmental: if an environmental search is made available the Home Inspector will consider this and will report on his findings in relation to the results of the search. At present an environmental search is not a required HIP document and is not therefore mandatory. Most conveyancers recommend that an environmental search is carried out and one may be included in the HIP as an authorised document.

Natural subsidence risk: the Home Inspector will consider the results of any environmental search, if provided, and will report them in the Home Condition Report. The Home Inspector will add their own opinion as to the likelihood of natural subsidence in their summary.

Mining: the Home Inspector will check the environmental search to see whether the property is in a mining area and will report his findings. The results of the local authority search will also be considered. Where the property is in a mining area a mining search may be included in the HIP as an authorised document.

Mineral extractions and quarrying: as for coal mining.

HIP tip: You can obtain a free online environmental check by visiting www.homecheck.co.uk. The results may not be relied upon for commercial purposes and cannot be included in the HIP. It will, however, give you an idea of any potential problems that could crop up in a full search.

Trees: the Home Inspector will check the local authority search for any Tree Preservation Orders. The site will be checked for trees, and whether any trees on the site pose a threat to the structure of the property, or present health and safety issues.

Structural movement: the Home Inspector will give an opinion as to whether the property has been subject to structural movement, whether this is historic and may be ignored, or whether it is ongoing and requires further investigation. The structural risks to the property will be considered, including the type of soil or clay the property is built upon, any trees in the vicinity and any perceived mining risks. The Home Condition Report summary will include a statement on potential risk of future movement.

Damp: an electric moisture meter will be used to test the property for dampness. The Home Inspector will comment on whether there is damp in the property, whether the damp is typical for the age and type of property and whether any further inspection or treatment is advised.

Note: see the separate section on timber and damp on page 112.

Timber defects: the Home Inspector will inspect visible timber in the property and loft areas for infestation by wood boring beetles. They will comment on whether infestation was found and whether any further inspection or treatment is advised. Any other timber defects such as rot will be included.

Note: see the separate section on timber and damp on page 112.

Energy efficiency: the Home Inspector will assess the property and report on how energy efficient it is.

Environmental risks

Flooding: the environmental search, if made, will advise whether the property is situated in a flood plain or an area affected by flooding. The report will detail the findings of the search and the HI will advise whether, in their opinion, the property is at risk from flooding.

Radon and radon protection measures: the environmental and local searches will reveal whether the property is in a radon affected area. If the property is in a radon affected area the report will include advice on what steps need to be taken. Radon is a naturally occurring radioactive gas found in rocks and soil. If radon gas is present in your area it can build up in homes causing a significant risk of lung cancer.

HIP tip: for further information on Radon Gas visit www.defra.gov.uk. There are simple measures to prevent the build up of radon gas in homes and a government grant may be available.

Contaminated land assessment: the environmental search will reveal whether the property is in an area likely to be affected by contaminated land. Some local authorities also keep a record of contaminated land. Land may be contaminated in many ways, properties have been built on land that has been found to be dangerous because toxic materials have been used or buried on or under the land.
If the land is not known to be contaminated the environmental search company will provide a certificate to this effect which will be included in the HIP.

Radio masts: the environmental search will report whether there is a radio mast in the area and whether it is visible from the property.

Statutory and other risks: the local authority search will include entries relating to planning law, including planning and building regulations consents and any breaches or enforcement notices registered.

HIP tip: the CLG web site includes a vast amount of information on current Planning and Building Regulations Law. Visit www.communities.gov.uk.

Listed buildings: the Home Inspector will check the search to see whether the building is listed and the results will be recorded in the Home Condition Report. If the building is listed the Home Inspector will consider this when carrying out the inspection and will check whether listed building consent has been obtained for any alterations to the property.

HIP tip: for advice on listed buildings visit: www.heritage.co.uk or www.culture.gov.uk. Your local authority will also be able to offer advice on listed buildings.

Conservation area: The local authority search will reveal whether the property is in a conservation area. If it is, planning restrictions will apply to the property, particularly in relation to alterations to the exterior of the property. The Home Inspector will consider this when inspecting the property.

HIP tip: For further information on conservation areas visit www.opsi.gov.uk. Your local authority will also be able to offer advice on conservation areas.

Party Wall Act 1996: Since 1 July 1997 this Act has obliged any person undertaking works of a structural nature to, or near, a party wall, such as installation of beams, damp proof course or other structural works, to notify all adjoining owners, irrespective of whether planning permission has been applied for or granted.

HIP tip: works undertaken prior to 1 July 1997 are exempt from the legislation contained in the Party Wall Act 1996.

Roads: the local authority search will reveal whether the road onto which the property abuts is adopted and maintained by the local authority. If access to the property is gained via an unadopted or private road the Home Inspector will refer this to the conveyancer to check that there is legal access to the property and adequate maintenance provisions for the upkeep of the road.

Rights of way: the local authority search will reveal whether the property is affected by any registered public footpaths, bridleways or roads used as a public footpath. The results will be listed in the report. The Home Inspector will check for any evidence of rights of way being exercised over the property that are not documented in the search and will refer his findings back to the conveyancer.

- What to do in the event of a complaint.

- What to do if you are the seller and believe that the report is incorrect.

THE HOME CONDITION REPORT AND SELLERS

The Home Condition Report will cover the areas laid out in the left hand column of the Home Condition Report checklist on pages 99–111. Use the checklist to inspect your property before the Home Condition Report is done and to draw up a schedule of work required to put the property into good condition before the Home Inspector calls.

TIMBER AND DAMP PROBLEMS

It can be difficult to tell whether your property suffers from damp or timber infestation as the problem is not always visible.

Damp

The most common cause of damp in buildings is condensation. Older buildings may be affected by rising damp where water from the ground rises up through the walls by capillary action. Damp can also be caused by rain penetrating into the property because of faulty guttering, leaking roofs or badly fitting doors and windows.

Treatment of rising damp
This usually involves the installation of a chemical damp proof course (DPC) which is injected into the walls. This work can be carried out only in a property which has suitable cavity walls. The old plaster must be removed and once the new damp proof course has been inserted the walls must be replastered using special salt retardant plaster.

Treatment of penetrative damp
This will involve identifying the problem, e.g. leaking roof, faulty guttering etc. and rectifying it. The affected area must then be allowed to dry out and may need to be treated with a suitable sealant.

Treatment of condensation
This is a more complex issue. You must first rule out other causes of damp which may be creating moisture within the building. Once you have rectified any rising damp or penetrative damp problems and condensation persists you will need to:

- Ventilate the bathroom immediately after a shower or bath by opening a window to the outside. Close the door to the rest of the house.

- Ventilate the kitchen when cooking in the same way as above.

- Do not dry clothes indoors and ensure tumble dryers are properly vented.

- If you must dry clothes indoors, ventilate the room by opening a window or door.

- Consider installing an extractor in the kitchen and bathroom where most moisture occurs.

- Changing fuel may help. Paraffin heaters cause the most condensation while electric heating is the driest.

- A domestic dehumidifier will help by removing water from the air.

- If the property is not double glazed consider installing secondary glazing or new double glazing.

- Install adequate roof insulation.

Timber problems

Woodworm

This is common in older properties and is caused by wood boring beetles. There are three types of woodworm in the UK the most common of which is the Furniture beetle. This type of beetle attacks softwoods and the attacks leave tiny holes in the surface of the wood. You may also spot small piles of dust on the affected timber.

The second type of beetle is the House Longhorn beetle which is rare in the UK, but is found in some parts of north Surrey. It is mostly found in softwood roof timbers and an attack can result in structural weakness. This beetle leaves a larger hole than the Furniture beetle.

The third type of wood boring beetle is the Deathwatch beetle which is common in the south of England. This beetle will develop rapidly in damp and decaying conditions, and affects both hardwood and softwood. Treatment for woodworm involves spraying the affected areas with a chemical spray or treating with a paste. This can be carried out as a DIY project or by a specialist company. Mortgage lenders will usually insist that any woodworm is treated by a specialist, and that a suitable guarantee is obtained and placed with the deeds.

Wet rot
Wet rot is caused by moisture penetrating into the timber. Exterior timber that has not been treated with a wood preservative or painted will soon rot. Interior timber can also be affected by damp, wet and condensation. To avoid wet rot it is important to treat timber regularly with an appropriate wood preservative or to paint it. Treatment will involve removing the rotten area, replacing it and then treating with an appropriate preservative, or painting it to avoid reoccurrence of the problem.

Dry rot
Dry rot is the most serious type of timber problem and is caused by a fungus. The affected timber will crack and may smell musty. Common problem areas are under floorboards and in chimney breasts where the problem may remain hidden for some time. Treatment is expensive as the affected wood must be completely removed and replaced. Adjacent areas must also be treated with a preservative to prevent the problem reoccurring.

Timber, damp reports and guarantees
If your property is an older one and you do not have a current timber and damp guarantee, you would be wise to obtain a specialist report and estimate before any Home Condition Report or Survey is carried out. The Home Inspector or surveyor will

almost certainly recommend in their report that a timber and damp inspection be carried out and if you can produce one at the inspection this will avoid delays. A timber and damp specialist company will usually provide a report and estimate free of charge.

THE HOME CONDITION REPORT AND BUYERS

Questions have been raised by industry stakeholders and the press as to whether buyers will feel confident enough to rely upon the results of a Home Condition Report that has been ordered and paid for by the seller.

In reality, the majority of buyers will be better informed with a Home Condition Report and will be entitled to seek damages from the Home Inspector for any problems which arise at a later date that should have been dealt with in the Home Condition Report. Currently around 80% of buyers do not have a detailed survey, choosing instead to rely upon their lender's standard mortgage valuation. The majority of buyers do not realise that the mortgage valuation, which typically costs in the region of £250, is often a cursory inspection at best and sometimes just a drive-by exercise. The mortgage valuation is carried out on behalf of the lender to ensure that the property is of sufficient worth to offer security for the loan the lender is considering. Valuers acting on behalf of the lender have a duty only to the lender and if a problem occurs later on it is only the lender that has the right of redress or compensation.

Most borrowers do not realise that, although they are obliged to pay for the lender's mortgage valuation, they are not entitled to claim damages from the lender or their surveyor if it later transpires that the survey was negligent.

All Home Inspectors must have suitable insurance to cover them against this potential liability. The certifying body must also carry 'insurance of last resort' to protect buyers from uninsured Home Inspectors.

The buyer and their lender have the same legal right to rely on the Home Condition Report as though they had personally commissioned and paid for it. However, the buyer is not legally obliged to rely upon the Home Condition Report and may still request a private survey or other inspections of the property if desired.

It is important to ensure that the Home Inspector is ABBE qualified and a member of one of the approved certifying schemes: see the directory at the end of the book for a list or check the member's register on the National Association of Home Inspectors' website *www.nalhi.org.uk*

HIP TIP

A buyer and their lender can rely on the results of the Home Condition Report in law and can seek legal redress and financial compensation from the Home Inspector for any negligence.

THE HOME CONDITION REPORT AND LENDERS

The Home Condition Report does not currently include a valuation of the property. Where the buyer is obtaining mortgage or loan finance the lender will still insist upon an additional mortgage valuation. Lenders will, with the seller's consent, be able to view the Home Condition Report which will be stored on a secure database. The results of the Home Condition Report may affect the lender's valuation of the property or their decision to lend at all. Lenders may insist on property 'defects' being rectified before proceeding to advance mortgage funds.

It is envisaged that Home Inspectors will eventually be able to take further qualifications to enable them to provide a property valuation at the same time as the Home Condition Report.

3

Property Sellers and the New HIP Law

THE EFFECT OF THE HIP ON SELLERS

The main effect of the HIP on sellers is that following its introduction, home owners will no longer be able to place their property on the market without incurring any up front costs. Traditionally, sellers have been able to market their property with estate agents on a 'no sale, no fee' basis. This fee arrangement meant that sellers could place their property on estate agents books merely to 'test the market'.

From 1 June 2007 homeowners must have a HIP in place before marketing their property. The HIP must include the required documents and may also contain the authorised documents (see Chapter 1 for a list of required and authorised documents). The cost of a basic HIP without a full Home Condition Report is likely to be in the region of £300–£400 and the cost of a HIP with a full Home Condition Report is likely to be in the region of £650–£850. The price of the individual HIP will depend upon the supplier, the location of the property and whether it is freehold/ leasehold or commonhold. It will cost more to provide a HIP for a large property, as it will take longer to inspect, and for leasehold/commonhold properties, as are there are many more documents to obtain.

It is expected that estate agents will continue to work on the same 'no sale, no fee' arrangement but sellers will incur the up front cost of the HIP when they put their property on the market. Some agents and HIP providers will allow the seller to defer the cost of the HIP until the sale is complete or, if the property does not sell, until it is withdrawn from the market. If a property fails to sell, and the seller withdraws it from the market, the seller stands to lose the cost of the HIP.

The HIP Regulations do not make the inclusion of a Home Condition Report mandatory. However, those sellers who do not include a Home Condition Report in their HIP may find that they are at a disadvantage when selling their homes. Research has shown that buyers are more likely to opt for properties that have a full HIP including the Home Condition Report.

Initial findings from the dry run, which is currently taking place to test the effect of the HIP and the full Home Condition Report, show that buyers like having this information before making an offer to buy. Independent feedback from the trials has revealed that buyers proceed more confidently and believe that the seller, having paid for the full HIP, is more committed to the sale. The findings also show that the HIP is reducing the amount of time taken from initial offer to exchange of contracts by 3–5 days.

Those sellers who choose to include a Home Condition Report in their HIP would be wise to ensure that their property is in tip top condition before the home inspection. The Home Condition Report is an in-depth inspection that will uncover any faults and defects in the property. Potential buyers will with the seller's consent be provided with the report free of charge and, if it reveals that the property is in poor condition, they may offer less than the asking price or they may be deterred from making an offer at all.

Sellers who intend to market their property with the benefit of a Home Condition Report will need to literally 'put their house in order' if they want to achieve their asking price. The first thing to do is to assess the condition of the property by using the check list contained in Chapter 2. Sellers who do not feel confident enough to make their own assessment should employ a general builder to give an opinion. During the assessment make a list of any defects or repairs that are required and obtain estimates from a professional builder or tradesman for any work that you are unable to tackle. Following the introduction of the HIP reliable tradesmen will be more in demand than ever before. Chapter 5 explains how to go about finding and employing reliable tradesmen.

Exempt properties

Many businesses and commercial sales will be exempt from the HIP Regulations. See Chapter 1 for a full list of the exemptions. It is important that you take professional legal advice before marketing your property without a HIP.

PREPARING FOR THE HOME CONDITION REPORT

It makes sense for a number of reasons to ensure that your property is in tip-top condition before the Home Inspector arrives. First impressions count and a good Home Condition Report will enable you to get the property on to the market more quickly and ensure it is well received by potential buyers. By putting the property into good repair before the Home Inspection you will also avoid the cost and inconvenience of subsequent reinspections.

Use the checklist in Chapter 2 to make a thorough inspection of your property both outside and inside. Note any areas that need repair or redecoration and consider whether this is a DIY or a professional job. Make a list of jobs that require a professional and a separate list for the DIY jobs which you can tackle yourself. Tackle only the jobs that you feel competent to handle. Nothing gives a worse impression than a botched DIY job.

If you are not confident in your ability to inspect your property it would be wise to arrange for a suitably qualified tradesman to give a professional opinion and to provide an estimate for any necessary works. Most tradesmen will offer this service for free and you should check this before arranging the appointment. Always obtain several opinions before proceeding. Chapter 5 gives advice on how to obtain estimates and choose reliable tradesmen.

Once you have made your inspection and obtained any estimates needed you have the choice of having the work done before marketing the property, or including the estimates in the HIP.

Estimates and repairs

Whilst it is galling to have to spend money on a property that you are selling, do bear in mind that a property that is in need of updating, repair or maintenance will create an unfavourable impression with the Home Inspector and prospective buyers.

The Home Condition Report will include full details of any defects or problems in the property. Buyers who have never seen a detailed survey are likely to be scared off by a property that has a long list of faults and potential health hazards. As a result you may find it much harder to sell a property with a poor Home Condition Report. The average buyer has little idea how much repair and maintenance work costs. Without estimates to guide them they may put forward unreasonably low offers or decide that there is too much work to do and not put an offer forward at all.

You must also bear in mind the fact that the buyer's mortgage lender may see the Home Condition Report. If it is unfavourable this could affect their valuation of the property and the amount they are prepared to lend on it.

By doing your homework, and producing estimates with your HIP, the buyer and their mortgage lender can see exactly how much it will cost to put the property into good repair and can take this into account when making an offer. Including estimates in the HIP may also save time and prevent delays later on in the transaction because, even where the buyer is happy to proceed without estimates, their lender may ask for them as a condition of the mortgage offer.

There is currently no legal requirement or obligation for you to put your property into good repair before selling it, or to obtain estimates for any work that needs to be done. You retain the option to market the property exactly as it stands.

PUTTING THE HIP TOGETHER

In addition to the Home Condition Report the HIP comprises a number of documents that may be in your possession or with your deeds. Try to collate as much of the following information as possible to pass to your HIP provider.

The title deeds

Prior to 2003 if a property was mortgaged, you could be certain that the mortgage lender would be holding the deeds. Since

December 2003 this is no longer the case and most lenders do not hold the title deeds for registered property. After December 2003 lenders either returned the title deeds to their borrowers for safe keeping or in some instances destroyed them.

If you don't have a mortgage on your property, and you don't hold the deeds yourself, you may find that your conveyancer has stored the deeds for you in their offices. If the property is a registered freehold the deeds will consist of a Land Certificate or a Charge Certificate. If the property is unregistered the deeds will consist of a bundle of legal documents including conveyances and mortgages. Quite often the deeds bundle includes vital information required by a buyer's conveyancer including leasehold documents, planning and building regulations consents, guarantees, road and drainage agreements etc. It is important that you give everything in your possession to your conveyancer or the company that will be preparing your HIP.

It is rare these days that property is not registered with the Land Registry, but if that is the case your conveyancer or HIP provider will need you to provide the original title deeds, or details of their whereabouts, including your mortgage account number if the deeds are held by your mortgage lender.

Note: if your deeds are held by a lender, your bank or your conveyancer you will need to write to them giving your consent for the deeds to be sent to your conveyancer or HIP provider.

Official copies of the register

If your property has been registered at the Land Registry your conveyancer or HIP provider must obtain official copies of the register and a copy of the filed plan. They will need you to provide the land registry title number. If you are unable to do so they can obtain this information from the Land Registry.

Planning documents

These may be held with the deeds. If you have altered or extended the property since you purchased it you should have the planning documents in your possession. Your local authority will be able to tell you what planning permissions and consents are registered against the property and will provide copies of any that are missing, for a small fee.

Guarantees and warranties

Any guarantees or warranties that relate to the property should be included in the HIP as authorised documents. These may include a new home warranty, timber and damp guarantees, central heating/boiler guarantees, double glazing guarantees, etc. You will be asked to provide the complete documentation required under the guarantee. This may mean providing the original specifications, order and proof of purchase or receipt.

Commonhold and leasehold properties

See the list provided in Chapter 1. Collate all the information in your possession. Your conveyancer or HIP provider will need to know the contact details of your landlord, management company or commonhold association.

Note: it is important that you ensure that your ground rent and maintenance charge are paid up to date as you will be asked to provide evidence of this.

THE HOME CONTENTS FORM/FIXTURES AND FITTINGS LIST

The Home Contents form/Fixtures and Fittings form, is usually of great interest to potential buyers. It comprises a list of everything at the property that is classed as a fixture or fitting. You simply tick a box to indicate whether the item is included, excluded, non-existent or available for sale by negotiation. Buyers do not usually want the expense of fitting new carpets and curtains and it can be a selling point if these are included. The Home Contents Form/ Fixtures and Fittings List may be included in the HIP as an authorised document.

THE PROPERTY USE FORM/PROPERTY INFORMATION FORM

The Property Use form/Property Information form/Preliminary Enquiries, is designed to be completed by the property owner. The form contains information regarding the property such as alterations or extensions, occupants, neighbour disputes, boundary responsibilities, rights of way, etc. The form which is an authorised HIP document should be completed as fully as possible as it will be required as part of the conveyancing process. It may take you time to collate all the information required.

Although the HIP law does not oblige you to include completed forms in the pack it would save considerable time later on if you were to do so.

HIP TIP

By completing the Property Use form fully and accurately, and including all the necessary enclosures, you will speed up your conveyancing.

CHOOSING A HIP PROVIDER

When choosing a HIP provider you should consider the quality of the finished product, the time it will take to prepare and the final cost. You must also consider whether the choice of HIP provider affects your ability to change your estate agent or conveyancer if you decide you are unhappy with their services.

The HIP can be delivered in various formats including paper, CD Rom, memory stick and on a secure website. The latter three are convenient from the agent's point of view as they will reduce storage and copying charges. However, not all potential buyers have access to computers or the internet and it is thought that many computers will not have the memory required to download the packs. It is important to choose a HIP provider that will be able to supply a paper copy, as a buyer is entitled to insist upon one.

As a seller you are entitled to stipulate whether you have any conditions that you wish potential buyers to agree to before providing them with a copy of the HIP. You could, for instance, include a condition prohibiting buyers from revealing information contained in the HIP to any third party other than their advisers.

Before ordering a HIP from your chosen provider check the small print in the contract carefully. The quality of the HIP will vary from supplier to supplier, as will the time taken to deliver it.

Remember, as the property owner, you are liable in law to include the correct documentation in the HIP.

What to ask your HIP provider

◆ When payment for the HIP is due.

◆ If the HIP is being provided on a deferred payment basis is there a cut off point for the sale to take place? Some providers may require payment after just three months if completion has not taken place. You could find yourself having to pay for the HIP before the property has been sold.

◆ Whether the contract ties you into the HIP provider for other services. Some agencies provide conveyancing, mortgage and insurance services. Look carefully at the cost and quality of the ancillary services before agreeing to proceed.

◆ Whether they offer an insurance policy that can be taken out to pay for abortive fees if the sale does not proceed to completion.

◆ Whether the contract to provide the HIP restricts your right to market your property elsewhere.

◆ Who has legal ownership of the HIP?

◆ Ask to see examples of HIPs the provider has prepared for other properties.

◆ Whether the contract guarantees a specific delivery time for the HIP to be produced.

◆ Is the HIP provider a member of a trade association such as the Association of HIP Providers (AHIPP)?

◆ The HIP provider will be responsible for storing and copying a number of original deeds and documents relating to your property including deeds, leases, guarantees and planning documents. You should check that they have adequate, fireproof storage facilities and proper professional indemnity insurance.

◆ What formats will the HIP be supplied in?

◆ What security measures will be taken to protect the HIP and your own details? With identity thefts increasing you need to ensure that your personal details will not be released to all and sundry.

Estate agents as HIP providers

The estate agent is an obvious contender to supply the HIP. As selling agents they will be responsible for ensuring the HIP is in place before marketing the property, for storing it and providing copies to potential buyers.

Estate agents may work with local Home Inspectors and conveyancers to provide the HIP in-house. Others will purchase the HIP from a commercial HIP supplier.

To protect consumers the HIP legislation makes it a legal requirement for estate agents to belong to an approved redress scheme. Dissatisfied consumers will be able to seek redress from estate agents for complaints that relate to the HIP. The scheme will award compensation where the complaint is upheld. Estate agents who refuse to join the redress scheme will be banned from trading under the Estate Agents Act 1979.

Solicitors and licensed conveyancers as HIP providers

Many firms of solicitors and licensed conveyancers will seek to provide HIPs to their clients. Legal firms are likely to have a better understanding of the HIP Regulations and more experience in providing the legal documentation required. Their profession naturally calls for attention to detail and they are used to complying with strict legal requirements.

Another plus is that conveyancing firms will usually be on the lenders' mortgage panel and, where deeds are held with the lender they will find it easier to obtain them. They also have a direct on-line route to the Land Registry and most have contracts with property search agencies to obtain searches quickly and inexpensively. Law firms are used to storing data, deeds and documents safely on behalf of clients and usually have a fireproof safe or strong room.

It is compulsory for solicitors and licensed conveyancers to be a member of their regulatory body. For solicitors this is the Law Society and for licensed conveyancers this is the Council of Licensed Conveyancers. It is also compulsory for solicitors and conveyancers to carry professional indemnity insurance.

Law firms may work with local Home Inspectors to prepare the HIP in-house, whilst others will work with commercial HIP providers. The Law Society is to provide a HIP product for solicitors to market to their clients.

Lenders as HIP providers
Mortgage lenders are expected to provide the HIP. Many lenders already offer survey and conveyancing services and the HIP will be a natural progression.

Commercial HIP suppliers

A number of companies have been set up to market the HIP direct to sellers, estate agents and the legal profession. Some of these companies are an alliance of legal firms, search agencies, estate agents and surveyors. Others are simply commercial firms with little experience in the property industry that have seen a potentially lucrative new product to market.

Before proceeding to order a HIP from a commercial HIP supplier you must exert caution. The HIP is a complicated product to prepare and deliver in accordance with the strict regulations surrounding it. You should ensure that the HIP provider belongs to the Association of Home Information Pack Providers (AHIPP) and that they have adequate professional indemnity insurance. Check also whether the HIP provider has any previous experience in the property industry. The HIP will be useful to the parties involved only if it consists of complete and concise documentation. Some HIP providers may provide a very basic HIP that will consist of little more than an expensive, decorative folder full of blank forms.

PAYING FOR THE HIP

Currently most estate agents and many conveyancers operate on a 'no sale no fee' basis. This method of charging allows sellers to place a property on the market without incurring any up front costs or financial liabilities. If the property fails to attract a buyer, or the seller withdraws the property from the market the estate agent will not charge a fee.

Before the HIP the burden of up front costs was borne by the buyer. With the advent of the HIP that is set to change and homeowners will no longer be allowed to market their property without immediately incurring the cost of the HIP.

There is no fixed price for the HIP, but it is estimated that it will cost in the region of £300–£400 without a Home Condition Report and £650–£800 with a Home Condition Report. The price will vary depending on the size of the property and whether it is freehold or leasehold. Each property is different and there will be many reasons for price variations. For instance, larger properties will cost more to inspect and leasehold properties require a great deal more documentation than freehold properties.

Competition to supply the HIP will be fierce and you should shop around for a HIP provider in the same way that you would shop around for a conveyancer or an estate agent.

Negative equity and financial hardship
Negative equity occurs when the amount required to repay the loan(s) on the property added to the selling costs exceed the amount you expect to sell the property for.

The cost of the HIP will significantly increase your sale costs. Before setting a market price it is important to check that the price you hope to achieve will be sufficient to repay all the mortgages and loans secured on the property, and to pay for your HIP and your legal costs.

To work out how much equity you have in your property you will need to obtain a mortgage redemption statement from your lender. You will also have to obtain a valuation of your property from a valuer or estate agent. The difference between the potential sale price and the amount owed on the property is called 'the equity'. You must ensure that you have enough equity, i.e. money left over after you have paid off the mortgage to pay your estate agent's fees, your HIP costs and your legal fees. See below for examples of positive equity (i.e. sufficient funds to sell the house and pay all the bills) and negative equity (i.e. insufficient funds to sell the house and pay all the bills):

Example A – positive equity

Sale price	£100,000
Less:	
Mortgage repayment	£ 95,000
Estate agent's fee	£ 2,000
Conveyancing fee	£ 500
HIP cost	£ 700
Total	£ 98,200
Equity	**£ 1,800**

The above example shows that this seller will realise enough money from the sale to pay off their mortgage and all costs.

Example B – negative equity

Sale price	£ 95,000
Less:	
Mortgage repayment	£ 95,200
Estate agent's fee	£ 2,000
Conveyancing fee	£ 500
HIP cost	£ 700
Total	£ 98,400
Negative equity	**£ 3,400**

The unlucky seller in example B has negative equity. If they want to proceed with the sale of their property they must find £3,400 from their own funds to pay off the balance of their mortgage and their selling fees.

The current HIP Regulations do not contain any exemptions for hardship. You may not sell your property without repaying all mortgages, loans and financial charges secured upon it. If you find yourself in negative equity and are forced to proceed with your sale try to negotiate with your lender(s) to allow you to sell the property and pay the shortfall back over a period of time. Alternatively, you will need to pay the shortfall from savings or by raising an unsecured loan.

HIP TIP

If you are in negative equity and can't afford to pay for a HIP speak to your mortgage lender. They may allow you to sell the property and repay the shortfall as an unsecured loan. The Citizens' Advice Bureau will be able to advise you with regard to debt problems. You will find the number in the directory at the back of this book.

PUTTING A PROPERTY ON THE MARKET

After the new HIP law comes into force on 1 June 2007 home-owners will not be allowed to advertise their property for sale, unless it is exempt from the HIP Regulations (see Chapter 1), either privately or through a selling agent, until the HIP is in place. Prior to 1 June 2007 sellers can market their property immediately either privately or via an estate agent.

Sellers who are marketing via an estate agent must wait for the HIP to be prepared, during which time the property must not be

marketed or advertised in any way. Sellers may, however, sell the
property privately provided that it is not placed on the open
market (see Chapter 1 – exemptions for private sales).

Delays in getting the property on to the market could mean that
you miss out on 'hot' buyers who are ready and able to proceed
immediately. Estate agents often have buyers queuing for property
in a particular area or for a particular type. In the past the agent
would have telephoned these buyers immediately they knew that a
property was coming on to the market. Occasionally, a sale would
be tied up even before the estate agent had prepared the property
details or advertised it. After the HIP is introduced proactive
agents will have their hands tied by red tape and any attempt to
inform potential buyers that a desirable property is coming onto
the market could result in that agent being banned from trading.

Will the HIP cause delays?
The majority of property professionals predict that the HIP will
cause a delay in getting a property to market.

Some HIP providers are forecasting that they will be able to
deliver a HIP on a registered freehold property within 3-5 days.
However, early results from the ongoing HIP trials have revealed
that the HIP is taking on average 14 days to prepare and up to 4
weeks in some areas. The reasons for the delay are mainly the
time taken to obtain the local authority search and delays in
obtaining leasehold documents. The Government is working with
local authorities to ensure that searches are produced promptly
and is also encouraging the use of personal search agencies. Until
these problems are resolved the Government has announced
transitional arrangements to allow properties to be marketed
without certain required documents (see Chapter 1).

Sellers can do much to speed up the delivery of the HIP by ensuring that they provide timely and accurate information to their conveyancer or HIP provider.

Selling costs

If you use an estate agent you will still have to pay the estate agent's fee for selling the property. You will also still need to appoint a conveyancer to act for you in the sale of the property and pay their fees for dealing with the conveyancing on the sale. It is unlikely that the basis of payment will change from the existing arrangements and you should still be able to pay most of these fees on legal completion.

Selling a property without an estate agent

If you are lucky enough to sell your property to a friend, neighbour, relative or an existing tenant, provided the property has not been advertised for sale on the open market, you will not have to produce a HIP. This exemption includes landlords such as local authorities and housing associations who are selling to existing tenants.

If you intend to sell your property without using an estate agent, and you advertise the property for sale on the open market you must still have a HIP in place before marketing your property.

Currently, it is relatively simple to sell your property privately without employing an estate agent. All you have to do is put an advertisement in the paper or on the internet, erect a 'For Sale' sign and hope for the best. If a buyer is found the conveyancer then takes over and does the rest.

Following the introduction of the HIP legislation, if you wish to sell privately you must first find a HIP supplier or attempt to put together a HIP yourself. Unless you are legally qualified do not attempt the latter option as the regulations are complex and you are liable to face legal action if you get it wrong. Once you have sourced a reliable HIP provider you are then responsible for supplying the HIP to potential buyers and keeping the HIP up to date. Chapter 6 sets out the ramifications of selling your property privately in more detail.

HIP TIP

You do not need to have a HIP if you sell privately to family, friends or a tenant already in occupation, provided that you have not advertised the property for sale on the open market.

Changing estate agents

Currently, you can change your estate agent if you are unhappy with them. When an estate agent takes your property onto their books they will generally meet the up front costs involved in selling your property. These costs include the initial property appraisal and valuation, preparing the property details, printing and postage costs, advertising and office and staff overheads. Because of this most estate agency contracts stipulate that you must allow them to market the property for a period of time. This can vary from eight weeks upwards. If you are unhappy with your estate agent and want to dismiss them you will have to check the contract you have signed. Once your contract period expires you are entitled to move to another agent. Chapter 6 includes detailed advice on dealing with estate agents.

Post-HIP considerations

Following the introduction of the HIP it may be more difficult to change your estate agent. When you decide to market your property the estate agents will usually be your first port of call. Because of this agents are in a good position to convince you to order your HIP from their agency. If you then proceed with that agent and order a HIP on a deferred payment basis, as outlined above, will you be able to end the contract if you are unhappy? It is likely that the HIP contract will contain a condition obliging you to pay for the HIP immediately if you leave the agent. It is also entirely possible that the contract could contain a clause giving ownership of the HIP to the agent, meaning that if you instructed another agent you would have to start all over again with another HIP.

There is also the consideration that the agent as HIP provider may have control of a number of important documents which belong to you including the lease, title documents, planning documents, guarantees etc. There is no doubt that following the introduction of the HIP there is potential for a disgruntled selling agent to cause considerable inconvenience and difficulty to any client who wishes to move to another agent.

When selling a property post-HIP it will be extremely important to consider the various options open to you when purchasing your HIP and to look very carefully at the small print contained in the HIP contract.

If you have purchased your HIP from your conveyancer or an independent HIP provider you should have no problem taking it with you to another agent. When entering into an agreement to purchase your HIP you should ensure that you retain legal ownership of it.

ABORTIVE SALES

Under the HIP legislation as the seller you are liable to provide a HIP. If you do not subsequently sell your property, or your sale falls through, you will not be able to claim a refund of the cost of the HIP unless you have entered into a 'no sale no fee' contract or have taken out insurance to protect you against this risk.

Research has revealed that many HIP providers intend to offer deferred payment schemes that will allow you to market your property with no up front costs. You must read the small print carefully or get your conveyancer to check it for you, as the schemes vary considerably. Set out below are details of some typical HIP schemes.

- ◆ Deferred payment option – you order the HIP and sign a legally binding credit agreement to pay for it at a later date. If the property has not sold and completed at the end of the deferred period you must pay the HIP provider out of your own pocket.

- ◆ Pay on completion option – you order the HIP and sign a legally binding agreement to pay for it out of the proceeds of sale. The small print may require you to pay for the HIP if you subsequently withdraw the property from the market or if the property does not sell.

- ◆ No sale no fee option – it is likely that only the largest companies will have the resources to offer this option. You order

the HIP and sign a legally binding agreement to pay for the HIP
on completion. If the sale does not proceed the HIP provider
does not get paid. There may be caveats in the small print which
you must read carefully, and the contract may oblige you to buy
other services such as mortgages, insurance, conveyancing and
removals from the supplier.

◆ Payment on delivery – you order the HIP and are obliged to pay
for it upon delivery.

It is still very early days in the HIP market and only the larger,
more organised companies have produced a HIP offering to date.

Withdrawing from the sale before exchange of contracts
The law that relates to making an offer to sell or buy a property
remains unchanged. Provided the initial offer is accepted on a
'subject to contract' basis you may still withdraw from the
transaction for any reason up to the point of unconditional
exchange of contracts. Prior to formal and unconditional
exchange of contracts the party that withdraws has no legal
liability towards the other party.

④

Property Buyers
and the New HIP Law

THE EFFECT OF THE HIP ON BUYERS

Traditionally it has been the buyer's lot to bear the brunt of the cost of property surveys and searches. Buying a property was a little like purchasing a ticket for the lottery, you paid your money and took your chances. Without the certainty of a formal contract you were forced to risk hundreds, sometimes thousands, of pounds on searches and surveys only to find that the purchase could not proceed because of a poor survey or a problem with the legal title.

The advent of the HIP will bring you far more clarity from the outset, and it is hoped that this will mean that fewer transactions fail as a result of survey and legal problems.

Buying a property and the HIP

In a nutshell, the changes the HIP will bring are as follows:

Before the HIP
- ◆ You would put forward an offer to purchase a property with little up front information.

- ◆ Once an offer had been made and accepted, subject to contract, you would then embark on more serious checks of the property, including arranging a survey and appointing a conveyancer to investigate the title to the property and make searches.

- From the moment you made an offer to purchase you would be expected to pay out for conveyancing fees, searches, surveys and mortgage fees. These costs often ran to hundreds of pounds and were not refundable if things went wrong.

- If you decided to proceed without a survey, relying only on a mortgage valuation, you would have had no legal redress against the lender or their valuer if the survey proved to be negligent.

- It was often several weeks down the line before a problem was revealed. By that time you would have invested time and money in the purchase and usually a chain of transactions would be reliant upon you proceeding.

- If, as a result of the problems, you withdrew before exchange of contracts, you lost the money you had spent and the chain collapsed.

- If the seller decided to gazump you or withdraw prior to exchange of contracts, you would lose all the money you had spent and the seller would have lost very little.

After the HIP

- Under the new HIP Regulations you will be entitled to view the HIP before making an offer to purchase. The cost of the HIP is met by the seller. The documents included in the HIP are set out in Chapter 1. The seller may include a Home Condition Report, a type of mid-range survey, in the HIP but is not obliged to do so. The seller or his estate agent are entitled to ask you to prove that you can afford the property and that it is the type of property you are interested in buying before supplying a copy of the HIP.

- You will be given much more information up front at very little cost. The estate agent or supplier of the HIP is entitled to charge you a reasonable fee for copying the HIP.

◆ In most cases the HIP should be available to view as soon as the property is put on the market. Some HIP documents may not be available immediately but the seller or his agent must order them and add them to the HIP as soon as possible (see Chapter 1). The information you receive should enable you to make a more informed offer for the property.

◆ If the HIP includes a Home Condition Report you will be able to check the physical condition of the property. You will also be able to see from the Energy Performance Certificate how much it costs to heat and light the property.

◆ You may be asked to provide evidence of a mortgage or finance before an offer is accepted. This is not compulsory under the new HIP law, but it is expected to be adopted by estate agents as best practice.

◆ If you withdraw from the purchase before exchange of contracts you will not have incurred search costs, as these will have been provided in the HIP. If the seller has chosen to include a Home Condition Report you could also save on survey fees.

◆ Previously, if a property had several interested buyers, each would be paying for separate searches. Once the HIP law is in place the same HIP can be supplied to as many potential buyers as necessary thus avoiding wasted money on duplicate searches.

◆ You will be able rely upon the contents of the HIP including the searches and, if supplied, the Home Condition Report. This means if a search provider or Home Inspector is found to have provided an incorrect or negligent search or report you will be entitled by law seek legal redress and financial compensation.

◆ You will be protected by an estate agents' redress scheme in relation to the HIP, which means that if you suffer loss as a result of an estate agent's breach of the HIP regulations you will be able to claim legal redress and financial compensation.

Buyer's entitlement to a copy of the HIP

Under the new HIP legislation you will be entitled by law to ask the seller or, if they are using one, the selling agent for a copy of the HIP relating to the property. As you will have seen from previous chapters the HIP contains a mine of information, including searches and an Energy Performance Certificate. Prior to the HIP legislation the buyer had to pay for the searches, and their inclusion in the HIP should save you around £150.

You can insist on being given a paper copy of the HIP although you may have to pay a small copying charge. The seller or selling agent is entitled to ask for evidence that you have the means to purchase the property, that it is the type of property you are seeking to purchase and you may be asked to agree to conditions in relation to the supply of the HIP.

Buyer beware

The HIP does not put the burden of proof on the seller and the law remains *caveat emptor*, which means let the buyer beware. It is your responsibility to make the appropriate checks and surveys before proceeding to exchange of contracts. Any offer you put forward on a property must still be made on a strictly subject to contract basis.

The HIP is designed to provide up front information for you to take away and have checked by legal experts, *not* to encourage you to proceed to buy a property without proper legal advice.

MAKING SENSE OF THE HIP

For the first time you will be presented with a HIP consisting of hundreds of pages of legal documents, searches, possibly the Home Condition Report and the Energy Performance Certificate. Legal terminology is often confusing and you may find that you do not understand much of what is written.

If you are concerned about anything you read in the HIP you have the option to take it to an independent conveyancer before making an offer. Remember, the estate agent acts for the seller so you should not rely upon the estate agent's explanations as to the contents of the HIP. The conveyancer will be able to check the contents of the HIP and explain them to you in plain English. They will probably charge a fee for this service, but it is worth the expense if you are planning to pay for additional surveys, or you have to pay a hefty mortgage application fee. By checking in advance for any problems that would prevent the purchase from going ahead you could save yourself hundreds of pounds in wasted valuation and mortgage application fees.

CONTENTS OF THE HIP

The HIP consists of a number of legal documents, searches and the Energy Performance Certificate. The HIP may also include a Home Condition Report, planning permissions, building regulations and consents, guarantees relating to the property, the Home Use Form and the Home Contents Form. The HIP must as a minimum include:

Official copies of the register and of the filed plan

This document is an extract from the Land Registry files and will give the title number of the property, details of who the owners are, details of what mortgages or loans are secured on the property and details of any restrictions or rights that affect the property. The filed plan will show the boundaries of the property edged red. Ownership of the boundaries may be marked with a 'T'.

Things to look out for in the Official copies and filed plan:
The filed plan will show the extent of the property edged in red. You should check that the plan is accurate. Take it with you when you go to view the property. It is important to know which boundaries belong to the property as you will be responsible for maintaining them. The filed plan may show the property boundaries, if not ask the seller which boundaries they have maintained during their ownership. If the plan does not seem accurate advise your conveyancer immediately.

Check the Proprietorship register of the official copies. This will show you who owns the property. If there are adults living at the property, who are not shown as owners in the Proprietorship register, then you should report this to your conveyancer who will arrange for them to sign a document releasing any rights in the property.

The Charges register will reveal any legally binding covenants that affect the property. These can restrict the use of the property and/or the land. For instance, many developers place restrictive covenants on properties that they have built forbidding TV or Satellite aerials, extensions and conservatories and many leases forbid pets.

Epitome of Title

If the property has not yet been registered with the Land Registry all the deeds that prove ownership to the property will be attached to a schedule called an Epitome of Title. This may include conveyances, wills, searches, marriage and death certificates and mortgages or loans. The deeds should show a good root of title at least 15 years old with an unbroken chain of events from the 'root of title deed' to the present day. It is your conveyancer's job to check the title to the property. The main conveyance document should include a full description of the property, details of any rights or restrictions that affect the property, and will usually include a plan showing the property and, if you are lucky, the boundaries that belong to the property.

Things to look out for in an Epitome of Title:
If a plan is included take this with you when you go to view the property and check that it is accurate. Check the ownership of the boundaries with the seller.

Read through the conveyances as they will reveal any restrictive covenants or conditions that restrict the use of the property (see official copies above).

Leasehold and commonhold documents
If the property is leasehold, or commonhold, a copy of the lease and associated documents will be included. See Chapter 1 for a full list. The lease is a lengthy, complicated document that details all the obligations/rights of the landlord and the tenant, and usually lists the restrictions and regulations that affect the property. The lease generally contains provisions for insurance and management of the property and the common parts and will also include a layout plan of the property. The leasehold or commonhold documents will also include information relating to the management of the development, the running costs incurred and the yearly maintenance fees payable by the tenants.

What to look out for in the lease and management/service charge accounts
From the documents supplied you should be able to assess how
much the yearly ground rent and management charges are,
whether the charges are paid up to date by the seller and whether
there are plans for major repair or works to the development that
would increase the charges. Your conveyancer is responsible for
checking the lease and leasehold/commonhold documents.

Searches

As a minimum requirement the HIP will include the local
authority search and a water authority search. It may also include
other searches as listed in Chapter 1. The local authority search
will reveal useful information such as whether the seller has
planning permission for that extension, or building regulation
consent for the loft conversion. You will also be able to see
whether there are any major road proposals planned for the area,
whether the property is a listed building, or is in a conservation
area, etc. You should note that the local authority search covers
only the property and not the surrounding land unless a separate
search is done. If the property is adjacent to open land you will
need to check with the local authority what the plans for that land
are. Your conveyancer is responsible for checking all the searches
and you can ask them to raise additional searches and enquiries if
you wish.

What to look out for in the local search
The search will reveal if the property is in a private or public
road. If the road is public the local authority pays for its
maintenance but if it is a private road the residents must pay for
its maintenance. Road maintenance can be costly and you may
want to find out more from the seller about the costs involved. If
the seller has extended/altered or added to the property the search

should reveal planning permissions and/or building consents. If you notice that the property has been altered or extended recently you should notify your conveyancer. Building regulations consent is also required for most conservatories and even for newly installed double glazing in some instances.

A Sale Statement

This will state the extent of the property being sold and whether there are any conditions that attach to the sale.

An Energy Performance Certificate

The Energy Performance Certificate will advise you how much it will cost to heat and light the property and will give the property an energy rating of A–G (see Chapter 2).

New build properties

With a new build property the HIP will include all of the documents referred to above with the exception of the Energy Performance Certificate. In place of the Energy Performance Certificate the HIP will include either an interim energy assessment or a Predicted Energy Assessment which provide much the same information as the Energy Performance Certificate.

The buyer's responsibility to check the HIP before proceeding

As the law remains 'caveat emptor' you are responsible for making all necessary checks and searches before proceeding to exchange of contracts. The HIP is provided for information purposes only and you must still employ a conveyancer to check the legal title and a surveyor to check the physical condition of the property.

The law remains *caveat emptor* – let the buyer beware. If in doubt the Royal Institute of Chartered Surveyors (RICS) website includes useful information on the types and costs of various surveys. There is also a useful directory of RICS qualified surveyors. Visit www.RICS.org. Full contact details are contained in the directory at the end of this book.

The Home Condition Report and the mortgage lender

Under the new HIP regulations provided the seller has given their consent your mortgage lender will be able to view the Home Condition Report if one has been included in the HIP. As a result they will have much more information about the property condition than they would normally get from a traditional mortgage valuation. A property with a poor Home Condition Report may be given a lower mortgage valuation and consequently this may affect the amount the lender is prepared to lend. If the Home Condition Report reveals defects in the property your lender may request estimates for the work and insist that the work is done before completion of the loan. Alternatively, they may make it a condition of the loan that part of the mortgage advance is retained by them until the work is completed.

Your lender will not, at present, rely upon the HCR as a mortgage valuation. This is because the Home Condition Report does not include a valuation of the property. Your lender will still insist upon a mortgage valuation being carried out. In most cases this will involve a physical inspection of the property by a qualified surveyor, although in some cases where the loan does not exceed 75% of the value of the property the lender may rely upon an automated valuation. As the borrower it will be your responsibility to pay for the mortgage valuation.

The legal content and the searches included in the HIP have always been available to your lender via the conveyancer. The conveyancer must provide the lender with a clear Report on Title before they will release funds.

The Home Condition Report and the buyer

If the Home Condition Report has shown defects in a property the Home Inspector will have given them a condition rating of 1–3 depending on how serious or urgent the problem is. The Home Inspector will also have included a summary of the defects and condition ratings given, and advice on whether problems need urgent attention, are ongoing or have stabilised.

If the Home Condition Report reveals defects in a property that you are interested in, before making an offer you will need to ask the seller or their agent whether the seller intends to remedy the defects or provide estimates for the work that needs to be done. If the seller intends to remedy the defects the property will be reinspected by the Home Inspector to ensure that the work has been carried out properly and any guarantees should be placed with the HIP. If the seller does not intend to remedy the defects, or provide estimates, it will be necessary to obtain estimates yourself before making your offer to purchase. You will need to ask the seller's permission to do this and the estate agent should arrange the necessary appointments.

For details of how to arrange estimates and deal with tradesmen see Chapter 5. Once you are in possession of the estimates you can consider whether you wish to proceed with the purchase at all and, if you do, you can try to negotiate a price which reflects the amount of money you will have to spend to put the property in order.

Remember, your lender may also see the Home Condition Report and the estimates and will take these into account when deciding how much money to lend on the property.

THE COST OF BUYING A HOUSE

You will still require a conveyancer to carry out the conveyancing for you and you would be wise to instruct one as soon as you decide to start looking for a property. You can then ask your conveyancer to check the contents of the HIP for you before putting in your final offer. The deeds can reveal important issues that may affect your decision to proceed with the purchase. For instance some properties have legal restrictions that prevent you from keeping pets, having a satellite dish or altering the property.

The provision of the HIP may save some time, but it is unlikely that it will reduce the standard conveyancing charges. You will also still have to pay for:

◆ Some searches that are not included in the HIP such as land registry searches, bankruptcy searches and any specialist searches the conveyancer advises.

◆ If the required or authorised searches are out of date you will have to pay for them to be renewed or updated.

◆ Land registry fees.

◆ Stamp duty.

◆ Telegraphic transfer fees.

◆ Mortgage valuation and mortgage application fees.

◆ Survey fees if you want an independent survey or if a Home Condition Report is not included in the HIP

Property searches

Some searches, including the local authority search, have a limited shelf life of three months. After that date the searches must be renewed or top-up insurance taken out.

Only the local authority and the water authority searches are required to be included in the HIP. They must not be more than three months old at the First Point of Marketing. However, there is no obligation on the part of the seller to update the searches if they are out of date by the time the property is sold.

In addition to the local authority search and water authority search most conveyancers recommend that an environmental search is carried out. If the property is in a mining area, a mining search will be needed. There are numerous conveyancing searches, and it depends on the type of property and its location as to which searches are necessary.

If the searches are out of date, or insufficient, further searches may be required. Your conveyancer will provide you with an estimate which will include details of the necessary searches and their costs.

Mortgage costs

As stated above the Home Condition Report, if provided, will not contain a valuation of the property and your lender will probably require a separate mortgage valuation. This may be by means of a traditional physical inspection or, if the loan is less than 75% of the purchase price, the lender may rely upon an automated valuation. Details will be provided when you complete your mortgage application. You will be expected to pay the cost of the mortgage valuation and any mortgage application fees.

Abortive purchases

The idea behind the HIP is to reduce the number of transactions that do not proceed due to adverse information coming to light after an offer has been made. Buyers will not be legally bound to proceed as long as their offer remains subject to contract. The Government is hoping that fewer transactions will fail because much of the information will be given to the buyer at the outset of the transaction, meaning that there will be fewer reasons for them to withdraw later on.

If you withdraw from the transaction prior to exchange of contracts you would not have any financial or legal liability to the seller. However, you would still have to pay your conveyancer's fees for the abortive work, unless they were working on a 'no sale no fee' basis, plus the cost of any additional searches or disbursements your conveyancer had incurred. You could also lose any mortgage valuation fees or mortgage application fees you have paid.

After contracts are legally and unconditionally exchanged you cannot withdraw from the purchase without serious legal implications and financial loss.

5

Getting Your Property in Order for a HIP

Let's face it, most of us panic when we have to call in a plumber, an electrician or a builder. Television programmes, such as *Watch Dog*, broadcast worrying stories of 'cowboy' tradesmen almost every week, alerting us to con artists who charge extortionate call-out fees or exaggerate the nature of the problem to inflate their bill.

The problem is how, as a layman, can you be certain if the tradesman you choose is genuine and that you really do need a new roof, central heating boiler or a complete rewire? This chapter will show you how to source reliable tradesmen, obtain accurate and honest estimates, and ensure that any work needed is carried out promptly and professionally.

It is hoped that the introduction of the Home Condition Report, albeit voluntary at present, will encourage property owners to put their property into good condition prior to marketing it. The Home Inspector will require evidence that work done to the property, particularly in relation to gas, electricity and heating systems, has been done to a proper standard by a qualified tradesman, meaning that dodgy DIY will no longer be acceptable.

FINDING RELIABLE TRADESMEN
It can be difficult to find good, reliable tradesmen and the best

course is often by word of mouth. Start by asking friends, relatives or neighbours for recommendations. Be prepared to wait for a recommended or quality tradesman, as good tradesmen are in demand and usually booked up weeks in advance.

A good builder or building company will, for a fee, carry out a building survey of your property, and provide you with general advice on its condition and any necessary repairs. Most builders will be able to carry out general repairs to the fabric of the building, including the roof, walls, guttering, doors, woodwork, etc., but you may need specialist companies for services, timber and damp treatment, etc.

HIP TIP

The Federation of Master Builders operates a free Find a Builder service on www.findabuilder.co.uk or phone 08000 152 522. The site covers all tradesmen including roofers, plumbers and general builders.

Choosing a builder

* Always obtain a firm, written quote.

* Don't be afraid to ask for references from past customers and details of their previous work. If the firm is local ask if you can visit previous sites to inspect work done.

* Obtain a quote for their hourly rate for any extra work that may arise.

* Request a firm date for starting and finishing the job. Get it in writing.

* Ask for a copy of their professional insurance cover.

- Check whether they will provide a guarantee for the finished job.

- Check whether the firm is a member of any trade organisation.

- Don't pay cash and try to avoid paying money in advance of completion of work.

- If you have agreed to pay in instalments don't pay until the work is done to your satisfaction.

- Arrange with the foreman to inspect the work carried out at the end of each day and point out anything you are unhappy with.

- If you are having a lot of work done inspect it regularly and draw up a 'snagging' list. This is a list of work that remains to be done or work you are not happy with. Insist the tradesman completes the work on the snagging list before you hand over the final payment.

- Always obtain a written receipt for monies paid.

- Pay on time.

- Ensure the area to be worked on is cleared and tidy. Don't expect the tradesman to clear up after you.

- Builders tend to start and finish early. Check what time they intend to arrive and leave.

- Offer refreshments or leave a tray with tea, coffee, milk and sugar available.

- Make toilet facilities available.

- If there is a lot of work to be done draw up a written contract. This should cover:
    - a full description of the work to be done, including any plans and details of materials agreed upon;

- stipulating who is to provide the materials;
- stating the agreed price, including any VAT, and an hourly rate for any additional work requested;
- start and finish dates;
- details of penalties for breach of contract;
- a schedule of when payments are due;
- actions to be taken in the case of dispute.

The contract should be signed by both parties and dated. Each party should keep a copy of the contract.

Keep all invoices for work and materials, and any planning or building regulations consents. These will need to be placed in the HIP eventually.

HIP TIP

If you intend to have a lot of work done ask the builder to enter into a binding agreement. The website of the Federation of Master Builders at www.fmb.org.uk contains useful advice including specimen building contracts.

PLANNING PERMISSION, BUILDING REGULATIONS, LISTED BUILDINGS AND RESTRICTIVE COVENANTS

Before starting work check with your builder, architect and local authority whether planning permission, listed building consent or building regulations consent are required. One of the most common causes of delay in conveyancing transactions is lack of necessary local authority or restrictive covenant consents for alterations to the property. The Home Inspector will be able to spot if you have had work done and will relay this information back to the conveyancer, who will then ask for the necessary consents. If you have already had work done, but not obtained consent, turn to Chapter 14 which deals with obtaining retrospective consent and/or indemnity insurance.

Many properties have legal restrictions called restrictive covenants imposed on them. These restrictions can prevent you from extending or altering the property. Your conveyancer will advise you whether your deeds contain any legal covenants or restrictions on the property.

TIMBER AND DAMP

Many companies deal with both timber and damp problems. A list of companies that operate nationally is included in the directory at the end of the book. Most will offer to provide the report and estimate for free.

It is important that you obtain at least three opinions from specialist timber and damp companies and an independent opinion from a general builder. Whilst the majority of timber and damp companies are *bona fide* it has been known for companies to advise more treatment than is strictly necessary.

Timber and damp companies will usually give a 25-year guarantee for the work that they have carried out. However, it is important to read the small print and keep all the documentation. When claiming under a timber and damp guarantee you will often be asked to produce the original specification, report and estimate as well as the guarantee. If the timber and damp company have not carried out the subsequent replastering you will also have to provide evidence that the plastering was carried out in the manner recommended in the report, otherwise the guarantee will be invalid. The benefit of the guarantee can usually be passed to a new owner but most companies require that the guarantee be assigned to the new owner on completion of the purchase. This usually involves sending the company a form of assignment document together with a fee.

Choosing a timber and damp specialist

◆ Obtain more than one estimate for any type of work you are considering.

◆ Ask how long the company has been operating. Try to choose one that has a proven track record. Most companies will offer a 25-year guarantee for damp and timber treatment – but this is only of value for as long as the company stays in business. It has been known for companies to operate for a year or two, liquidate the original firm and start up under another name. This makes the company difficult to trace and allows them to avoid their responsibility under the guarantees they have given.

◆ Ask whether the guarantee can be assigned to a new property owner. It is pointless having a guarantee if the incoming owner cannot claim on it. Read the assignment procedure carefully and keep all documents including estimates.

◆ Ask if the company can provide the replastering that will be necessary after work has been completed. This has to be done using a special type of plaster and, unless you can show that the replastering was carried out to the company's specification the guarantee will be invalid.

Check whether you have any guarantees for timber and damp with your deeds. If so ask the original company to reinspect and give a report. If you do hold guarantees for timber and damp you should ensure that the company still exists and that the benefit can be assigned to a buyer, as this question will be raised in pre-contract enquiries.

HIP TIP

When obtaining estimates for timber and damp work check how long the company has operated. Most give 25-year guarantees, but these are worthless if the company ceases to trade.

ENERGY INSTALLATIONS

Electricity

Electrical wiring should be inspected at least every ten years. If you suspect the electrical system in your property is outdated have it checked by a qualified electrician with a National Inspection Council for Electrical Installation Contracting (NICEIC) qualification.

HIP TIP

A list of qualified electrical contractors can be found on the NICEIC website www.niceic.org.uk together with useful advice on saving and using electricity safely.

Gas

Gas installations should be installed by a Confederation for the Registration of Gas Installers (CORGI) qualified gas contractor and a certificate should be supplied to confirm this.

HIP TIP

A list of CORGI contractors can be obtained from the CORGI website www.corgi-gas-safety.com. If you have gas central heating or a gas appliance the Home Inspector will almost certainly recommend a CORGI inspection.

Oil

Oil installations should be installed by and checked by a qualified Oil Fired Technical Association (OFTEC) contractor and a certificate should be supplied to confirm this.

HIP TIP

The OFTEC website www.oftec.co.uk includes a list of OFTEC members. OFTEC members must be trained to Government standards and carry indemnity insurance.

DOORS, WINDOWS AND GLAZING

Since 1 April 2002 building regulations require that all new glazing installations comply with improved thermal performance standards. New glazing products must be installed by a FENSA (Fenestration Self Assessment Scheme) registered installer or a certificate must be obtained from the local authority building control.

Under current building regulations certain windows and doors should be made of toughened glass. Your builder or architect will be able to advise you whether your doors and windows comply with current building regulations. If you have had glazing or a conservatory installed since 1 April 2002 and do not have a FENSA certificate you will need to obtain a certificate from the local authority.

HIP TIP

For a list of FENSA registered companies visit www.fensa.co.uk or the Glass and Glazing Federation at www.ggf.org.uk

ENERGY EFFICIENCY

Information on energy efficiency can be obtained from the Energy Saving Trust. For more details visit their websites www.est.co.uk and www.saveenergy.co.uk. The following are ways to improve the energy efficiency of your property.

Cavity wall insulation

This is the most effective way to save energy and can reduce heat loss through the walls by up to 60%. The insulation is injected into the cavity between the walls and the treatment is quick, efficient and mess free. Cavity wall insulation is relatively inexpensive and a Government grant may be available. You should ensure that the company you use is a member of the Cavity Insulation Guarantee Agency (CIGA). If you use a professional CIGA member the work will be guaranteed for 25 years by CIGA.

HIP TIP

To find a CIGA registered installer and find out about grants visit the CIGA website at www.ciga.co.uk or contact your local Energy Efficiency Advice centre on 0800 512 012.

Loft insulation

By insulating your loft to the recommended depth of 270mm (10 inches) you can save up to a third of your heating costs. It is fairly simple to install loft insulation yourself and the materials can be bought from most DIY stores. Alternatively, your local Energy

Efficiency Advice centre will be able to recommend a reliable installer and advise you whether you are eligible for a grant.

HIP TIP

You can obtain details of your local Energy Efficiency Advice Centre by entering your post code on the Energy Savings Trust website www.est.org.uk or by phoning 0800 915 7722.

Draught proofing

Up to 20% of all heat loss in the average home is through ventilation and draughts. Draught proofing is a simple and easy way to make your home more energy efficient and reduce heating bills. Most DIY stores carry a wide variety of draught proofing products and they are relatively simple to install. There may be grants available to help you pay for the cost of draught proofing: contact your local Energy Efficiency Advice centre as above. If you decide to appoint a professional to install your draught proofing ensure that they are a member of the Draught Proofing Advisory Association Limited.

HIP TIP

For advice on draught proofing products, availability of grants and a local members list contact the Draught Proofing Advisory Association Ltd on 01428 654011, or visit their web site www.dpaa.co.uk

Tank and pipe insulation

Insulation can help to reduce heating bills by keeping water hot for longer. Simply by installing a British Standard jacket to your hot water cylinder you can cut heat loss by up to 75%. These jackets are sold by most DIY stores, and are inexpensive and easy to fit. Your tank jacket should be at least 3″ thick to provide the best insulation.

Double glazing

This reduces heat loss through your windows by up to 50%. If your property does not have double glazing consider fitting it, or installing secondary glazing. For older or period style properties double glazing may not be an option. If this is the case invest in heavy curtains with thermal linings to reduce heat loss through windows.

DRAINS

The property owner is responsible for the private part of the drainage system that runs from the property to the main drain or public sewer. Your local authority is responsible for the public sewerage system. If you live in a row of houses you may share a private drainage system with your neighbours. This will be documented in your deeds, which should contain an obligation on the property owner to keep the drains in good repair and to grant a right of access onto the land for neighbours to carry out repairs.

If you suspect your drains are blocked lift the manhole or inspection cover to check whether you can locate the blockage and clear it. If this does not work you will have to call in a plumber or drainage expert. See the tips below for choosing a reliable plumber. When the problem appears to be with a neighbouring property you will need to notify your neighbours that you think there is a problem and ask them to deal with it. If the drainage is shared there is usually a clause in the deeds obliging all the property owners using that drainage system to pay a proportion of the cost of the repairs.

The local authority is responsible for dealing with problems with the public drains and sewers although they are not responsible for the cost of clearing blockages caused by property owners.

FINDING A RELIABLE PLUMBER

+ Ask friends and relatives for recommendations.

+ The Institute of Plumbing and Heating Engineering has a directory of registered members. You can search for a local registered plumber by entering your post code.

+ Prepare a list of the work you want done and ensure that you give a written copy to the plumber.

+ Try to obtain at least three written quotes. Ask the company to ensure that any call-out fee or additional charges for labour and parts are included.

+ Request a firm start date in writing and ask how long the job will take.

+ Ask whether a guarantee will be provided for the finished job.

+ Ask what the complaints procedure is if things go wrong.

+ Do not pay in cash and ensure that you obtain a written receipt once the work is finished.

HIP TIP

Members of the Institute of Plumbing and Heating Engineering (IPHE) work to a code of professional standards and are vetted by the Institute to ensure that they have the necessary skills and professional standards. Further advice and a directory of members can be found on their web site www.iphe.org.uk

ROOFS

You or your builder may be able to replace or repair the odd slipped tile or cracked slate, but you will need the specialist services of a roofing contractor for more serious work.

How to find and choose a reliable roofing contractor:

- Ask friends and neighbours for recommendations.

- The National Federation of Roofing Contractors Ltd (NFRC) has a member's directory on its website www.nfrc.co.uk

- Try to obtain three written estimates. Check that the cost includes all labour and materials.

- Ask what the hourly rate/travel costs will be if additional work is needed.

- Check whether there is a guarantee for completed work.

- Ask to see a copy of the contractor's public and employee liability insurance.

- Obtain a firm start date in writing and ask how long the job will take.

- Ask whether scaffolding is needed and whether the contractor will provide it. As the property owner you are responsible for obtaining any local authority consent for scaffolding to be erected on the public pavement or road. You must also obtain permission from your neighbour if the scaffolding affects or attaches to neighbouring property.

- Ask what the complaints procedure is if things go wrong.

- Check whether a skip will be needed and whether the contractor will supply this. If the skip has to be deposited on the public pavement or road you must seek permission from the local authority and highways department.

HIP TIP

The National Federation of Roofing Contractors (NFRC) members operate under the Federation's Code of Practice. They vet their members closely and offer a back-up guarantee for work done and have a complaints procedure if things go wrong.

Thatched roofs

These require specialist advice. Properties with thatched roofs are generally listed, so your first port of call should be the Conservation Officer at the local authority. They should be able to supply you with a list of Master Thatchers.

There does not appear to be a national organisation or body for thatchers, but there is a number of regional Thatching County Associations, most of which have standards for their members and dispute procedures. Your local authority or library should be able to provide details of the association for your area.

HIP TIP

For advice on thatched roofs generally the website www.thatch.org provides much useful information, including tips on insurance and local authority grants.

Note: for those who do not have access to the internet, full contact details for all of the organisations mentioned in this chapter are included in the directory at the end of this book.

6

Estate Agents, Property Marketing and HIPs

THE ESTATE AGENCY PROFESSION AND HIPs

The majority of estate agency firms today are made up of qualified and dedicated staff who work long hours in an often frustrating and difficult industry. The introduction of vocational training and qualifications has improved the professional image of estate agency and the services it offers.

Whilst it is still not compulsory for an estate agent to be licensed or belong to a regulatory body, many choose to become a member of one of the voluntary bodies such as the National Association of Estate Agents (NAEA) or the Royal Institute of Chartered Surveyors (RICS). The introduction of HIPs will require all estate agents to belong to a compulsory redress scheme in relation to HIPs.

The way in which estate agents operate will change dramatically after the introduction of HIPs. The main reason for this is that whilst the HIP Regulations make it the property owner's responsibility, to arrange and pay for the HIP, once an agent is appointed they become the 'responsible person' under the regulations and are liable for any breach of the regulations in relation to the HIP.

ESTATE AGENTS' DUTIES UNDER THE HIP REGULATIONS

Estate agents must also become familiar with the HIP Regulations, particularly if they intend to supply the HIP to their clients. When taking a new property onto the market agents will need to be able to advise their clients whether a HIP is required or whether one of the many exemptions apply.

The documents to be included in the HIP must be checked to ensure they are not out of date at the First Point of Marketing and the HIP index must be correctly updated when documents are added or removed. Estate agents must know what documents are required, authorised and prohibited from inclusion in the HIP. They must also be aware of what documents may be removed or replaced from the HIP and those documents that may not be removed from the HIP under any circumstances.

Estate agents will also have to gain a working knowledge of the Home Condition Report and the legal documents contained in the HIP to enable them to respond to queries from potential buyers. Agency staff will need to be trained to copy lengthy legal documents and to accurately reproduce detailed legal plans.

Under the new regulations agents will also be obliged to include the Energy Performance Certificate or, as a minimum, the two Energy Performance graphs on their sales particulars.

Storing and reproducing copies of the HIP

Estate agents will be responsible for storing the HIP and providing copies to potential buyers. Some HIP providers are making provisions for the HIP to be stored on a CD or secure website which will save on storage space. However, the current regulations stipulate that at least one original copy of the HIP is in the possession of the selling agent. The regulations also stipulate that enforcement action can be taken up to six months after the estate agent was responsible for the HIP, meaning that agents must ensure that they store a copy of the HIP for each property that they take on the market for at least six months.

As the HIP will comprise important legal documents of a sensitive and personal nature estate agents must put in place measures to ensure that the HIP is stored in a secure and fireproof way. The estate agent must also judge at what point the HIP is supplied to the buyer and whether to allow potential buyers to take the HIP away with them, or whether to insist that it may only be viewed in the office. For instance, will the HIP be given out to every person who wanders in off the street expressing a vague interest in a property, or will the estate agent insist that the HIP is displayed only to potential buyers who register with the agent and prove identity?

Conditions of providing the HIP to potential buyers
The regulations provide that the estate agent may ask potential buyers for evidence that they can afford the property and that it is the type of property they are interested in buying. The estate agent does not have to provide a copy of the HIP to a potential buyer where it is evident that they could not afford the property, that it is not the type of property they are looking for, or if they know that the seller would not be prepared to sell the property to them. Estate agents will tread a fine line here and must ensure that they do not breach any of the discrimination laws.

The discrimination laws and the HIP

Estate agents will have to put in place new procedures to qualify potential buyers without committing any discrimination offence. A reasonable reason to refuse to supply a copy of the HIP to a potential buyer would be because the property is in a sheltered or retirement development where the buyer has to be of a certain age, or where the property has an agricultural restriction and requires the buyer to have an agricultural occupation. The seller or estate agent must not refuse to supply a copy of the HIP on the grounds of race, sex, age, political or religious reasons, etc.

Time limit to provide an 'authentic' copy of the HIP

Potential buyers and law enforcement agencies are entitled to request a copy of the HIP unless disqualified from doing so as mentioned above. The estate agent cannot refuse to supply a copy of the HIP to a law enforcement agency. The estate agent must produce an authentic copy to the potential buyer within 14 days of the request and to enforcement agencies within seven days from the request.

The copy must be exactly the same as the current original HIP to be an authentic copy and if documents have been removed, amended or updated in the original HIP then the copy must also be updated. The potential buyer can insist upon a paper copy of the HIP and, as 40% of the population still do not own a home computer, it is likely that demand for paper copies will be high.

Protection of the seller when supplying the HIP

Identity theft is a serious problem in the UK today and the information contained in the HIP would be of immense value to this type of criminal. The HIP will contain the seller's full name and address and may contain their partner's name, names and ages of all occupiers at the property, their address and post code, and details of their mortgage lender(s). It could also contain a layout plan of the interior of the property and other details relating to the security of the property, such as whether the property has a security system or alarm. Although the Home Condition Report is prohibited from disclosing personal data or security information relating to the property, this information could be contained in the legal title documents and the Property Use and Home Contents forms. This information is all grist to the criminal mill and estate agents will need to be careful to whom they release it.

The estate agents' redress scheme

For the first time the HIP law makes it a legal requirement for an estate agent to belong to a redress scheme in relation to the HIP. At present only 40% of estate agents are members of the voluntary Ombudsman for Estate Agents Scheme. This has, in the past, made it difficult for consumers to complain or obtain financial compensation against estate agents without resorting to legal action.

The redress scheme will deal with complaints about estate agents relating to acts or omissions in relation to the HIP. This will include any advice given by an estate agent as to whether a HIP is or is not required. The scheme will be able to award financial compensation to consumers where complaints are upheld.

In addition the redress scheme can pass complaints about estate agents to the OFT. This means that estate agents could be banned from trading for serious or persistent breaches of the HIP regulations.

The Estate Agents Act 1979

The estate agency profession is also governed by the Estate Agents Act 1979 which is enforced by the Office of Fair Trading. Among other things the Estate Agents Act 1979 governs how estate agents deal with their clients' property, money, and the way in which properties are described and marketed. An estate agent is no longer allowed to give a false or misleading description of a property.

The estate agent's role

The estate agent plays an important role in the sale or purchase of a property. They are not just responsible for finding a buyer for the property, but also for checking the chain, monitoring progress and helping with problems throughout to ensure that the transaction goes through. A good estate agent will keep up the impetus of a transaction by making regular progress calls to the conveyancers, mortgage lender and clients.

As with most professions there is the occasional rogue agent who hits the headlines and plunges the rest of the profession into disrepute. It is important that you choose your estate agent wisely to avoid pitfalls and problems with your property sale or purchase.

MARKETING YOUR PROPERTY

Before you can market your property you will need to have it valued. Most estate agents will offer to provide this service free and without obligation. Begin by making a shortlist of at least three of your preferred estate agents and obtain a property valuation from each of them.

An estate agent or 'property lister' will visit your home and carry out a valuation inspection. Try to be present during the visit so that you can point out positive aspects of your property such as a south facing garden, a high specification kitchen, proximity to local schools and amenities, etc. Some agents will return to their office to discuss the valuation with colleagues before presenting it to you, whilst others will give you a valuation on the spot and attempt to pressure you into instructing them. Do not be bullied into giving an instruction until you have compared all the valuations and carried out your own research.

Finding out the true value of your property

Valuing property is not an exact science and you may receive widely varying valuations from different agents. When valuing property the estate agent takes into account a number of factors such as:

- current market conditions;
- age of the property;
- condition;
- accommodation;
- locality;
- amenities;
- the price at which a similar property in your area has sold for.

Once a valuation has been reached the agent will generally telephone to advise their opinion on the current market value of your home and will then confirm it in writing. You are not obliged to accept the agent's valuation and it is best to do some homework yourself before deciding upon the market price.

There is a number of ways in which you can obtain information on the potential value of your home:

- Study the local papers to see what price similar property is being marketed for in your area.

- Visit estate agents and ask for copies of details of properties similar to yours in your locality. Ask whether they have sold similar property to yours recently and if so at what price.

- Visit the Land Registry website www.landreg.gov.uk which gives information on house prices based on the sale price at completion.

- There is a number of other websites that give property price information including www.upmystreet.com or www.houseprices.co.uk

HIP TIP

The Land Registry website www.landreg.gov.uk gives information on house prices at the point of completion. This is more accurate than comparing prices on property websites where houses may have been over-priced by the seller or marketing agent.

Once you have received the valuation of your property you need to consider what price you want to market the property for. If you are not in a hurry to sell you may be prepared to wait for a sale and try a higher price than the agent has recommended. Bear in mind that buyers rarely offer the asking price for a property and will usually try a lower offer. If you set the price higher initially and receive no interest you can always reduce the price later on. However, if you set the price too low and are inundated with offers it is far more difficult to increase the asking price.

Some estate agents give inflated valuations in order to win sales instructions. Do not be flattered by the higher valuation, or tempted to place your property with the agent who gives you the highest valuation. You will be disappointed when the property fails to attract interest at the inflated valuation and you are forced to reduce your asking price after several fruitless weeks.

Following the introduction of the HIP this dubious tactic may become less popular with estate agents who are funding the considerable up front cost of the HIP, as it tends to delay sales and lead to disgruntled sellers taking their business elsewhere.

If your property is unusual or unique the estate agent may feel unable to give an accurate valuation and may advise marketing on an 'offers in the region of' or 'offers in excess of' basis.

CHOOSING AN ESTATE AGENT

The best way to choose an agent is by personal recommendation, so ask for recommendations from friends and relatives. Try to choose an estate agent who specialises in your type of property and ensure that they belong to one of the voluntary regulatory schemes outlined in this chapter.

◆ Ask friends and relatives for a recommendation.

◆ The National Association of Estate Agents' website contains a directory of members. You can locate an NAEA member in your area simply by typing in your post code.

◆ Obtain details of all estate agents in your area from the property pages of your local paper or from *Yellow Pages.*

◆ Draw up a list and visit or telephone each agent in turn. Ask to register as a potential buyer and request details of property similar

Estate agent checklist	Estate agent	Marks out of ten
Office		
Is it conveniently located for walk-in trade? Is the window display attractive and up to date? Does the office appear well run and tidy? Were the phones ringing? Did the office equipment and computers appear modern and up to date?		
Staff		
How were you greeted? Were the staff polite, friendly and professional? Did they appear motivated and eager to sell? Were they too pushy? Were they too busy? Did they display any professional qualifications?		
Property particulars		
Were they well presented and easy to read? Did they include a colour photograph? Were they accurate?		
Additional services		
Do they offer additional services such as HIPs, mortgages, insurance and removals? Are these optional?		
Information technology		
Do they advertise property on the internet? Will they email or text details of new property coming on to the market to buyers?		
Local paper		
Do they advertise in the local paper? If so how often? Are the photographs in colour?		
Sold boards		
Check the local area and count the number of sold boards for each agent. This is usually a good indication of how many properties they are selling in your area.		
Complaints procedure		
Do they belong to a regulatory body that will help you if things go wrong?		
Total points scored		

to yours. Some agents specialise in a certain type of property, for instance older or period property, bungalows, flats, etc. If your property does not fall into the estate agent's specialised category cross them off your list. Next, using the checklist opposite, rate each firm on your list with marks out of ten.

ESTATE AGENTS COMPLAINTS PROCEDURE

Estate agents are not currently obliged to belong to a regulatory body. They are governed by the Estate Agents Act 1979 which sets out strict guidelines relating to the agent's conduct when selling property.

There is a number of voluntary regulatory bodies which estate agents may belong to. These include the National Association of Estate Agents (NAEA), the Royal Institute of Chartered Surveyors (RICS), the Ombudsman for Estate Agents (OEA) and the Housing Ombudsman.

The OEA is a voluntary organisation to whom dissatisfied consumers can turn if they experience problems with an OEA member. The OEA can make awards, binding on the agent concerned, of up to £25,000.

The NAEA has campaigned for some time for the mandatory licensing or regulation of estate agencies, but to date the Government has failed to address this issue. Provided you instruct an agent who belongs to one of the regulatory bodies detailed above you will be able to ask that regulatory body to deal with any complaints you may have against the estate agent.

ESTATE AGENTS' CHARGES

Estate agents usually charge a fixed percentage of the sale price achieved plus VAT where applicable. Charges can vary from 1% to 3% and it is worth shopping around before agreeing to a price. If an agent is keen to sell your property they may be prepared to negotiate a discount, or they may offer a discount if you agree to have a 'for sale' board. Most will charge a discounted fee for a sole agency instruction. Do check the small print in the contract as some agents charge additional fees for advertising and brochures.

Generally estate agents work on a 'no sale no fee' basis. Their fee becomes due upon exchange of contracts, although most will wait for payment until legal completion.

ESTATE AGENTS' CONTRACTS

Check the small print before signing as the contract will be legally binding upon you. If in doubt ask your conveyancer to look through it before you sign it.

Contracts vary but should cover the following as a minimum.

Personal interest in the property

Estate agents must by law disclose in writing any personal interest they, or their agency, have in a property that they are marketing or purchasing.

The right to cancel the contract

The contract should state whether you or the estate agent has the right to cancel the contract and under what conditions.

How long you are bound by the contract

The contract should state how long you are bound by it. Agents will require a reasonable length of time to sell the property, usually six to eight weeks. Try not to agree to a longer period than this as it will prevent you from moving to another agent if you are dissatisfied.

Sole agency, sole selling rights and multi-agency

You have a choice when instructing an agent whether to grant that agency the right to sell the property without competition or whether you intend to instruct several agents. Be very careful what you agree to as you could end up paying the agent's fee twice.

Sole agency

When you grant sole agency to the estate agent you are agreeing not to instruct any other estate agent during the term of the contract. If you subsequently instruct another agent during the term of your contract, and the new agent sells the property, you will have to pay both agents a fee. To avoid this ensure the contract has expired before instructing another agent. This does not apply where you sell the property privately. If you find a buyer yourself without an agent you do not have to pay the agent's fees. Many agents collaborate with other firms in the area and share details with other offices. In this way you can obtain the benefit of a multi-agency agreement at sole agency prices.

Sole selling rights

If you grant the estate agent sole selling rights you must pay their fee if the property is sold, by any means, during the term of the contract. Even where the property is sold via another agent or privately to friends, relatives or neighbours you must pay the fee.

To avoid this make sure the contract has expired before instructing another agent or agreeing a private sale.

Multi-agency

With a multiple agency contract you may employ several estate agents to work for you and/or sell the property privately. Only the estate agent who sells the property is entitled to claim payment. If you sell the property privately you are not liable for the agent's fees.

Ready, willing and able purchaser

Beware this term and do not agree to it. It obliges you to pay the agent's fee for finding a buyer who is ready, willing and able to exchange unconditional contracts *even if* you decide you do not want to proceed and you withdraw from the sale before contracts are exchanged.

HIP TIP

Before signing an estate agent's contract ensure you understand it and ask your conveyancer to check it over if you are in doubt. If you move agents make sure the contract period has ended otherwise you could end up paying both agents.

The agent's charges

These should be set out clearly in the contract as a fixed sum, e.g. £1,500 or as a percentage of the sale price. Details of any extra payments such as VAT and any charges for advertising or providing a 'for sale' board should be included.

MARKETING WITH AN ESTATE AGENT

An estate agent may employ one or all of the following methods to sell your property:

- Mailing list – agents keep a register of interested buyers and mail out details of new property coming onto the market each week. Many now text or email new property details to buyers.

- Media advertising – local or national newspaper advertising. Ask if your property will be advertised in the local or national press and how often. This can be made a term of the contract.

- Internet websites – most estate agency firms now belong to an internet property portal and upload property details onto a website. Check if the estate agent will display your property on an internet website and ask how often this is updated.

- 'For sale' boards – generate local and 'drive by' interest.

SELLING YOUR PROPERTY WITHOUT AN ESTATE AGENT

The new HIP legislation will make it more difficult for you to sell your property without an agent. This is because you must be able to provide a copy of the HIP to all potential buyers on demand. If you choose not to instruct an estate agent to sell the property then you alone are responsible for ensuring that the HIP is in place and that authentic copies are available for potential buyers. There are penalties for breaching the HIP Regulations and fixed fines can be enforced.

It will, however, be possible to obtain a HIP from sources other than the estate agent. Many solicitors and conveyancing firms will provide the HIP, lenders may do so and there are companies that have been set up specifically for this purpose. As stated before it cannot be stressed enough that the quality of the HIP is paramount if you are to avoid legal action for breach of the regulations.

Property shops

In the past you would have had the choice of marketing privately, through an estate agent or via one of the property shops that have sprung up on the high street and on the internet. However, the law relating to property shops and companies that claim not to be estate agents, but offer a service to enable sellers to market their homes privately, is being reviewed at present. The Government has plans to deem those companies that offer property for sale, whether they are solicitors or conveyancing firms, internet property sites or local independent companies, as estate agents for the purposes of the Estate Agents Act 1979 and the HIPs legislation. This means that they will be governed by the same strict rules as estate agents, obliged to become a member of a regulatory scheme and subject to the HIPs Regulations.

You should bear in mind that if you sell your property privately you will have to pay for the HIP and any marketing costs up front, with no guarantee of a sale.

If you choose not to employ an estate agent you will need to check the chain yourself and will have to rely upon your conveyancer for updates. Once a sale is underway you will find that the other conveyancers in the chain will not speak to you directly as this could create a conflict of interest.

If you intend to sell a residential property on the open market after 1 June 2007 you must have a HIP in place before putting the property on the market. Some residential properties are exempt from the HIP legislation. See Chapter 1. In Chapter 3 you will find details of where to obtain a HIP.

Private marketing methods

'For sale' board

Erecting a 'for sale' board is a cheap and easy way to advertise the fact that your property is for sale. It is simple to construct a 'for sale' notice. Most printing firms will be able to make a professional board to your specifications. The board should include your contact telephone numbers and the words 'viewing by appointment only', unless you want the world and his wife knocking at your door at all times of the day and night.

Media advertising

It is relatively inexpensive to advertise a property for sale in the local newspapers. Draft your property description carefully as adverts are charged on a word or line basis. Placing an advert in the weekly newspapers such as *Dalton's Weekly* or *Loot*, merits consideration as they reach a wider market and may be picked up by buyers wishing to relocate.

Property shops

There is a number of independent property shops on the high street and on the internet that will offer to put you in touch with potential buyers for a small registration fee. If you are using a high street firm check what you will get for your money. Ask whether they mail details to prospective buyers. If so how many buyers do they have registered? Is their mailing list up to date? How many properties have they sold in the past three months?

Internet sites

If you are using a property internet site to market your property you will probably pay a one-off registration fee and be asked to upload a photograph and property details onto the site. Before

Example property details

12 Anywhere Place, Nottingham

Entrance porch leading to:

- *Sitting room 12' x 15'* Window to front, radiator.
- *Dining room 12' x 13'* Window facing garden, radiator.
- *Kitchen 11' x 10'* Fitted units, window and door to garden, radiator.
- *Downstairs cloakroom* fitted with low level w.c., wash hand basin and radiator.

Stairs leading to first floor:

- *Bedroom 1 12' x 15'* Fitted wardrobe, window to front, radiator.
- *Bedroom 2 12' x 13'* Window to side, radiator.
- *Bathroom 10' x 10'* Bath with shower over, w.c. and pedestal sink. Window to rear, radiator.

The property has oil central heating, electricity, telephone, mains water and drainage.

Council Tax Band: C

Price: £120,000 or near offer

Seller: Mr J. Jones

Contact Details:

you register ask for details of the number of visitors to the site each month and check on the search engines whether the site is highly ranked. An internet site is worth using only if a buyer is able to find it.

Property particulars
If you are selling your property privately you will need to prepare a set of property details. Keep your details brief and to the point. State the room, the room size, windows, radiators, etc. Avoid flowery descriptions. Note that from 1 June 2007 property sales particulars must include a copy of the Energy Performance Certificate or the two Energy Performance graphs.

Although the description opposite is not particularly enticing from a marketing point of view it is factual and unlikely to lead to disputes later on.

Confirming a private sale
If you sell your property privately, without an estate agent, you will need to take the following actions as soon as an offer is confirmed.

◆ Ask the buyer to confirm their offer in writing, subject to contract, and to provide the name, address and telephone number of their conveyancer.

◆ Before accepting the offer you will need to find out whether the buyer is in a position to proceed. Ask your buyer to confirm:
  – whether they have a property to sell;
  – if so whether the property is sold, subject to contract. If the buyer has a property to sell, and does not have a buyer for it, you may want to wait until the chain is complete before

going further. You will also have to consider whether you will continue to market the property during this period;

— whether they require mortgage finance and whether this has been agreed in principle. Do not be afraid to ask for written evidence that your buyer has the deposit available and their mortgage arranged.

◆ It is important that you check each link of the chain to make sure that the chain is complete. If your buyer has a property to sell, and claims that the chain is complete, you can check this by phoning their estate agent or buyer and asking them to confirm this. Do this with every member in the chain, both above and below you.

◆ Only when the chain is complete and you have evidence that your buyer has their finance arranged should you confirm your acceptance of the offer, subject to contract. Do this in writing and include details of your own conveyancer's name, address and telephone number.

◆ Write to your conveyancer advising them of the sale. In the letter give the sale price agreed and any conditions or timescales you have agreed with the buyer. Include the contact details for the buyer's conveyancer and advise your conveyancer that this is a private sale. Ask your conveyancer to confirm receipt of your letter and to write to the buyer's conveyancer to start the ball rolling.

How to Achieve a Successful Sale

How do you define a successful sale? To me a successful sale is one where the property does not take forever to sell, where I achieve the price I was hoping to achieve and where the conveyancing proceeds smoothly and without a hitch to legal completion. Sadly, this is rarely the case and most of us experience some problems when selling our property.

If you have worked through the book thus far, you will have carried out your research, chosen an estate agent, settled on a marketing price and your property is on the market at last. If you are selling post-HIP Regulations your HIP will be in place and you may be looking forward to sitting back, putting your feet up and waiting for the first interested punter to arrive. Wrong! If you want to achieve a quick sale and a good price now is definitely not the time to relax.

Achieving a successful sale depends upon being motivated, organised and concentrating on each stage as it arises, i.e. preparing the property for market, dealing with viewers, negotiating offers and sealing the deal. This chapter will show you how to present your property at its best to potential buyers, how to get the best from your estate agent and how to negotiate when the offers come rolling in.

HOW TO GIVE YOUR PROPERTY BUYER APPEAL
If you have followed the advice in the earlier chapters of this book

your property should already be in good structural repair and condition. You must now prepare it to be viewed by an onslaught (hopefully) of discriminating potential buyers.

Most of us are unused to thinking of our home as a commodity to be sold. Décor, clutter, the arrangement of our furniture is personal to us, and it is what creates a home. However, when selling a property you need to appeal to the widest audience possible and this means that you must learn to view your property objectively. If you find you are unable to consider your property with an impartial eye ask an honest friend to look around the property with you, to comment on smells, décor, room arrangements, etc. Once you have completed this task you can then set about depersonalising your home so that viewers can imagine their own belongings in the setting that you create for them.

Outside

The exterior of the property should welcome the prospective buyer and invite them in to view. First impressions count so make sure that the approach to your property appears attractive and well cared for. I always take an informal look at the outside of a property before making an appointment to view and I am sure I am not alone. If your property does not have 'kerb appeal' potential buyers will simply drive past and on to the next property.

Declutter

Remove any clutter such as bikes, prams, toys, dustbins, etc. to the back garden or to a temporary location. If there is limited parking space, or your car has seen better days, park it elsewhere to give viewers room to park on the drive. New tarmac or gravel can transform a tatty exterior.

Clean up
Clean the windows and exterior paintwork and polish the door furniture. Add a new welcome mat to the porch.

Neat and tidy
Mow the lawn, trim the hedges and add a hanging basket, window box or tubs of seasonal plants and flowers. Remove moss and weeds from paths and patios and wash down with an appropriate cleaner.

Make it bright
If the viewing is during the evening ensure there is adequate outside lighting and that it is switched on.

Inside

Spring clean
A clean home will appeal to all buyers whatever the price range or style of the property. Give the property a spring clean from top to bottom, paying particular attention to kitchen, toilet and bathroom.

Make it smell nice
Bad smells deter buyers. Invest in some subtle air fresheners. Wash the dog, put those smelly old trainers in the bin, and avoid cooking strong-smelling food such as fish and garlic before a viewing.

Flooring
If your carpets are soiled or stained either have them professionally cleaned, or invest in a new Berber style carpet in a neutral colour. If you can't afford a new carpet consider taking up the old carpet, and stripping and varnishing the floor boards.

Replace any damp or dirty carpets in the toilet or bathroom with vinyl or tiles.

Curtains
Have heavy curtains dry cleaned, clean any blinds, and wash or replace grubby net curtains. If the property is not overlooked consider taking down the nets to allow more light into the property.

Lighting
Good lighting is important and your home should be well lit even in the daytime. During the dark winter days and nights table lamps and candles will give a cosy glow and, if you have a fireplace, light the fire.

Add some flowers and plants
Fresh flowers and potted plants are universally popular and create a cheerful, cared for and homely atmosphere.

Music
Turn the telly off and put a relaxing CD on the stereo – classical or easy listening jazz are best. Keep the sound turned down.

Interior décor
Interior décor should be kept light and neutral throughout. Although white walls will make a room seem larger it can appear cold. Instead use a palette of soft creams in varying shades on walls, and a smart white gloss on paintwork such as skirting boards and window sills.

In the kitchen
Kitchens and bathrooms sell houses so if you are planning to spend money these are the rooms to invest in. If your kitchen cabinets are

well laid out and in good repair but looking a bit tired, consider replacing or painting the doors and add some new handles. Old tiles can be repainted and use a grout whitener on dirty grouting.

Create a lifestyle
It is becoming somewhat of a cliché, but buyers are very impressionable and it has been proved they will buy into a 'successful lifestyle'. To create an impression of that upwardly mobile lifestyle think of the interior décor features in glossy magazines and the Sunday supplements:

- Replace tatty appliances that are displayed on worktops, such as kettles, toasters, coffee machines, etc. with new ones – you can take them with you when you move.

- Buy new tea towels, washing up bowl, sink tidy, etc. in co-ordinating colours to match your kitchen.

- Display pots of fresh herbs on window sills.

- Fill a wine rack full of good quality wine – you can drink it when you exchange contracts.

- Have some freshly brewed coffee on the go.

- Fill an attractive bowl with exotic fruit such as pineapples, mangoes, lemons and limes, or vegetables such as peppers and tomatoes.

- Lay the dining table for a meal with your best cutlery and crockery, and add a flower arrangement and some candles.

- If your sofa is sagging, tatty or covered in dog hairs have it professionally cleaned or invest in a new throw and some scatter cushions.

- Buy some classy coffee table books and magazines to leave on the coffee table.

- Your bed linen should match the décor and be pristine. Cover crumpled duvet covers that are past their best with a smart, new quilt or throw and add some toning cushions.

If you are at a loss for ideas go and have a look around the home departments of the major department stores for inspiration.

Appliances

Whether or not you are including appliances in the sale they should be clean and sparkling. If your oven and hob or cooker have seen better days consider having them professionally cleaned. White goods that are scratched can be repaired with white enamel paint.

The bathroom and toilet

Should be sparkling clean and smell fresh. Clean and polish taps. Use a descaling product to get rid of lime scale. Old tiles can be smartened up with a coat of tile paint and use grout whitener to brighten up grubby grout. Change the toilet seat and bath panels if they have seen better days. Install a new shower curtain, some thick fluffy towels, expensive guest soaps and some attractive bottles and jars of lotions and potions.

Keep it clutter free

Keep clutter to a minimum and avoid hanging lots of small pictures and photographs on the walls. Try displaying one print that tones with the room colour and is large enough to provide a focal point without swamping the room. To create an impression of light and space hang an attractive mirror opposite a window.

Give them room to move

Make sure that there is easy access to and from each room to allow viewers to move around freely. Check that you know where the keys to doors and windows are, and ensure that they open and close easily.

Give it an identity

Viewers should be able to identify rooms immediately. Furnish each room according to its proposed use or description in the estate agent's details. It sounds obvious, but if a room is referred to as a kitchen/breakfast room you need to show the buyer that there is room to eat in there. Install a table and chairs, or at least a couple of stools and a breakfast bar. Bedrooms should include a bed, preferably a double if there is space.

Period features

If the property is an older style or period property the buyer may be looking for original period features. If these have been removed or covered up consider reinstating them. You can purchase reclaimed period doors, skirting boards, floors, picture rails, in fact just about everything from a period reclamation centre.

HIP TIP

Visit a show home on a new development to see how the properties are presented. You will note that light, neutral colours on walls, carpets and curtains are used to make the property appear larger and to allow the viewer to imagine their own belongings there. Colour and interest are added with prints on the walls, and accessories such as vases of flowers and cushions.

Canny developers often use scaled down furniture in small rooms to make them appear larger.

HOW TO DEAL WITH VIEWINGS

Whether you sell your property via an estate agent or privately you must try to be available when a buyer wants to view the property. Many buyers can view only outside of working hours, during the evenings and at weekends. While this may not always be convenient it is important to make a concerted effort to be available for every viewing appointment that is offered. Give your estate agent a set of keys to the property and if you are not available ask them to accompany the buyer on the viewing. Stipulate to the estate agent that they must never allow the keys to your property to be given out on loan to potential buyers.

Check that your estate agent has all your contact numbers including your mobile number, home and work numbers and your email address.

Remember, you may get only one chance. The buyer may be looking at several properties and if yours is unavailable to view they may simply buy elsewhere.

How to impress potential buyers

Be ready for viewers
Showing potential buyers around your home can be a nerve-wracking inconvenience. Once you place your property on the market you will need to be prepared for a viewing at any time. Don't scramble out of the door in the morning leaving the washing up in the sink and the bed unmade. A buyer may want to view at short notice: if you leave the house clean and tidy you can arrange for the estate agent to show viewers around in your absence. Consider the case scenario below.

Case scenario

It is Saturday morning and you are looking forward to a nice lie in, a big fried breakfast and a day reading the papers or lounging in front of the television watching the football. Suddenly, the telephone rings. It is your estate agent. Mr and Mrs Newlywed have seen the details of your property and would like to view it immediately as they are in the area today only. Would it be possible for them to come around now? You look around you, the place is in a state, the house smells of fried food and you haven't washed or shaved. You decline and ask them to make a more convenient appointment. The estate agent makes an appointment for them to view the property three doors away. Mr and Mrs Beprepared are at home; they have kept the property tidy and are ready for an immediate viewing. Mr and Mrs Newlywed are delighted with the attitude of Mr and Mrs Beprepared and love the house. They put in an offer immediately. You never hear from them again. Next time the estate agent has a keen buyer in the office they don't bother to phone you.

Keep the property clean and tidy

When a buyer is coming to view ensure the house is clean and tidy. Clear away any clutter and have a quick whiz around with the vacuum and the duster. Put some fresh flowers in a vase. Polish the taps, mirrors and glass, and put fresh towels in the bathroom and toilet. If you have been cooking or have pets, open the doors and windows to allow strong odours to dissipate, or use an air freshener.

Make your viewers welcome

Lay a tray for tea and coffee and offer refreshments when viewers arrive. Welcoming potential buyers in this way allows you to overcome any initial shyness and relax tension. You will have more time to chat naturally about your home and its good points over a cuppa.

Be prepared with information

Have details about the area to hand. Viewers may ask what the schools in the area are like, whether there is local transport and what amenities are nearby. Your local library will have details of local schools and playgroups, and you can obtain bus and train timetables from your local station.

HIP TIP

A list of good schools in your area can be found on www.goodschoolsguide.co.uk – you can search by town, post code and age range. You can also obtain details on schools, colleges and universities from www.directgov.uk

Make space

Try to present an empty house as it appears larger, and offers less distraction. Pack the kids/pets/other half off to the park or to grandparents for an hour or so.

How to conduct a successful viewing

◆ Dress smart/casual. There is no point selling the viewers a 'life style' of the young, upwardly mobile professional if you open the door wearing a baggy track suit and grubby trainers.

◆ Greet the viewers cordially and introduce yourself – remember they may end up buying your property.

◆ Ensure that you have a copy of the estate agent's particulars to hand to deal with any questions the viewer may have.

◆ Be confident, show them into each room and state what room you are in, e.g. 'This is the main bedroom, second bedroom, etc.'

so that they can check this against the description in the agent's details.

Once you are all in the room point out any positive aspects and play down any negative issues. Try not to chatter too much or to seem over-eager. Make a list of the positive attributes of your property to use as an aide mémoire when showing your home. Every property is different, but here are a few examples of positive phrases you could use, if they apply:

◆ Kitchen: a view over the garden, quality fitted units, appliances included, easy to clean, well laid out, cosy and warm, the hub of the home, space and/or plumbing for dishwasher/washing machine, breakfast bar or eating area.

◆ Dining room: light and airy, warm and cosy. Open plan kitchen/ dining rooms allow you to talk to guests and keep an eye on the kids while cooking a meal. Private kitchen/dining rooms allow you to dine in peace away from the rest of the household. 'A lovely room at Christmas and for special occasions.' A large dining room: 'We had 20 people in here last Christmas.' A small dining room: 'Perfect for cosy suppers.'

◆ Sitting room: doors/windows to garden, point out any nice views. Open fireplace, plenty of plug sockets for TV and stereo, flooring to remain.

◆ Bathroom/cloakrooms: recently fitted or refurbished suite. Downstairs cloakroom/bathroom useful for kids, visitors and elderly relatives. En suite bathroom – peace and quiet away from the family, heated towel rails, power shower.

◆ Bedrooms: double bedroom, spacious, light and airy, views, built in cupboards.

◆ General positive attributes to point out: central heating, separate immersion with lagged hot water tank, good loft/cavity wall insulation, double glazing, period features, open fireplaces, recent work done, guarantees available, low maintenance features such as UPVC windows, landscaped or easy to maintain gardens, good natural light, low council tax charges, good bus/train routes, good local schools, safe community, items included in the sale.

◆ Good position: if you have found a property to buy and the chain is complete mention this. Tell the buyer if you are able to move quickly – this may be a plus, but stress that you are flexible just in case they are not ready to move just yet.

Building a rapport with viewers

Once you have shown the viewers around offer refreshments and ask if they would like to wander around the property alone while you make the tea. Try to build a rapport with potential buyers as no one wants to deal with an off-hand or aggressive seller.

Keep safe

A note of caution – while most buyers are genuine there are always some opportunists out there and it is sensible to keep a close but discreet eye on viewers. Lock away small, valuable items such as jewellery, handbags and money. Never allow anyone into your home without a prior appointment and always ask for identification.

Obtaining useful information from viewers

Once the viewing is over, and the potential buyers are enjoying the refreshments you have provided, you can use this time to glean very useful information that will assist you later on in negotiations. See the list of questions below, but do try to bring them into the conversation naturally:

- Do you have a property to sell? – If so is it sold?
- When were you hoping to move?
- Would you need a mortgage to buy?
- Have you arranged your mortgage?
- Have you seen many properties?
- Do you have many more properties to view?

Try to remember the answers and write them down afterwards. Avoid giving out too much information about your own situation at this stage as knowledge is power. If you tell potential buyers that you are under pressure to move quickly they may use this information to offer a lower price. Likewise, if you intimate that you are in no particular hurry to sell and they need to move quickly you may dissuade them from making an offer.

NEGOTIATING THE SALE PRICE

Good news – you have an offer on the table; bad news – it is not the one you were hoping for. Don't despair and whatever you do don't be offended, angry or dismiss it out of hand. Under the Estate Agents Act 1979 agents must put *all* offers forward to you.

Most buyers will put in an offer lower than the asking price to test the water. That does not mean they will not increase their offer and you will need to learn how to haggle.

Negotiating strategies

- Mention the property was valued by three separate firms of professional estate agents.

- Ask why the buyer thinks the property is not worth the asking price. Do they have concrete reasons for their lower offer or are they just being cheeky?

- Point out that you checked the Land Registry website and similar properties in your neighbourhood have achieved the price you are asking.

- Confirm that you have rectified or intend to rectify any defects in the property revealed in the Home Condition Report.

- Offer to include additional items in the sale such as carpets, curtains and kitchen appliances if the asking price is paid.

- Offer a quick sale or an extended completion date to suit the buyer's circumstances.

- Agree to take the property off the market for a fixed period.

- Stress your own good position (e.g. no onward chain or being prepared to move into temporary accommodation).

Don't accept a lower offer until you or your selling agent has checked:

- Whether the buyer has a property to sell.
- Whether the buyer is in a chain and if the chain is complete.
- Whether the buyer needs a mortgage.
- Has a mortgage offer been agreed in principle?
- Does the buyer have the balance of the price readily available?
- Is the buyer able to proceed at the pace you require?

Accepting a lower offer

Consider accepting a lower offer only if the buyer is in a good position to proceed. If you wish to make a counter offer ask your estate agent for advice on what would be an acceptable counter offer. Remember, the estate agent is working for you and their fee is likely to be a percentage of the total purchase price, so they should want to achieve the best offer for you. Bear in mind that many estate agents sell products to buyers including mortgages, insurance, removals and conveyancing. They can gain a considerable amount of additional revenue by selling these lucrative extras and this may sway them into persuading you to accept that buyer's offer. Always ask the estate agent whether they are selling additional products to the buyer before accepting a lower offer. If you find out that the estate agent is making money from the buyers you may be able to negotiate a fee reduction to help offset the lower sale price.

If you decide to accept a lower offer try to use it as a bargaining point to move at the pace you want to. For instance, you could agree to the lower offer provided the buyer completes by a certain date.

It can sometimes take several days or weeks for an offer to be made and accepted. Try to be patient and always be polite; if the sale proceeds you are going to be dealing with the buyer for several weeks if not months.

HIP TIP

Use bargaining points to get your asking price. Offer to include carpets and curtains or to take the property off the market if your asking price is paid.

CONFIRMATION OF THE SALE

As soon as you accept an offer for your property the estate agent will complete the 'particulars of sale'. They will need to know the name and contact details of your conveyancer. The buyer will also be asked to provide details of their conveyancer, mortgage or mortgage broker and, if they are selling, their selling agent. This information will enable your estate agent to check the chain if they have not already done so. Copies of the particulars of sale are sent to you, your conveyancer, the buyer and their conveyancer.

Once the conveyancers receive their copy of the particulars of sale they then begin the conveyancing process. The estate agent will continue to check the progress of the chain, either by telephoning the conveyancers involved or, if available, by checking an online progress website. A good agent will endeavour to smooth out any problems that occur and should keep you advised of progress up to the point of exchange. At exchange of contracts the estate agents send their invoice to your conveyancer who, with your permission, will pay it on legal completion.

Remember to telephone your conveyancer to confirm that you wish to proceed with the sale. Ask them to telephone you once they have received the estate agent's particulars and made contact with the buyer's conveyancer. As the old saying goes, 'there is many a slip between cup and lip'. Don't assume that if you hear nothing all is going to plan. By checking with your conveyancer and your estate agent on a regular weekly basis you can forestall any problems or delays.

8

Conveyancing and the HIP

This chapter looks at how to find the perfect conveyancer, conveyancing costs and how the HIP will alter the conveyancing procedure.

There is a bewilderingly large number of solicitors and licensed conveyancer firms in the United Kingdom. Law is one of the most oversubscribed professions of our time and conveyancing is one of the most popular specialist subjects. This chapter will explain what conveyancing means, the different types of conveyancing firms and how to select the perfect conveyancer for you.

SO WHAT EXACTLY IS CONVEYANCING?
Conveyancing is the legal term for transferring land or property from one person to another. It is usually carried out by a firm of solicitors or licensed conveyancers, but can be done by an individual. While the basic conveyancing procedure appears fairly straightforward, do not be fooled: English property law is complex. Lenders will insist that you use a qualified conveyancing firm if you are taking out or repaying a mortgage.

The legal profession is much maligned, and is often accused of archaic practices and a failure to communicate. Whilst this is still true for some, many firms now use sophisticated technology to streamline conveyancing procedures and some offer online or email progress reporting. Experienced conveyancers are used to coping with deadlines, chains of transactions, stressed-out clients, and ensuring that paperwork and money are delivered correctly and on time. A good conveyancer can make or break a property deal and it is important to ensure that you choose the right conveyancer for you.

What is the difference between solicitors and licensed conveyancers?

Solicitors
Solicitors must qualify under Law Society training rules. In order to qualify they must complete:

♦ Academic training, usually by obtaining a degree or similar qualification.

♦ Vocational training known as the Legal Practice Course (LPC).

♦ A training contract in a firm of solicitors.

Once a solicitor has qualified they are entitled to practise as an employed solicitor. They may not set up a solicitor's practice of their own until they have been qualified for a period of at least three years.

Solicitors are governed and monitored by the Law Society. To comply with Law Society rules all solicitors must hold a current practice certificate and legal indemnity insurance which must be renewed each year. Solicitors are bound by strict rules and regulations, particularly in relation to clients' money. They must keep their knowledge up to date by completing a set number of hours of Continuing Professional Development (CPD), and evidence of completion of the required number of CPD hours must be submitted to and approved by the Law Society.

A solicitor is entitled to practise in all areas of law, but most choose to specialise in one particular area.

Solicitors' firms vary widely from one-partner firms, called sole practitioners, to very large firms with many partners.

Licensed conveyancers
Licensed conveyancers are governed by the Council for Licensed Conveyancers. A licensed conveyancer specialises solely in property law. In order to qualify as a licensed conveyancer they must:

◆ Complete the CLC training course.
◆ Pass the CLC examinations.
◆ Complete two years' supervised practical experience (this can be done whilst studying).
◆ Undergo relevant conveyancing experience in the three months following the passing of exams.

Once the conveyancer has passed the necessary exams, completed the two years' practical training and the three months' conveyancing experience, they will be granted a limited licence. The licence must be renewed each year. A limited licence allows a conveyancer to work as an employed licensed conveyancer.

Before a licensed conveyancer is allowed to set up their own firm they must have held a limited licence for at least three consecutive years.

The rules governing licensed conveyancers are similar to those governing solicitors. As with solicitors, licensed conveyancer firms vary from one partner firms to large firms with many partners.

HOW TO CHOOSE A SOLICITOR OR A LICENSED CONVEYANCER

Solicitors and licensed conveyancers basically provide the same conveyancing service. As you read above, they are both governed by strict rules relating to their professional standards. There are robust complaints procedures in place and if a solicitor or licensed conveyancer is in serious breach of conduct they can lose their right to practise.

The main difference between a firm of solicitors and a firm of licensed conveyancers is that the former will be able to offer a range of legal services in addition to conveyancing. If you are looking for a firm that will be able to act for you in other matters such as wills, probate, divorce, family law, business law, etc. you may wish to instruct a firm of solicitors. Licensed conveyancers specialise solely in conveyancing work.

Points to consider when choosing a conveyancing firm

The number of partners in the firm
If you are buying or selling, and have a mortgage, ideally you should choose a firm with at least two to three partners. Your conveyancer will also be required to act for your mortgage lender and some lenders stipulate that the firm has at least two or three partners. If in doubt, check with your lender whether your chosen firm is on their recommended panel. A smaller firm may offer a more personal and bespoke service, but what happens if the sole principal is on holiday or away ill?

Who will actually carry out the conveyancing?
Do not assume when you employ a firm of solicitors or licensed conveyancers that your conveyancing will be done by a qualified solicitor or licensed conveyancer. Often conveyancing work is carried out by legal executives or experienced conveyancing staff under the supervision of a solicitor or partner. Professional rules stipulate that the firm must tell you in the initial client care letter who will actually do the work and who the supervising partner is.

Are they Lexcel accredited?
The Lexcel accreditation is granted only to solicitors who offer the highest quality of management and customer care.

Do they specialise in conveyancing?
Check that the conveyancer who will act for you specialises in conveyancing. There is nothing more frustrating than finding that your conveyancer is in the middle of a protracted court case when you need them to exchange contracts.

What will they charge?
Conveyancers' fees vary widely. Shop around to obtain estimates

and ensure that you get them in writing. Many firms now offer an instant online quote service. These can be found by simply typing conveyancing into one of the major search engines such as Google. See below on how to compare estimates.

Communication

One of the most frequent complaints about property lawyers is lack of communication. Check how the conveyancer will communicate with you and other parties in the chain (mail, email, telephone, fax, etc.) and how often you may expect to hear from them.

Empathy

It is important that you are able to build a good rapport with your conveyancer from the start. Do they appear to listen to you and understand your needs? Will you have one conveyancer who deals with you from start to finish, or will you have to deal with a different person each time?

Experience and accuracy

Your conveyancer should be experienced in conveyancing and accurate in preparing the necessary legal documents. Check your initial correspondence and estimate carefully. Have they got it right?

Speed

Ask your conveyancer how quickly they will be able to complete your transaction. Remember, they will not be able to guarantee a date because this depends on the other parties in the chain. If your conveyancer appears under pressure they may have too many clients to deal with, which could slow your transaction down.

COMPARING CONVEYANCING ESTIMATES

Comparing conveyancing estimates is very difficult for the layman. Conveyancing firms set out their estimates in different ways and hidden extras are often included in the small print. It is important to read the estimate and any terms and conditions very carefully. What may seem a cheap estimate can end up very expensive once all the extras are added on.

Some pointers to consider when comparing conveyancing estimates:

- Ensure you obtain at least three estimates, in writing, and read the small print carefully. Most firms will quote a fixed fee for a 'standard' conveyancing transaction, but will charge extra if the transaction becomes more complicated or protracted.

- Some firms will charge extra for acting for your mortgage lender, photocopying, postage and telephone calls, professional indemnity insurance, expedition fees, etc. etc. Check whether these are included in the estimate.

- Ask what the hourly charging rate is for additional work. One of the problems the conveyancer has when providing the quote is the limited information available at the outset of the transaction. This means that the conveyancer is able to give an estimate only on the facts as known.

- Ask the firm to confirm in writing that the estimate includes everything you will need to take you to completion.

- Give the conveyancer as much information as possible about your transaction.

The introduction of the HIP should improve the accuracy of estimates provided by conveyancers, as they will have more information about the type of property you are buying or selling at a much earlier stage. As a general rule of thumb you can expect to pay more for leasehold, commonhold, shared ownership and share of the freehold, new build and unregistered property transactions as these involve more work than a standard freehold registered property.

THE CONVEYANCING ESTIMATE EXPLAINED

The estimate will be broken down to show the labour costs and the disbursements separately.

Labour charges

These are the fees that the conveyancer charges for carrying out the conveyancing on your behalf and on behalf of a lender. Typically they are described as:

♦ Professional or conveyancing fees.

♦ Fees for acting for your lender (where you are obtaining or repaying a mortgage the conveyancer will be asked to act for the lender and you must pay the fee. Some conveyancers include this in the overall fee).

♦ Petty disbursements – this is an additional notional charge made by the conveyancer to cover the cost of telephone calls, photocopying, faxes and postage.

♦ Completing the Stamp Duty Land Tax form (SDLT) – the Government requires buyers to complete and submit this form on completion. The form is lengthy and complicated. Most conveyancers offer to complete it on behalf of the client for an additional fee.

- Indemnity insurance – some conveyancers require their clients to make a contribution towards their indemnity insurance.

- Expedition fees – some firms charge extra for giving priority to an urgent transaction.

- File storage – conveyancers must store your file for a minimum of six years and some charge for this.

Disbursements

The conveyancer is obliged to collect money on behalf of a number of third parties. These charges are known as 'disbursements'. Typically these would include the following.

Search fees

- Local authority search – the fee varies from one local authority to another. The average is £150, but you can find out the exact search fee from your conveyancer or from the land charges department of the local authority. Some conveyancers use personal search companies as they are usually cheaper and quicker.

- Water authority search – fees also vary from one water authority to another. The average is £35.25, but you can find out the exact search fee from your conveyancer or from the local water authority.

- Environmental search fees – vary depending on the type of search and the search company used. The average would be £30, but your conveyancer would confirm this.

- Mining search – average £25.

- Bankruptcy search – £1 per name if posted, £2 per name if faxed or sent online.

- Land Charges search – £4 each.

Other fees

♦ Value Added Tax – currently charged at 17.5% of the conveyancer's professional fees. There is no VAT on HM Land Registry fees or Stamp Duty. VAT is payable on some searches but not on others.

♦ Land Registry fees – are payable by the buyer and are charged on the purchase price on a sliding scale:

Current Land Registry Fee Scale		
£0 – 50,000		£ 40
£50,001 – 80,000		£ 60
£80,001 – 100,000		£100
£100,001 – 200,000		£150
£200,001 – 500,000		£220
£500,001 – 1,000,000		£420
£1,000,000 and over		£700

♦ Stamp Duty Land Tax – is payable by the buyer and is charged as a percentage of the purchase price. Some areas which have been designated by the Government as disadvantaged are stamp duty exempt.

Current Stamp Duty Land Tax on residential property	
0 – £125,000	NIL
Over £125,000 – 250,000	1%
Over £250,000 – 500,000	3%
Over £500,000	4%

♦ Fees payable to the landlord/management company – these charges are laid down by the landlord or the management company. If you are selling, then you would pay the charge for procuring the pre-contract information. This charge can vary enormously, but an average would be £150. If you are buying, you would pay the fee on completion for registering the Transfer Notice and any Deed of Covenant. Again this charge varies enormously, but an average would be £150.

◆ Ground rent/management charges – these are not strictly a conveyancing expense, but should be included in your budget if you are buying a leasehold property. If the seller has paid the ground rent and maintenance charges in advance they will reclaim them from you and they may appear on the conveyancer's final statement. If you are buying a new leasehold property you will be liable to pay the ground rent/management charges from the date of completion up to the end of the next chargeable period. Ground rent is usually charged quarterly and payable in advance. Maintenance charges are usually charged yearly in advance; charges are generally estimated and a balancing statement is made at the end of the year. Some management companies allow tenants to pay the fees monthly in advance.

◆ Telegraphic Transfer (TT) fee – this is a bank charge for transferring money electronically from one bank to another. Buyers will pay at least one TT fee for the transfer of the money to the seller's conveyancer. Sellers will also usually pay at least one TT fee for the transfer of the money to repay an existing mortgage. The charges vary, but an average would be £35.

HIP TIP

Check www.hmrc.gov.uk/so/current_sdlt_rates for the current Stamp Duty Land Tax rates. The Inland Revenue site also lists the Stamp Duty exempt areas. You can check if your property is exempt by entering your post code.

The cost of disbursements on a property transaction can vary widely for a number of reasons. Some properties require more searches and enquiries than others and, if you are selling a leasehold or commonhold property, the buyer's conveyancer will ask for additional information which must be obtained from the landlord or management company. Following the introduction of the HIP the local authority search, water search and the leasehold/ commonhold information will be contained within the HIP.

If you are selling a leasehold or commonhold property you will usually be asked to pay for the cost of obtaining the pre-contract information from the landlord or management company. If you are buying a leasehold or commonhold property you will be asked to pay any fees due to the landlord or management company for registering a notice of the transfer of the property into your name. You may also have to pay a separate fee to the landlord/ management company for the registration of your mortgage details.

HIP TIP

Shopping around for a conveyancer can save you hundreds of pounds. Conveyancing Marketing Services will do the hard work for you by searching for the best conveyancing quotes that match your criteria and then delivering your selection of quotes instantly on line and by email. They also provide a free quote-beating service: www.conveyancing-cms.co.uk

HOW TO ENSURE YOU GET GOOD SERVICE FROM YOUR CONVEYANCER

◆ Ask friends and family for personal recommendations.

◆ Check whether the firm has a website and if so read any client feedback published.

- Ask whether the firm adheres to a 'service charter'. If so request a copy and check the service offered. As a minimum firms should specify:
  - how quickly telephone calls will be answered;
  - how soon calls will be returned;
  - how quickly emails/incoming post will be dealt with;
  - how quickly client enquiries will be answered;
  - when clients will be updated.

- Telephone the firm on several occasions to check how quickly the telephone is answered and whether the receptionist is friendly and efficient.

- Ask what the firm's opening hours are. Many firms still offer a strict 9am–5 pm policy and close for lunch, whilst others are open from 8am to 8pm and at weekends.

- Ask to speak to the person who will be dealing with your case. How many tries does it take you to get through? Is the person helpful, friendly and empathetic?

- Ask whether the firm operates an online or email tracking system. Many modern firms now operate systems where you can view or receive electronic updates 24/7.

- Does the firm work on a 'no completion, no fee' basis?

- Can they provide insurance to pay for legal expenses if the matter does not proceed?

- How quickly does the initial client care letter and written estimate arrive? Are all the details correctly spelled and typed, does it appear professional?

LOCAL *v* DISTANCE CONVEYANCERS

Most towns will have a good choice of conveyancing firms. Check

Yellow Pages, the Law Society's directory of solicitors at www.lawsociety.org.uk and www.theclc.gov.uk for the CLC directory of licensed conveyancers. Entering the words 'conveyancing quotes' into one of the main internet search engines such as Google will provide details of hundreds of firms offering conveyancing at very competitive rates – but remember to get the quote in writing and read the small print.

Using a local conveyancing firm

◆ You should be able to meet your conveyancer in person.

◆ You can hand-deliver and collect urgent or important documents.

◆ You should be able to attend in person to have contracts and complicated issues explained to you.

◆ They should have local knowledge of the area.

◆ They may know and have a rapport with the other local conveyancers and estate agents.

Using an online or distance conveyancing firm

◆ They are often cheaper than local firms.

◆ You may not need to visit in person.

◆ They generally have automated systems to make the conveyancing procedure more efficient and streamlined.

◆ They often offer online tracking and automatic email or text updates.

◆ They tend to correspond more by email, speeding up the transaction.

◆ They are often open outside normal office hours.

As you have seen there is more to choosing the perfect conveyancer than you would expect and it pays to start looking early, before you have sold or found the property of your dreams.

As soon as you have decided upon your conveyancer call them and tell them that you would like them to act for you. Confirm this in writing. There is much to be done in the early days and the conveyancer can get everything organised so that as soon as you are ready to proceed with your transaction they can act immediately.

HIP TIP

As soon as you have decided on a conveyancer ask them to act for you in writing. Having a conveyancer ready to move will impress your buyer or seller, and the estate agent, and save valuable time later on.

9

HIPs and the Conveyancing Process

The introduction of the Home Information Pack will alter the current conveyancing system to a small degree, but it is not expected to have a huge impact on either the speed or the cost of the actual conveyancing process.

Whether the HIP is useful to a conveyancer will depend upon the quality of preparation, the extent and accuracy of the documentation included and the age of some of the documents. A HIP that has been well prepared to include current title documents, completed Property Use and Home Contents (or their equivalent) forms and current searches will be of enormous use to the conveyancer, who will simply need to check the contents and the contract. Conversely, a HIP that is badly prepared, inaccurate, incomplete and out of date will be a waste of time and money.

In this chapter we look at the current conveyancing procedure and how that will be affected by the introduction of the HIP.

THE SALE PROCEDURE

Instructing a conveyancer

Now	After the HIP
You instruct your conveyancer when you have made a firm offer for a property and it has been accepted.	Your conveyancer is involved in the preparation of your HIP and instructed by you as soon as you decide to place your property on the market.

The first step to take in any property transaction is to select and instruct your conveyancer. There is much to do in the early stages of a sale even before a buyer is found. Your conveyancer must obtain your written instructions to act for you, satisfy money laundering and proof of identity regulations, and obtain the title deeds and paperwork relating to your property.

Currently, most sellers wait to receive a firm offer on their property before instructing a conveyancer as they are wary of incurring any costs before a sale has been agreed. This reluctance to instruct a conveyancer can delay the transaction by several weeks. The answer is to find a conveyancer who will work on a 'no sale, no fee' basis.

By instructing a conveyancer early on you can call on their expertise to decipher the estate agent's contract and the HIP contract. Following the introduction of the HIP it is hoped that sellers will be motivated to find and instruct a conveyancer at the point of marketing. The conveyancer who is involved in producing the legal content of the HIP can then carry on that work once the property is sold. Using the same conveyancer for the HIP and the conveyancing should save time and money.

HIP TIP

Instructing your conveyancer early on in the transaction could avoid delays at a later stage. Ask your conveyancer to advise you on the estate agent's and the HIP contracts in addition to carrying out your conveyancing.

Confirming instructions in writing

Now	After the HIP
Your conveyancer sends you a client care letter and the Property Information/Fixture and Fittings forms when you ask them to act for you. The forms must be completed by you and returned with the various enclosures such as guarantees and planning documents. There may be a delay in returning the forms if you cannot locate all the necessary paperwork.	Your conveyancer sends you a client care letter and Property Use/Home Contents forms when you ask them to act for you. You may already have completed the forms for inclusion in the HIP and located any necessary guarantees and planning documents earlier on before the property was put on the market. This means that you can sign and return the instructions to your conveyancer immediately.

Once you have asked your conveyancer to act for you they will send you an initial confirmation of those instructions and an estimate. This is called a client care letter. The client care letter will usually contain the following information:

- the name of the person acting for you and any assistant;
- direct contact details;
- money laundering and client identification procedure;
- estimate;
- complaints procedure;
- when and how payment of fees and disbursements is due.

You will usually be sent two copies and asked to sign and return one copy. When you are selling a property the client care letter will also usually include the Property Information form and the Fixtures and Fittings form (or the Property Use form and the Home Contents form as they will be known post-HIP). As part of the conveyancing process you must complete these forms. The Property Information form/Property Use form is a set of standard questions dealing with:

* details of all residents at the property;
* property address;
* tenure (i.e. freehold/leasehold/commonhold);
* planning and building regulations;
* alterations to the property;
* guarantees;
* neighbour or other disputes;
* rights of way and access to the property;
* maintenance costs;
* boundaries;
* services connected.

The Fixtures and Fittings form/Home Contents form is a standard form listing all the fixtures and fittings at the property. You state whether the items listed are included in the sale, excluded or non-existent. You are obliged by law to complete the forms accurately as they form a part of the contract. There are additional Property Information forms and Property Use forms to be completed in respect of leasehold and commonhold properties.

Prior to the introduction of the HIP, the Property Information form and the Fixtures and Fittings form were sent out by the conveyancer with the client care letter. The conveyancer then waited for the signed letter and forms to come back before applying for the deeds needed to prepare the draft contract. This meant that it could take several weeks from when the offer was made and accepted for your conveyancer to receive the deeds and prepare the draft contract. After the HIP is introduced the title information, Property Use form and the Home Contents form may be included in the HIP. Upon receipt of the HIP your conveyancer should have sufficient information to prepare the contract and despatch it to your buyer's conveyancer immediately an offer is accepted.

Your conveyancer cannot start to work for you until you confirm your instructions in writing. Make sure your conveyancer knows where to obtain your deeds as lenders can take up to 28 days to despatch deeds.

Obtaining the deeds

Now	After the HIP
Your conveyancer waits for you to return the signed client care letter and forms and then writes to your lender applying for the deeds to the property. Provided your conveyancer is on their panel the lender despatches the deeds within 28 days. Some lenders will ask for their borrower's written consent to release the deeds and will make a deeds production charge. If the deeds are not with the lender your conveyancer will obtain them from you, your bank or former conveyancer. You will need to provide written consent. For registered land your conveyancer will obtain official copies of the register from the Land Registry.	The deeds may have been obtained before the property was marketed and details included in the HIP. The official copies of the register and filed plan will have been obtained and included in the HIP.

Since October 2003 the majority of lenders do not hold deeds to registered freehold property. However, if the property is unregistered, leasehold or commonhold it is likely that the lender still holds some or all of the deeds. Your conveyancer will need the name and address of your lender and your mortgage account number. They will then write to your lender, requesting that the deeds be sent to them on loan. Lenders are naturally cautious about releasing deeds because they represent security for the mortgage and are very difficult to replace or recreate if lost. Your lender will send deeds only to a conveyancer who is on their approved panel. Lenders can take several days if not weeks to send deeds and may ask for your written consent. If your conveyancer or HIP provider is not on your lender's approved panel they will send the deeds to an approved panel conveyancer, who will produce certified copies of the deeds and send them to your conveyancer or HIP provider. Likewise, if you are in arrears with your mortgage payments, your lender will not release the deeds but will arrange for their own conveyancer to send copies. You are obliged to pay the costs of your lender's panel conveyancer for this service. Most lenders charge a deeds production fee and a fee for the mortgage repayment.

Official copies of the register and of the filed plan
If the property is registered land your conveyancer will also apply to the Land Registry for official copies of the register and the filed plan. The Land Registry normally despatches these within 24 hours of the request.

Preparing the contract

Now	After the HIP
The contract is prepared after a formal offer has been made and accepted. This is usually confirmed by the estate agent's particulars. To prepare the contract your conveyancer requires the deeds, official copies of the register, filed plan, Property Information form and Fixtures and Fittings form.	The contract procedure will be the same following the HIP. Your conveyancer may not need to send as much information to your buyer's conveyancer as some of the information may already be contained in the HIP. Your conveyancer should be able to produce the contract more quickly as they will have all the information needed in the HIP.

Preparing the contract

Once your conveyancer has received the title deeds, the official copies of the register and the filed plan they will prepare a draft contract. The contract will set out:

♦ names and addresses of the seller and the buyer;
♦ names and addresses of both sets of conveyancers;
♦ the price;
♦ the deposit to be paid on exchange of contracts;
♦ the postal address and the legal address of the property;
♦ the tenure;
♦ the title number;
♦ covenants and legal restrictions to which the property will remain subject;
♦ any special conditions;
♦ the standard conditions of sale.

There is no provision for a draft contract to be included in the HIP although the Sale Statement does include some of the information.

Sending the contract pack to the buyer's conveyancer

Once the draft contract has been prepared your conveyancer will send two copies to your buyer's conveyancer for approval. Under current procedure they would usually enclose with the pack as much information about the property as they had been able to gather, including the Property Information form, the Fixtures and Fittings form, any relevant copy deeds such as conveyances or leases, copies of guarantees and planning documents, etc. relating to the property. If your buyer's conveyancer has been provided with a HIP they may already have copies of the Home Contents form, the Property Use form, guarantees, planning permissions, etc. and your conveyancer will not need to send them again.

Dealing with additional pre-contract enquiries

Now	After the HIP
Your conveyancer sends out the contract pack and then sits back and waits for any additional queries or enquiries to be made. Your buyer's conveyancer examines the pack and sends copies of relevant documents to your buyer, enquiring whether they have any questions or queries. Additional enquiries are then sent to your conveyancer who then sends them on to you for answers or to outside authorities such as the leaseholder/management company. This stage is one of the main causes of delay in property transactions.	The HIP provider has the opportunity together with the property owner to gather information before a buyer is even found. Sometimes this information can take weeks to gather: leasehold information from landlords/management companies, planning consents from local authorities, missing documents, insurance policies to deal with title defects, etc. If all this information is put into the HIP there will be fewer preliminary enquiries and the time taken to get to exchange of contracts could be lessened considerably. If, however, the HIP contains the bare bones of information required then it will have been a waste of time and money.

It seems that no matter how much information is gathered and sent to a buyer's conveyancer they will usually make additional enquiries. These may result from the documentation they have received, specific queries that the buyer wants answered or they may be standard enquiries. Either way, your conveyancer must answer them and must refer them to you before doing so.

HIP TIP

The HIP has the potential to reduce the pre-contract enquiry stage from several weeks to just days if properly prepared.

Preparing to sign the contract

Now	After the HIP
Once your buyer's conveyancer has received answers to their enquiries they will approve the contract and send one copy back to your conveyancer, who will then write a standard report explaining the terms of the contract and send it to you to sign and return.	This stage will not change.

Getting ready for exchange of contracts

Now	After the HIP
When both sets of conveyancers are holding a contract signed by their clients, and your buyer's conveyancer has cleared funds for the deposit, they will notify each other and start to discuss completion dates. Your views will be sought on convenient dates.	This stage will not change.

Exchanging contracts and completing the sale

Now	After the HIP
When the chain is ready and completion dates are agreed the conveyancers will exchange contracts. They will then make arrangements to complete on the completion day.	These stages will not change.

Exchange of contracts is usually done by telephone using a Law Society formula to ensure all the parties in the chain are legally committed to the transaction at exactly the same time. After exchange of contracts has taken place the sale is legally binding upon both you and your buyer.

Arranging completion

Traditionally, the time period between exchange of contracts and completion was 28 days. However, it may be more or less to suit the parties involved and these days completion often takes place a week or so after exchange. Between exchange of contracts and completion your conveyancer will obtain a redemption statement from your lender(s), obtain the estate agent's invoice and prepare a final completion statement to send to you. A final deed called the Transfer is sent to you for signature. This document must be returned to your conveyancer before completion. Your buyer's conveyancer will send another set of enquiries called Requisitions on Title which your conveyancer must answer and return. Requisitions on Title include practical information such as where the keys will be left on completion and the bank account details to send the completion money to.

Completion day

On the day of completion your buyer's conveyancer will transfer the purchase price into your conveyancer's client account. This is done by an electronic bank transfer and can take minutes or several hours to arrive. Once the money is committed to the bank's system the conveyancers have no control over the time it takes to arrive at the other end. This is entirely dependent upon the efficiency of the bank's systems. When the funds are received your conveyancer will confirm completion to you and your estate agent and authorise the release of the keys.

HIP TIP

Completion funds can take hours to move through the various banks in the chain. Don't book your removal van too early, otherwise you will be waiting around for the keys and may have to pay additional removal charges.

After completion

Once completion has taken place your conveyancer repays the mortgage(s) on the property and arranges for the mortgage entry to be removed from the Charges Register. With your permission they pay their own and the estate agent's invoice from the proceeds of sale and then send any balance to you.

THE PURCHASE PROCEDURE

Instructing a conveyancer

Now	After the HIP
Most people do not usually instruct a conveyancer until they have found the property they want to buy and had an offer accepted, subject to contract.	You should instruct your conveyancer as soon as you decide to buy a property. By instructing your conveyancer to act straightaway you can ask them to check the HIP for you before you make a firm offer for the property. Your conveyancer can then alert you to any potential problems that would affect your decision to buy or withdraw your offer.

Confirming instructions in writing

Now	After the HIP
A client care letter is sent to you as soon as you confirm that you wish the conveyancer to act for you. At this point your conveyancer usually asks for a deposit of around £200 to pay for searches. Your conveyancer will also usually deal with obtaining proof of identity from you.	The process will be the same. If you have instructed your conveyancer early on it could save time later in the procedure. If the HIP contains useful up to date searches your conveyancer may not need to collect such a large deposit.

Client care letter

The procedure is the same as detailed above for the seller. Currently your conveyancer will ask you for a deposit in the region of £200 to cover the cost of the initial searches. However, if the HIP contains up to date searches you may not need to pay such a large deposit. Your conveyancer may still ask for a deposit from you as there may be additional searches and minor disbursements to pay for.

Examining the contract pack and searches

Now	After the HIP
Currently your conveyancer waits to receive the contract pack from your seller's conveyancer before doing any work. This is usually to ensure that your seller is genuinely proceeding with the sale to you and because the pack contains plans which your conveyancer uses for the searches. Once the pack is received your conveyancer will check the contract and the legal title, raise pre-contract enquiries and make the necessary searches.	If your conveyancer has been supplied with the HIP they will have more up front knowledge of the property. They can check whether the searches in the HIP are current and whether they need to update them or make further searches. The HIP will include a plan which will enable them to apply immediately for any additional searches. They can also start to prepare their additional pre-contract enquiries as much of the contract information will be included in the HIP.

HIP TIP

With the introduction of the HIP your conveyancer should be able to move forward more quickly. They will be able to see what searches have been obtained, whether they are current, and if new searches are necessary they can apply immediately as the HIP contains all the necessary information and plans.

Raising additional enquiries

Now	After the HIP
Currently your conveyancer knows little of the property until the contract pack is received. They are then presented with a pile of information about 20 cms thick to wade through. They will sift carefully, checking the contract, legal title, estate agent's particulars, Property Information form, Fixtures and Fittings form and any survey. If they are lucky all this will have been sent with the contract pack. It is often the case that this information will arrive piecemeal over the course of several days or weeks, which means that your conveyancer constantly has to revisit the file and raise enquiries piecemeal.	Your conveyancer will be in possession of the HIP. They can check the legal title, the searches, the Home Condition Report (if supplied) and any leasehold, commonhold or additional information immediately. As soon as a sale is confirmed they can start to prepare their additional enquiries. When they get the contract pack they will then just need to check the contract and any additional information sent. This should enable the additional enquiries to be sent out more quickly. The HIP presents a more efficient system for your conveyancer, as they will receive the majority of the information at the outset.

Approving the contract

Once your conveyancer is satisfied with the contract and the replies to their searches and enquiries they will 'approve' the contract and return one copy to your seller's conveyancer.

The mortgage offer

Now	After the HIP
Currently most people obtain an informal mortgage agreement from a lender and wait to apply for a formal mortgage once their offer has been accepted on a property. Some people do not even research the amount they can borrow or speak to a lender until they have found a property to buy. This can cause delays and problems if their application is declined or they cannot borrow a sufficient amount. Some buyers also continue to shop around for a good mortgage deal even after their offer to buy has been accepted. This causes delays in the chain. Once your application for a mortgage is sent to your lender they must then carry out credit checks, get confirmation of your earnings and obtain a mortgage valuation. This is often the longest process in the conveyancing transaction and can sometimes take weeks, especially if you are self-employed or have complicated circumstances.	The HIP regulations place no obligation on you to obtain a mortgage agreement in advance of making an offer on a property. However, it is thought that sellers and estate agents will demand to see a mortgage offer in principle before agreeing to accept a formal offer to purchase. If your seller has paid out money up front for the HIP they will want to be sure that you are serious about your offer and that you are in a position to proceed with the purchase. If potential buyers are forced to obtain a mortgage agreement in principle this should speed up the process of the mortgage offer being made as the lender should already have made credit checks and ensured that the borrower is earning sufficient money to repay the loan. The Home Condition Report (if supplied) does not contain a valuation, so a mortgage valuation will still be necessary, although with the Home Condition Report this may be reduced to an automated valuation in some cases. Again this would save time as surveyors get busy and it can take days if not weeks for survey appointments to be carried out.

HIP TIP

It is expected that after the HIP sellers and estate agents will require sight of a mortgage agreement in principle before accepting an offer to buy.

The contract report and signing of the contract

Now	After the HIP
Once your conveyancer has approved the contract and has received your mortgage offer they will prepare a detailed report on the contract and pre-contract documents. This will be sent to you with the contract to sign. The contract report pack generally includes other documents for signature, such as the mortgage documents and the Stamp Duty Land Tax form. You must then read the report, sign and return the documents and put your conveyancer in funds for the deposit.	This stage will not change.

Exchanging contracts

Now	After the HIP
When your conveyancer is holding the signed contract, mortgage deeds, Stamp Duty Land Tax form and cleared funds for the deposit they are ready to exchange. They will notify your seller's conveyancer and suggest a completion date. When the date is agreed they will exchange contracts by phone as detailed above.	This stage will remain the same.

Arranging completion and completion day

Now	After the HIP
After contracts are exchanged your conveyancer applies for the final searches, raises Requisitions on Title, drafts the Transfer, sends a Report on Title to the lender requesting funds, places any necessary insurance on risk and prepares a completion statement to send to you. On the day of completion your conveyancer checks that they have received all the funds and arranges a telegraphic transfer of the completion money to your seller's conveyancer.	These stages remain unchanged.

After completion

Your conveyancer will send off the Stamp Duty Land Tax form and Stamp Duty to the Inland Revenue who will then send a certificate to confirm the duty has been paid. Your conveyancer then sends an application to the Land Registry to register you as the new owner and your mortgage company as the new lender. Once registration is completed your conveyancer sends your lender whatever deeds they require and the remainder are sent to you or stored at the conveyancer's office at your request.

HIP TIP

It is clear from the information in the above boxes that the HIP will be of most benefit in the early stages of the transaction prior to exchange of contracts. If prepared properly and completely, the HIP could save considerable time at the initial stages of searches and pre-contract enquiries. If, in addition to the HIP, the seller and their agent insist on a mortgage agreement in principle before acceptance of offer, this will create further time-saving and add more certainty to the transaction.

10

How to Find and Secure Your Dream Property

Buying a new property, whether for investment or to live in, can prove a life-changing and challenging experience. The decisions you make now may dictate where you will be living for the foreseeable future. Quite possibly, you are about to spend the most money you have ever spent. For most of us buying a property is usually the largest financial investment we make during our life times.

If you plan your investment wisely you should secure a comfortable home to live in and an asset that will appreciate in value during your ownership. However, before you set sail on your voyage of adventure you need to embark upon a little research.

BEING PREPARED

To avoid disappointment and stress you must be realistic about what you can afford and where you want to live. Insisting that you want a two-bedroom house with a garden in area A when you can only afford a one-bedroom flat in area B will inevitably lead to frustration and heartache.

Before you even start to look for that dream home it is important to put in some ground work. The first thing to do is to find out whether you are able to obtain a mortgage and how much you can afford to borrow. I have acted for many disappointed buyers who have found their dream home, only to find that they can't get the mortgage they need because of a poor credit history or insufficient earnings.

Finally, once you find your dream home it is important to ensure that you secure it. The only sure-fire way to do this is to get to exchange of contracts as fast as possible, for it is only once contracts are unconditionally exchanged that you can be sure that the property is yours.

A little time spent in preparation while you are still looking for a property will pay off later on. Start by sourcing your mortgage, choose and instruct your conveyancer and get the initial paperwork out of the way, so that as soon as your offer to buy is accepted you can concentrate on pushing forward to exchange of contracts.

CAN YOU GET A MORTGAGE?

The very first question you must ask yourself is whether you are eligible to obtain a mortgage. This will depend on the following:

Your earnings

The lender will take into account your gross pay, that is your salary before tax and national insurance are deducted. Lenders do not usually take into account overtime or bonus payments unless your employer will confirm that they are guaranteed. Self-employed people are generally asked to provide at least three years' audited accounts as proof of income.

Your credit history

The lender will carry out a credit search. This will show up any credit problems you have had in the past, including bad debts, late payments and County Court Judgements. The lender's conveyancer will also carry out a Land Charges search before releasing funds which will show if you have been or are in the process of being made bankrupt.

References

The lender will take up references with your existing mortgage company or your landlord if you are currently renting a property.

Your credit score

Your credit score depends on your circumstances, such as how long you have lived in your present property, how long you have been in your current employment, your previous credit history and how much deposit you have been able to save.

The value of the property

Before a lender will agree to lend on a property they will carry out their own valuation to make sure it is good security for the loan.

CAN YOU AFFORD TO REPAY A MORTGAGE?

It is important that you check that you will be able to afford the repayments and that you take into account the possibility of future interest rate rises and loss of earnings due to redundancy, sickness or starting a family. Before proceeding with a mortgage you should complete an estimated monthly budget as follows:

Monthly budget calculator

Mortgage repayment	£
Life insurance	£
Building and contents insurance	£
Council tax	£
Water rates	£
Electricity/gas/oil	£
Credit cards/loan payments	£
Food	£
Travel costs	£
Car costs	£
TV licence/cable	£
Entertainment	£
Savings for holidays	£
Pension contributions	£
Total costs:	£
Total net income:	£

FINDING OUT HOW MUCH YOU CAN BORROW

Lenders calculate the amount they are prepared to lend you on a multiple of your gross salary. This varies from lender to lender and it makes sense to shop around as some are prepared to lend more than others.

Traditionally, lenders have been very cautious when calculating the amount they were prepared to lend. Although interest rates have steadily reduced over the past few years, and are currently low at around 5.5% they have started to rise again. Interest rates climbed as high as 15% in the 1990s. Unless you have taken out a fixed rate mortgage, interest rate rises can have a catastrophic

effect on your ability to make your mortgage payments. As a
result many people lose their homes when interest rates start to
climb. To avoid this lenders err on the side of caution when
lending money and employ a strict calculation when deciding how
much a borrower can afford to pay back each month.

The lender's calculations

The amount a lender would lend, until very recently, was typically
from two-and-a-half to three-and-a-half times the main earner's
income before tax, plus one times any second earner's income or
two-and-a-half times the joint income of the borrowers. Lenders
calculate your income on your basic pay before tax, and will
usually take into consideration only half of any overtime,
commission or bonus pay and then only if it is guaranteed by
your employers. The calculation does vary from lender to lender
and some will lend more than others. Lenders are required to lend
responsibly and may reduce the amount they are prepared to lend
you if you already have high outgoings such as credit card or loan
repayments.

A specialist mortgage adviser will be able to advise you of the
amount each lender is prepared to lend. Mortgage advisers have a
duty to make reasonable enquiries to ensure that you can afford
the mortgage they recommend. Further details of mortgages,
mortgage advisers and how to source a mortgage are contained in
Chapter 11.

First time buyers

With the average price of a first time buyer's property soaring to
around £120,000, first time buyers are finding it increasingly
difficult to get on to the property ladder and most find they are

not earning enough to satisfy the lender's mortgage calculations. As a property chain must start somewhere this lack of first time buyers causes stagnation in the property market.

Added to this, first time buyers must also find a hefty deposit to put towards their property purchase. Although some lenders will lend 100% of the property value most lenders require you to pay a deposit of at least 5% of the purchase price. With legal, survey and removal costs added this means that the average first time buyer must save around £7,500 and that is assuming that no Stamp Duty is payable and that they will not be having an independent survey. A combination of low earnings and student debt repayments often means that first time buyers are unable to save the necessary deposit and legal fees, which exacerbates the problem.

To buy a property worth £120,000 with a 95% mortgage you would have to borrow £114,000 on mortgage. Taking a calculation of one earner at three times their income this means that the main earner must be earning £38,000 per annum to qualify for a mortgage. The average first time buyer does not earn anywhere near this amount and, even if buying jointly with a partner or spouse, the couple would have to earn around £45,600 per annum to qualify for the two-and-a-half times joint income.

How much lenders will charge

As mentioned above some lenders will lend 100% of the valuation of the property, and some will even lend in excess of this amount to include the cost of the fees and mortgage costs. Generally, the higher the percentage of the loan to the value of the property the higher the interest rate will be. High percentage mortgages pose higher risks to the lender, and as a result you may have additional costs to pay, such as application fees and mortgage guarantee or indemnity premiums.

Very recently lenders have started to change the way in which they calculate the sum they are prepared to lend. Rather than relying on a 'one size fits all' calculation they have begun to assess how much you can realistically afford to pay. Low interest rates mean low monthly repayments and, as a result of the continuing stability of bank interest rates, lenders are increasing the amounts they will lend. With increased multiples it is important to ensure that you don't overstretch your budget, particularly if interest rates subsequently begin to rise. By increasing the amount they are prepared to lend, lenders hope to encourage the first time buyer on to the property ladder.

MORTGAGE COSTS

There is a number of costs associated with obtaining a mortgage and these should be set out in the Key Facts Indicator (KFI) supplied by your mortgage adviser. Further details of the KFI are contained in Chapter 12.

Mortgage guarantee/indemnity policy premiums

With a high loan to value mortgage, a mortgage guarantee or indemnity policy is taken out by your lender to protect them in the event that you fail to make the mortgage repayments. You have to pay the premium, which is a one-off premium, paid when the mortgage is taken out. The premiums can be quite high, sometimes as much as 1% of the loan, although some lenders allow you to add this to your mortgage. When a mortgage guarantee policy is taken out by the lender, the insurance company pays up if the lender has to repossess your property and it does not sell for enough to pay off the mortgage. The policy does not carry any benefit to you and many borrowers have been pursued by these insurance companies to make good their loss.

Mortgage application fees

Some lenders charge a mortgage application fee to cover the cost of administration of the loan. Generally, these are paid when applying for the loan and are not refundable – even if the lender ultimately refuses to grant the mortgage. The fees vary from around £250 up to £1,000 plus. Mortgage application fees have risen steeply in recent months as lenders seek to claw back some of the profits they lose on the cheap mortgage products they offer.

Mortgage valuation fees

When you take out a mortgage the lender will insist that one of their panel valuers provides a valuation of the property. To do this the valuer will arrange to inspect the property. You must pay for the cost of the valuation even if the mortgage application does not proceed. The valuation is carried out purely for the lender's purposes to enable them to decide whether to grant you the mortgage and if so how much. The lender does not have to tell you the contents of the valuation, although some will provide you with a copy. If the valuation proves to be inaccurate or negligent you have no right in law to sue the lender or their valuer.

A mortgage valuation is not an extensive survey, sometimes the valuer does not even visit or go inside the property.

CALCULATING YOUR DEPOSIT

When calculating the amount of deposit you have available to put towards a property do not forget to deduct the costs of the transaction as follows:

◆ mortgage application fee;
◆ mortgage valuation fee;
◆ mortgage adviser fee;
◆ conveyancer's legal fees;
◆ Stamp Duty and disbursements;
◆ removal costs;
◆ sundry costs (connection of services, ground rent, maintenance charges, etc.).

Do not cut your budget to the bone – always allow for last minute costs.

Once you have collated the above information you can then assess how much you can afford to pay for your property. See the example below:

Example – purchase price calculator		
Mortgage	£114,000	+
Deposit	£ 7,500	equals
Total	£121,500	less
Costs	£ 1,500	equals
Purchase price	**£120,000**	

Now that you have found out how much you can afford to pay for a property you can begin your detective work to find out what that sum will buy you in the neighbourhood you want to live in.

HIP TIP

www.yourmortgage.co.uk contains a useful mortgage calculator that you can use to find out how much the monthly repayments would be for the amount you want to borrow.

HOW TO FIND THE RIGHT LOCATION

Property prices can vary hugely from one locality to another, particularly in London and other major cities. You may be lucky enough to have *carte blanche* in deciding where you want to live, but most of us are restricted in some way. Consider the following points before making your decision:

Work

Do you need to be able to drive to work? If so you will have to consider road connections and driving time. If you will be commuting by car try to replicate your journey in peak hour traffic. A journey that I make regularly will be fairly hassle-free and take me about an hour at the weekend. However, during rush hour the traffic is a nightmare and it can take up to two hours.

Public transport

Do you rely upon public transport to get you to work, the children to school or just to get you to the shops? If so, make enquiries to find what public transport is available. The local library should have details of rail and bus timetables or visit www.traveline.org.uk for a national database of rail, bus and coach travel.

Working from home

If you intend to work from home and use the internet you will need to check whether Broadband is available. In some areas the telephone system is hopeless and would make working from home very difficult. BT will be able to advise whether Broadband is available (visit www.bt.com).

Schools

Many parents now choose to move into the catchment area of

good schools. Before doing so check with the school what the catchment area is and whether your child will automatically be entitled to a place if you live within the catchment area. The local library will have details of schools in the area and copies of Ofsted reports. Visit www.goodschoolsguide.co.uk for a list of public information on schools in the UK.

Local amenities

If you don't drive you will need to find out whether there are shops, doctors, dentists, post office, etc. within walking distance. Do you want to take a bus ride every time you need a pint of milk or a loaf of bread?

Nightlife

Where are the nearest pubs, clubs and restaurants? If this is important to you, or you have teenagers, easy access to nightlife means that you won't spend your life ferrying the kids to and fro or bust your budget on taxis every weekend.

Community

Some areas enjoy a thriving community with vibrant pubs, clubs, colleges, places of worship, playgroups, etc. If a good community is important to you check the local pubs and the library for details of clubs or college classes, places of worship, playgroups, etc.

Running costs

If you are on a tight budget you may need to consider the running costs of the property. The seller should be able to give you a good indication of the costs of heating, lighting, water rates, council tax, etc.

CONSIDERING DIFFERENT TYPES OF PROPERTY

New build properties

If you are particularly interested in looking at newly built properties you may want to consider whether the property will have a New Homes Warranty, how long the development will continue after you have moved in, what the off-road parking arrangements are and whether the development prices are increasing in line with second-hand properties.

'Right to buy' and 'shared ownership' properties

If you cannot afford to buy a property on the open market there is a number of Government schemes that aim to help you. Full details are available on the CLG website. Current schemes include the following.

Right to buy properties

This scheme allows qualifying council or housing association tenants to purchase the property they are renting from their local council or housing association. Some schemes offer discounts on the price of the property. You will need to check with your landlord whether you qualify. As you would be purchasing the property as a tenant, your landlord is not obliged to provide you with a HIP and you must therefore pay for the usual searches and survey on the property.

Shared ownership properties

This type of scheme is usually run by local authorities or housing associations. Generally, you purchase a share in the property and the local authority or housing association purchases the remaining share. You pay a mortgage on the share you have purchased and rent on the share the local authority or housing association has purchased. You then have the option to purchase additional shares in the property until you own the whole property. This type of scheme is usually beneficial for people on low incomes who do not qualify for a sufficient mortgage to purchase a property outright. Details of shared ownership schemes can be obtained from your local authority.

The Homebuy scheme

This scheme has been introduced by the Government to help people onto the property ladder. It is a form of shared ownership which enables you to buy a share of a property if you are a social tenant, a key worker or a first time buyer. You do not pay rent on the share you do not own, but if you sell the property the landlord is entitled to a share of the sale proceeds. For instance if you own 50% and the landlord owns 50%, when you come to sell, the landlord would be entitled to 50% of the sale price of the property including any increase in value since the property was purchased. To check whether you are eligible for the Homebuy scheme visit the DCLG website at www.communities.gov.uk and type 'Homebuy scheme' into the search browser. The website includes a list of local Homebuy agents who aim to provide a one-stop shop for advice on the Homebuy scheme.

IS THE PROPERTY SUITABLE SECURITY FOR A MORTGAGE?

Some lenders will not lend on certain types of property and if you are in doubt you should first check with your lender. Typically, problems may arise with the following types of properties:

◆ Leasehold properties where the remaining term of the lease is less than 60 years. Most leases are for 99 or 999 years. If the lease has less than 60 years left to run the seller may be able to obtain an extension of the lease from the landlord. However, be warned: this is a lengthy procedure.

◆ Properties which are not expected to remain habitable for at least 60 years from the time when the loan is granted.

◆ Properties which are not structurally sound.

◆ Properties with defective leases (N.B. this could not be identified until your conveyancer had studied the lease).

◆ Freehold flats.

◆ Flying freeholds. Lenders will lend on some properties that have flying freeholds (i.e. where part of the property is situated over or under the adjoining or adjacent property). The lender's decision depends on how much of the property is affected by the flying freehold. Again this is something your conveyancer would be able to advise you and your lender upon. N.B. There is a type of insurance that covers problems with flying freeholds.

VISITING THE AREA

HIP TIP

You can gain information about a locality from the library, local papers or visit www.upmystreet.com where you can view property prices, crime reports and search for just about everything using a post code.

When you have decided where you want to buy, the next thing to do is visit the area and walk around. Do this both during the week and at the weekend and try to visit at different times of the day. This will give you a feel for the locality. Ask yourself the following questions:

- Would you feel safe walking home at night?

- Are the properties in the area well maintained?

- Do the shops appear successful? Shops that appear seedy and are shuttered may indicate a high crime level. When good shops close and bargain bucket shops open it indicates an area is on the slide. Likewise, good shops and new restaurants opening indicate an area is on the up.

- Is there a lot of graffiti or evidence of vandalism?

- What is the traffic like?

- Is there a lot of noise from roads, trains, planes?

- Is there a lot of noise from the street – particularly when the pubs and clubs turn out?

- Are there factories or businesses nearby that create pollution or smells?

- Are there electricity pylons or other potential health hazards?

- Is there a lot of development going on in the area?

- Are those open fields and spaces likely to be built upon?

- Are there any major plans for new road or rail networks?

- What types of occupants live in the area? If the area is predominantly occupied by singles or elderly couples would you feel happy living there with a young family?

As you explore the area make a list of any streets or roads that you would particularly like to live in and those that you would definitely not like to live in. Include notes to remind you how you came to your decision, e.g. Flowers Road – good place to live, bus stop and shops nearby, Graffiti Street – no good, nightclub at one end of the road and kebab shop at the other, front gardens full of litter and properties vandalised.

REFINING YOUR SEARCH

By now you are well on your way to finding the perfect property. You should know how much you can afford to pay and the area you want to live in. The next thing to do is to assess your property needs. Using the examples below, take a sheet of paper and draw two columns, one entitled 'must haves' i.e. the basic necessities in a property that you absolutely could not live without and the second column 'wish list'. If you add your contact details you can then give this list to estate agents when you register with them. Be warned though, most estate agents will send you everything in your price range – whether it suits your criteria or not.

FINDING A PROPERTY

Now that you have completed your list, it is time to burn some shoe leather and hit the streets. Take several copies of your list with you. Explore every avenue in your search, leave no stone unturned. You never know where that perfect property might be lurking.

Estate agents

As a buyer you will not have to pay any estate agent fees for their services as these are paid by the seller. Make a list of every estate agent within ten miles of the area you wish to buy in. Obtain details from *Yellow Pages* and the local newspaper. Visit as many agents as possible and try to build a rapport. If you can't visit, phone to register with them and then send them your list. Ask them to inform you immediately if any property that meets your

Property Requirements List

Mandy and James Hopeful

Address: 19 Everhopeful Gardens,

London

Telephone:

Email:

Mobile:

Price range: £110 – 120,000

Position: first time buyers.

Deposit available: £6,000

Mortgage arranged in principle with the
Done Searching Building Society

Conveyancer: Mr B. Cautious,
Cautious and Partners,
19 Anywhere Road, London
Tel:
Fax:
Email:

Must have	Wish list
Area/Location:	Area/Location:
Public transport	Nice local restaurants
Good local playgroup	Designer shops
Local shops and amenities	
School catchment area for St Stephens	
Number of bedrooms: 3	4
Number of reception rooms: 1	2
Number of bathrooms: 1	Upstairs bathroom Separate toilet downstairs
Some outside space	Big garden
Parking	Garage
Study	Home office

criteria comes on to the market. Furnish the agents with a copy of your mortgage certificate, details of your deposit, your conveyancer's contact details and your timescale. Call in or telephone at least once a week to check whether anything new is coming on to the market.

Adverts
Buy all the local newspapers and scan the estate agents' adverts for any properties you might have missed or overlooked. Be on the look out for properties that are advertised for sale privately. Some national weeklies such as *Dalton's Weekly* and *Loot* advertise property for sale.

Property boards
Check 'for sale' and 'sold' boards in the area you wish to purchase in and approach the estate agent or the property owner if it is a private board. Just because a property board indicates the property is sold does not mean that it is. Always check, the board may be old, the sale may have fallen through.

Leaflets
Leaflet-drop specific areas. Prepare some leaflets indicating that you are interested in buying property in that area. Give your name and telephone number, but do not mention prices. Be aware that after the HIP comes into force if your purchase results from a

leaflet-drop and the seller has never marketed the property they may not be obliged to provide you with a HIP. You would therefore have to add the cost of searches and survey into your calculations. In this scenario the seller would be saving not only the cost of the HIP but estate agency fees and you may be able to negotiate a price reduction because of this.

Other ideas

Check the local post office and supermarket notice boards. Put a notice on the board detailing your property requirements.

Write to all the conveyancing firms in the area. Many law firms sell property on behalf of their clients.

If you are moving into a new area consider appointing a relocation agent to find a property for you. A relocation agent will work exclusively for you – not the seller. Their charges are in the region of 1.5% of the property purchase price. For further information contact the Association of Relocation Agents (www.relocationagents.com).

HOW TO MAKE THE MOST OF VIEWINGS

Unless you are naturally curious, viewing properties is a necessary evil in your pursuit of a dream home. Sort the wheat from the chaff by checking your property requirements list and perhaps having a look at the property from the outside. Estate agents will encourage you to view as many properties as possible as viewings impress their sellers. It is a waste of your time and the seller's time to view a property that is out of your price range or does not meet your requirements. That said, you will need to set aside time for viewing. Put together a short-list of the properties that appeal to you and approach the estate agent or the seller to make an appointment to view.

Try not to cram too many appointments into one day; viewings often take longer than you expect and you will end up stressed and running late for appointments. After you have seen more than about three properties they will start to blur into one another and it will be difficult to remember one property from another.

When viewing property you should dress smartly and arrive on time. Ensure you have a copy of the estate agent's particulars and your property requirements list with you. Introduce yourself to the seller or the estate agent and remember to be polite – whatever you think of the property. Keep your thoughts, whether positive or negative, to yourself.

Show homes

When viewing a show home do not be bamboozled by the smart, new décor, the modern kitchen and bathroom and the nicely co-ordinated accessories. It is important to check the actual room sizes and the overall square footage of the house and the garden. Developers are expert in making properties appear larger than they are with clever décor and undersized furniture. You should also check what similar properties are selling for second-hand in the area. Many developers offer 'deals' when selling new property, particularly at the start of the development. The developer may offer to pay Stamp Duty and legal fees, or to include carpets and curtains, some even offer to pay your 5% deposit. Do not be fooled, all of these offers are built into the price. Some new property can lose value in the early years because of this.

Objective viewing

With the advent of the HIP you will be able to view the Home Condition Report (if one has been provided), which will give you an objective view on the condition of the property at the time the report was done. You should however keep your eyes and ears open during the viewing.

To avoid getting in a muddle when you are viewing several properties take along a viewing checklist such as the one overleaf.

Try to look past the décor of the property, and the carpets and curtains. Redecorating and fitting new flooring is relatively cheap compared with installing central heating, double glazing, rewiring, replastering ceilings and walls, fitting a new kitchen and bathroom or installing a new damp proof course. If you notice that the property has tenants or occupants other than the seller you should notify your conveyancer otherwise you may find you have inherited the previous owner's tenants.

Relating with the seller

If the seller or occupant is unfriendly and negative about the property or the sale, it may be that the property is being sold as a result of a divorce or relationship split, or the occupant may be renting the property and not wish to leave. An unwilling seller can delay a property transaction for weeks or even months, and you will need to quiz the estate agent carefully to find out the exact circumstances of the sale and then pass this information on to your conveyancer.

Never criticise a property or make plans for major alterations when you are viewing a property for the first time. Wait until you

Viewing checklist

Property address:

Seller's name:

Estate agent:
Telephone number:
Email:

Asking price:

Type of property:
Detached/semi/terraced/flat/maisonette
Council tax band:
Council tax:
Water rates:
Leasehold charges:
Average heating/lighting costs:

Tenure: freehold/leasehold/commonhold
Length of lease (if any):

Outside area:
Locality:
Garden:
Off road parking:
Garage: single/double

Inside:
Number of reception rooms:
Number of bedrooms:
Number of bathrooms/toilets:
Kitchen comments:
Bathroom comments:
Double glazed throughout: yes/no

Central heating: oil/gas/electricity/other

Open fire: yes/no

General décor comments:

Property condition:

Exterior: (if the exterior of the property is shabby and in need of maintenance it may mean that the property has not been well maintained in general)

Interior:

○ Is it cold?

○ Does it have central heating?

○ Is it bright or is it dark and gloomy?

○ How is the kitchen laid out?

○ Are the kitchen units in good condition?

○ Is there independent access to the bathroom?

○ Is the bathroom suite in good condition?

○ Are the ceilings in good condition – look for cracks that have been papered over or polystyrene tiles.

○ Are the walls in good condition?

○ Does it smell of damp?

○ Is it double glazed?

○ Does the wiring appear modern?

○ Has it been let out? Who is living there?

○ Is the person showing the property the owner?

○ Is the owner or occupant friendly and positive about the sale?

are outside to make notes and observations. Always let the estate agent know your thoughts, good or bad, so that they can relay them back to the seller.

MAKING AN OFFER

Making an offer to purchase a property is a serious commitment and should not be treated lightly. I recently heard of a couple who viewed several properties over the course of a weekend and put offers in on all of them just to see what would happen. Imagine the disappointment and frustration of the sellers when they learned that the eagerly awaited offer was not serious. This type of behaviour will earn you no respect with the estate agents and you will be dismissed as a time waster.

Make an offer to purchase only once you are sure that you wish to proceed to buy that property. Remember, all offers should be made on a strictly subject-to-contract basis. The Law Society has expressed fears that buyers will be encouraged to enter into a formal contract to purchase simply on the strength of the information contained in the HIP. Never sign a contract to purchase a property without going through the proper channels and taking the advice of a qualified conveyancer.

Asking the right questions

To put forward an offer to purchase you must first let the estate agent or the seller, if a private sale, know that you are interested. Register your interest as soon as possible; you never know how many other potential buyers are interested in the property. You then need to decide whether you are going to offer the asking price or put in a lower offer. It is fairly common practice for buyers to put forward an offer of less than the asking price but before you do this ask a few questions.

- Try to find out the seller's position. Has the property been on the market long? Have they found somewhere to buy? If the property has been on the market for a while and the seller has found something to buy they might be more amenable to accepting an offer. If the property has only just come onto the market and the seller is still looking for a property to buy they are less likely to grab the first offer they receive.

- Has there been much interest in the property? Or any other offers? You need to find out if there are any potential rivals out there. If there has been a lot of interest in the property and several offers you may want to jump in and offer the asking price to thwart the competition.

When calculating your offer you need to consider the following points:

- How the price of the property compares with similar properties you have viewed. Are the sellers asking more – if so, why?

- Is the property in good condition? Did the Home Condition Report (if provided) point out any serious defects? What is the cost of putting those defects right?

- Ask the estate agent whether the seller is open to offers. If so, how much would the estate agent consider a reasonable offer? Remember they act for the seller and are paid a commission that is a percentage of the sale price.

- Ask your conveyancer for advice. They may have acted in the sale or purchase of similar properties and generally have a good feel for the local market.

How to make your offer

When you have decided how much you are prepared to pay, put your offer forward to the estate agent or, if there is no agent, direct to the seller. You will stand a better chance of your offer being accepted if you are in a good position to proceed.

When putting forward an offer:

◆ Provide the estate agent/seller with a copy of your mortgage certificate and evidence of your deposit. Do not state you are a cash buyer if you need to arrange finance or sell a property. These things will be checked by the estate agent and the conveyancer.

◆ State your own position, e.g. first time buyer, property sold subject to contract, property still on the market – be honest as the estate agent will check the chain.

◆ The timescale you want to move to.

◆ Full contact details of your conveyancer and your mortgage company or mortgage adviser.

◆ Details of your estate agent if you are selling a property.

OFFER ACCEPTED

Thankfully, your offer has been accepted and you are ready to race towards exchange of contracts and completion.

What to do next

Insist that the property be taken off the market, the 'for sale' board be removed and all marketing of the property ceased. If there is a picture of the property in the estate agent's window ask them to take it out, and if it is advertised on a website ask for it to be removed – and then check that it has. You do not want your rivals sniffing around and putting in higher offers after your offer has been accepted.

If there has been a lot of interest in the property and you are very concerned about other offers being made on it consider asking the seller to enter into a 'lock out' agreement. Basically, this is an agreement given by the seller not to proceed with other offers. Your conveyancer will be able to draw up such an agreement for you.

Next steps

Instruct your conveyancer. Telephone and write to your conveyancer to confirm you are proceeding with the purchase, give the name and contact details of the estate agent, the seller's name and the postal address of the property. If you have a HIP and have not already given this to your conveyancer you should forward it to them now.

♦ Apply for your mortgage. You will now need to make a formal mortgage application.

♦ Arrange a survey if you have decided to have a private survey carried out.

♦ Ensure your deposit funds are ready. Move savings from notice accounts into an instant access account.

♦ Turn to Chapter 12 and follow The Move Master Plan.

11

HIPs and Mortgages

Currently around 70% of the UK population are homeowners and around 11.5 million of us have a mortgage on our property. Within this thriving mortgage market there is a vast choice of mortgage products from an estimated 155 different mortgage lenders.

THE COUNCIL OF MORTGAGE LENDERS

The Council of Mortgage Lenders (CML) is the trade association that represents 98% of all lenders operating in the UK today. The CML has voiced concern at the planned introduction of HIPs from the outset.

Lenders' difficulties with the HIP

One very contentious issue is whether lenders will accept the Home Condition Report rather than insisting upon an additional mortgage valuation. The Government is keen for them to do so, as a second valuation introduces further cost into the home-buying process.

One of the main stumbling blocks to the Home Condition Report being accepted by lenders is the lack of a property valuation. Before they will lend on a property lenders must be certain that it will provide adequate security for the mortgage. To do this they employ a qualified valuer, at your expense, to value the property on their behalf.

If the valuation later proves incorrect the lender can confidently seek redress against the surveyor and be certain that their insurance company will meet any claim.

Lenders are an extremely powerful group in the UK property industry. They have devised the procedures outlined above to ensure that when money is loaned it is repaid. Understandably, they are reluctant to move into any new area that could undermine their security.

Traditionally the lender's mortgage valuation would be carried out by a surveyor who would visit the property to carry out a brief survey. The surveyor would then form a valuation of the property based on the property condition and the surveyor's knowledge of housing prices in that area.

Recently lenders have been able to use Automated Valuation Models (AVMs) to value property. The information as to the property's value is gleaned from a database. This type of valuation is generally used where the loan to property value ratio is less than 75%. Not all lenders are geared up to use these AVMs and still rely upon a physical valuation of the property.

One of the reasons given by Government in its decision to change the status of the Home Condition Report from a required document to an authorised document was the fact that lenders are not yet ready to move to AVMs and need more time to prepare.

In the future the Government hopes that the lender will rely upon the Home Condition Report for the physical inspection of the property and an AVM for the valuation. This would mean that only one physical survey of the property would need to be carried out thus saving time and money for the consumer.

While lenders are not prepared to rely upon the Home Condition Report at present it is likely to be of considerable interest to them. The condition of the property has a direct bearing on the security of the loan. Lenders may refer the Home Condition Report to their panel surveyor for advice which could have the effect of increasing the panel surveyor's fee. If this happens it could mean that in the future we see mortgage offers with an increased number of mortgage conditions relating to the property condition. You may also find that your lender insists that defects notified in the Home Condition Report are put right either before or after completion and that mortgage funds are retained until the work is carried out to the lender's satisfaction.

In the following paragraphs we take a look at mortgages generally.

WHAT IS A MORTGAGE?

A mortgage is a type of loan granted by a bank or a building society, known as the 'lender' or 'mortgagor'. The mortgage is usually granted for a long period, traditionally 25 years, and this period is known as the 'mortgage term'. The person borrowing the money is called the borrower, or the 'mortgagee'. As a borrower you offer the lender your property as security for the loan and sign a legal document, known as a 'mortgage' or 'legal charge'. This document, which must be signed in the presence of a witness, is the contract between you and the lender. Your conveyancer will register the mortgage or legal charge at the Land Registry and this creates a charge over your property to your lender for the period of the mortgage term.

The legal charge gives your lender certain rights over your property. These rights will be set out in full in the mortgage offer which you should read carefully. Your conveyancer should also explain the mortgage offer to you and the consequences of mortgaging your home. The majority of property owners are untroubled by these rights and it is only when problems arise that the extensive rights of the lender become evident.

A MORTGAGE LENDER'S RIGHTS OVER YOUR PROPERTY

Listed below are just some of the rights you give to your lender when granting a legal charge over your property:

- The right to enter and inspect your property to ensure it is being properly maintained.

- The right to serve notice on you to put your property into good repair, or to arrange for the property to be put into good condition at your expense, if you have failed to do so.

- The right to insure the property, at your expense, should you fail to do so.

- The right, subject to a court order, to sell your property if the mortgage payments are not made on time.

- The right, in the event of a dispute, to appoint a surveyor, estate agent or legal representative to act for them at your expense.

- The right to apply money from any insurance policies or repayment vehicles that you have assigned to your lender to repay your mortgage at the end of the term, or upon your death if you do not survive the full term.

- The right to use the proceeds of the sale to repay not only the mortgage but any other loans you have with your lender whether secured or unsecured. This right is not included in every mortgage, but is common in bank mortgages.

◆ The right to send the balance of the proceeds of sale after repayment of your first mortgage to any second or subsequent mortgagee who holds a registered charge over your property.

Remember, your home is at risk if you take out a mortgage on the property and cannot meet the mortgage repayments.

What is a 'CAT' standard mortgage?

To assist consumers when choosing a mortgage the Government has put in placed standards relating to:

◆ charges (C);
◆ access (A);
◆ terms (T).

The Key Facts Indicator (see below) will state whether the mortgage is CAT standard or not. CAT standards are voluntary and do not apply to all mortgages. The requirements for a CAT standard mortgage are as follows:

Charges
◆ The interest must be calculated on a daily basis.

◆ Every regular payment and overpayment you make must be credited to your mortgage account immediately.

◆ The lender is not allowed to charge you a mortgage indemnity fee.

◆ The lender must disclose all fees up front before you take out the loan.

◆ If you are using a mortgage adviser they may not charge you a fee for arranging a CAT standard mortgage.

With variable loan rates:

◆ The lender must not charge you an arrangement fee.

◆ The variable rate of interest must not exceed 2% above the Bank of England base rate.

◆ If the Bank of England base rate decreases, your mortgage interest rate must be decreased and the payment adjustment must be made within one calendar month.

◆ The lender must allow you to pay off all or part of the mortgage at any time without an early repayment penalty.

With fixed and capped rate loans:

◆ The lender or mortgage adviser must not charge you more than £150 for the booking fee.

◆ If the lender sets an early redemption charge this must not be more than 1% of the total outstanding on the loan for each year of the fixed period – and it must reduce monthly.

◆ The lender is not allowed to charge you a redemption penalty once the fixed or capped rate period finishes.

◆ The lender must not charge you a redemption penalty if you stay with the same lender when you move home.

Access:
If there is a minimum amount you must borrow to qualify for the loan this should not exceed £10,000.

◆ Any customer must be allowed to apply for the mortgage.

◆ The lender must not use any special selection rules and must apply their normal lending criteria.

◆ The lender must allow you to continue with your CAT standard mortgage when you move home – provided that the lender is satisfied that your new home meets their lending criteria.

◆ The lender must allow you to choose the day of the month on which you make your regular monthly mortgage payment.

◆ The lender must allow you to make early repayments at any time.

Terms

◆ The advertising and promotion of the mortgage must be fair and easy to understand.

◆ The lender or mortgage adviser must not insist that you purchase other products, such as insurance, to qualify for the mortgage.

◆ The lender must give you at least six months' notice if they can no longer offer you a CAT standard mortgage.

◆ The lender must allow you to pay interest only on the outstanding mortgage debt at the normal rate should you fall into arrears with your mortgage.

HIP TIP

The Council of Mortgage Lender's website www.cml.org.uk contains a useful mortgage calculator and repayment table. There are downloadable guides including what to do if you are in mortgage arrears.

CHOOSING THE RIGHT LENDER FOR YOU

There are currently around 155 lending institutions in the UK chiefly consisting of banks and building societies. There are other types of mortgage lenders known as centralised lenders. Many lenders are familiar high street names with local branches. Others operate entirely online or through independent financial advisers, mortgage packagers and mortgage brokers. The type of lender you choose will largely depend upon your circumstances and how good a mortgage risk you are.

Mortgage sources

Outlined below are the main mortgage sources in the UK today:

High street banks and building societies

Usually these have a range of mortgage, investment and insurance products. They often employ in-house mortgage advisers to sell their products. These advisers will be able to give you advice on their company's products, and prepare mortgage illustrations for you to enable you to shop around and compare. As most banks and building societies offer only their own mortgage products, their advisers are called 'tied' advisers. Some banks and building societies do offer other mortgage provider products and are called 'multi-tied' advisers.

Online mortgage sites and lenders

A search on the word 'mortgages' on one of the main internet search engines, such as Google, will produce literally millions of results. The results displayed will include sites that act as a host for many different types of lender and allow you to compare from a much wider range of mortgage providers. These sites often offer useful information on mortgage, life and investment products, and allow you to compare interest rates and products and get instant mortgage quotes online. Most lenders now have their own web site and some give you the facility to apply for a mortgage online.

Whilst these sites are a useful source of information it is best to seek the advice of a qualified mortgage adviser before proceeding.

Independent financial advisers (IFA) and mortgage brokers

An IFA is qualified to offer advice on a wide range of financial products. Mortgage brokers or mortgage advisers are qualified to offer advice on mortgages. The IFA or mortgage adviser may operate independently or within firms of estate agents. They should have a wide knowledge of the mortgage market and may have access to mortgage deals that are unavailable on the high street. If you are self-employed, or have a poor credit history, a good IFA or mortgage adviser may be able to secure you a mortgage where you have failed to do so.

Centralised lenders

These are large companies that specialise in mortgages and do not have a high street presence. These lenders often specialise in certain types of mortgage such as buy-to-let, adverse credit and high loan to value mortgages. They lend mostly through mortgage packagers, IFAs and mortgage advisers.

Employee schemes

Some employers offer discounted mortgages to employees. If you work for a bank, building society, insurance company or large company it is worth enquiring whether your company offer such a scheme.

DIFFERENT TYPES OF MORTGAGE

Mortgage lenders compete fiercely with one another, and are constantly introducing new and innovative mortgage products to attract borrowers. There are literally thousands of different mortgage deals available for the increasingly confused consumer to wade through. While on the one hand this is a good thing, as the consumer is able to tailor a mortgage to their specific needs, on the other hand it is impossible to compare all the different mortgages on offer unless you are a mortgage expert.

The following paragraphs will help you to understand the various types of mortgage that are available in the mortgage market today.

This chapter is for general guidance only. Before entering into a mortgage you should seek specialist advice from an IFA or mortgage adviser who is registered with the Financial Services Authority.

The repayment mortgage

Also known as a 'capital and interest' mortgage. With a repayment mortgage the lender looks at the sum borrowed, known as the 'capital', and calculates the interest that will accrue on that sum during the term of the mortgage. The lender then calculates how much you must pay each month to make sure that the mortgage is completely repaid at the end of the mortgage term. Each month your mortgage payment will consist of part interest and part capital. In the early years you are mostly paying off the interest and will not see much of a decrease in the loan. See the examples below:

*Example A	
You borrow	£100,000 (capital)
Add interest	£125,000 (interest)
Total	**£225,000** (total loan)

Divide the total loan of £225,000 by the mortgage term of say 25 yrs = £9,000 per annum loan repayments to make. Dividing the

£9,000 loan repayments into 12 equal monthly instalments would mean a monthly repayment of £750 per month.

The interest only mortgage

With an interest only mortgage the lender calculates the interest on the mortgage during the mortgage term. The lender then calculates how much the monthly repayment will be to pay off the interest only part of the mortgage. You make the mortgage repayments for the term of the loan. At the end of the loan you have paid off the interest, but still owe the full amount of the mortgage that you originally borrowed.

*Example B

You borrow	£100,000 (capital)
The interest on the loan is	£125,000 (interest)

You will be paying only the interest so you divide the £125,000 interest sum by the mortgage term of say 25 years = £5,000 per annum mortgage repayments to make. You then divide this into 12 equal monthly repayments = £416.67 each month.

You can see from the examples above that with a repayment mortgage you have a higher monthly payment, but at the end of the term you will have paid off both the capital and interest of the mortgage and will owe the lender nothing. With an interest only mortgage you will have a lower monthly payment, but at the end of the term you will have only paid the interest off and still owe the lender the full amount of the capital that you borrowed.

---

*The above examples are simple illustrations and do not in any way represent actual interest charges or repayment figures.

Advantages and disadvantages

Repayment mortgage
With a repayment mortgage you have the certainty that at the end of the mortgage term you will have nothing more to pay. You may have to pay a higher monthly payment in the early years.

Interest only mortgage
With an interest only mortgage you may have the benefit of lower monthly mortgage payments. At the end of the mortgage term you will still owe the full amount of the mortgage.

With an interest only mortgage some lenders will insist, and all will recommend, that you take out a savings plan to pay off the mortgage at the end of the term. This type of plan is called a 'repayment vehicle'. With the added cost of the savings plan the total monthly mortgage spend is often similar to the cost of the repayment mortgage.

Different types of repayment plans are discussed later in this chapter. Relying on a repayment plan to pay off your mortgage at the end of the term can be hit-and-miss. Some plans have done very well in the past and have provided at least enough to repay the mortgage whilst others have performed badly. If a repayment plan performs badly then it may not provide enough money to pay off the mortgage at the end of the term and you, the borrower, must make up the shortfall.

MORTGAGE INTEREST RATES

With the majority of mortgages in the UK you must pay interest to the lender. Individual lenders set the interest rate they intend to charge you based on the current Bank of England base rate and what their competitors are charging. Interest rates may go up or down throughout the term of your mortgage.

Interest rate options

There are two main interest options when choosing how to repay your mortgage.

Variable rate of interest

With this type of mortgage the interest rate charged on your mortgage can fluctuate throughout the term of the mortgage. A rise or fall in interest rates is usually triggered by a rise or fall in the Bank of England base rate. With a variable rate of interest you cannot predict what your monthly repayments will be. You will reap the benefit when interest rates fall, but conversely you will have to pay more when they rise.

Fixed rate of interest

Most lenders offer a 'fixed rate' product. This allows you to fix the rate of interest you will pay on the mortgage for an agreed number of years. The fixed rate period can vary from just one to two years up to a fix for the entire term of the mortgage. During the fixed rate period you can be sure that your monthly mortgage repayments will not increase if interest rates rise, but equally your mortgage repayments will not decrease if interest rates fall. Once the fixed rate period ends the mortgage will usually revert to the lender's variable interest rate. Some fixed rate deals will tie you into the mortgage for a further period after the benefit of the lower fixed rate has ended. If this is the case, and you wish to change mortgages at the end of the advantageous fixed rate period, you cannot do so without incurring a hefty 'early redemption penalty'.

Further mortgage options

Lending institutions set out their stalls attractively to entice borrowers. 'Discounted' mortgages, 'cash backs' and 'payment holidays' are just some of the new and innovative mortgage products to hit the market in recent years. In my experience I have found the old adage 'there is no such thing as a free lunch' to be true. If a lender is offering a benefit, whether it is a lower interest rate initially, cash back, free legal fees or survey fees, ultimately you will pay for that benefit. It is important to read the small print and to understand the facts before entering into a mortgage.

HIP TIP

The Financial Services Authority (FSA) website contains comparative tables that will allow you to compare various products, including standard mortgages, from different providers (visit www.fsa.gov.uk/tables). The FSA also publishes a number of useful leaflets relating to mortgages which are available online, or call 0845 456 1555.

THE KEY FACTS INDICATOR: KFI

Fortunately it is now easier to compare mortgages and understand the total costs of the mortgage over the lifetime of the loan. By law a lender or mortgage adviser, who is regulated by the FSA, must provide you with a Key Facts Illustrator (KFI). Read the KFI carefully as it gives an illustration of the mortgage, and details the features and costs associated with that particular product. The KFI should include the following details:

♦ The purpose of the KFI and permission to use it to compare mortgages.

♦ The service the mortgage adviser will provide.

♦ Confirmation of the information you have given to the mortgage adviser.

- The name of the lender and details of the mortgage including the interest rate, whether there are any restrictions and whether the mortgage deal obliges you to buy other products.

- The total amount the mortgage will cost you to repay at the current mortgage rate.

- The monthly repayments.

- How a rise in interest rates will affect the mortgage – to help you to decide whether you need a fixed rate mortgage.

- The fees payable to the lender and/or the mortgage adviser, when the payments are due and whether they can be refunded.

- Whether you must buy insurance products from the lender and whether the lender will charge you if you buy insurance products elsewhere.

- Whether the mortgage includes penalties for early repayment and what those penalties might be.

- Whether the mortgage has additional features such as payment holidays, flexible repayments which allow you to overpay or underpay the mortgage, etc.

- Any commission your mortgage adviser will receive from the lender.

- Where you can obtain additional information about mortgages.

The KFI enables you to see how a particular mortgage product will affect you in the long term as well as the short term. When you receive the formal written offer of mortgage it will contain an updated version of the KFI, which you should compare with the original to make sure you have been given the correct mortgage.

TYPES OF MORTGAGE PRODUCTS

Listed below are some of the different types of mortgage deals available.

Reduced or discounted interest rates

Lenders offer a product with an interest rate that is lower than their standard mortgage rate. Your repayments will vary with a rise or fall in the general interest rates, but will remain lower than the lender's standard interest rate for the period of the discount. The lower rate is usually offered for a fixed period after which the interest rate will increase to the lender's standard variable interest rate. It is often the case that the fixed low interest period is for a fairly short term and, when the lower fixed rate ends, you find you are tied into the higher, variable rate mortgage for a further fixed period. If this is the case you cannot repay your mortgage or switch to a better deal without incurring an early repayment penalty. Thus you are obliged to pay the higher interest rate for the remainder of the 'tie in' period.

Fixed interest rates

With this type of mortgage the interest rate on your mortgage is fixed for a set period. By fixing the interest rate you can guarantee that your monthly mortgage payment will not change during the fixed rate period. The down side is that you are usually tied into a variable rate mortgage for a period after the fixed rate has ended. During the fixed rate period the amount of interest charged cannot increase or decrease. You benefit if the general interest rate increases but if, as in recent years, interest rates decrease you are tied into a high fixed rate mortgage to your detriment.

Capped/collared interest rates

With a capped interest mortgage the lender guarantees that the interest rate on your mortgage will not rise above a fixed level, but it will decrease if their standard mortgage interest rate decreases. With this type of mortgage you have the certainty of knowing your mortgage repayments will not increase, but the added benefit of knowing that if interest rates decrease you will benefit. With a collared interest rate the lender stipulates that the interest rate cannot fall below a certain level.

Tracker interest rates

The lender offers an interest rate that tracks the Bank of England or some other base rate. With this type of mortgage the lender guarantees that the interest rate will not exceed or drop below the stipulated base rate by more than a specified amount. Mortgage repayments can go up or down.

Current account/offset mortgages

These mortgages are linked to your current account or a savings account. They work on the principle that the debt owed on the mortgage is reduced by the credit balance in your account before the interest on the mortgage is worked out. Each month the amount of credit in your account is subtracted from the mortgage debt and mortgage interest is paid on the balance only. Thus, if the amount in your current account or savings account increases, your mortgage repayments decrease and as your balance/savings decrease your mortgage repayments increase. This type of mortgage may be of advantage to regular savers and higher rate tax payers. If you link your savings to your mortgage you do not get interest on your savings, but you pay less interest on your mortgage.

Flexible mortgages

This type of mortgage allows you to overpay or underpay the mortgage at certain times. You may also be given a mortgage 'overdraft' that you are allowed to draw upon. These products can offer the flexibility to alter your mortgage payments to suit your circumstances and to repay the loan early, without penalty, if you choose to. Flexible mortgages can be useful if you are self-employed and your income fluctuates or if you want to pay your loan off quickly.

Self certified mortgages

This type of mortgage allows you to certify your income, without proof. The interest rate is usually higher and you are generally required to pay a deposit of at least 25% of the purchase price. The lender relies upon you to provide a true and honest statement of income. If you overstate your income you may end up with a mortgage you cannot afford and be subject to criminal proceedings for fraud.

MORTGAGE REGULATION

The Financial Services Authority is responsible for the regulation of the majority of mortgage sales. It is important to ensure that the firm you are dealing with is registered by the FSA. The FSA has a complaints and compensation procedure to protect borrowers.

FSA members must comply with the FSA regulations which are published on the FSA website. If you later encounter problems because of an FSA registered mortgage adviser there is a complaints and compensation procedure to protect you.

FSA members have the following obligations to their clients:

◆ They must provide clear information to you about mortgages and mortgage services in a standard Key Facts Illustration (KFI).

◆ Advertising and marketing material must be unambiguous and must include price information, including the mortgage annual percentage rate (APR).

◆ The advice you are given must be based on your specific needs and circumstances.

◆ Their charges must not be excessive and all the mortgage fees you will have to pay must be set out in the KFI.

◆ You will receive greater protection should you fall into mortgage arrears.

HIP TIP

Check whether your mortgage adviser is registered with the FSA on their website www.fsa.gov.uk/consumer or call 0845 606 1234. The FSA also publishes a guide to making a complaint about financial services which can be obtained on the consumer website or their Leafletline.

MORTGAGE RELATED INSURANCE

There are numerous insurance products related to mortgages, and it can sometimes seem as though you are signing your life away as you complete a myriad forms and sign hosts of direct debits.

Some of the more common insurance products are illustrated below.

Buildings insurance

When you purchase a property with a mortgage your lender will insist that you take out buildings insurance. Their mortgage valuer will state how much your property should be insured for. This is called the reinstatement value. This figure does not reflect the market value of your property, but rather the cost of reinstating it should it be completely destroyed. Your lender may insist that they are jointly named on your policy document and it is generally a condition of the mortgage offer that you provide them with a copy of the insurance policy each year. Buildings insurance is designed to cover your property against major risks to the structure and fabric such as fire, flood, subsidence, etc. In the event that your property is destroyed or damaged the insurance company pays out a sum of money to repair or reinstate the property. Your lender will almost certainly offer to arrange the buildings insurance for you, at your expense, but do not accept until you have shopped around as the cost of insuring via your lender is usually more expensive.

Contents insurance

This is usually taken out jointly with buildings insurance. Contents insurance is designed to insure personal belongings that are not covered by building insurance. It is not usually a condition of the mortgage offer that you have contents insurance. It is your own decision whether you require contents insurance and if so, how much.

Life assurance

When buying a property with the aid of a mortgage you must consider what will happen to the property, and any dependants living with you, if you die before the mortgage is repaid. If you are the sole borrower, upon your death your lender would expect the mortgage to be repaid in full more or less immediately. If you have not taken out sufficient life assurance to repay your mortgage when you die, your lender will expect the loan to be repaid from your estate (i.e. your assets after death). For most of us our home is our major asset and forms the majority of our estate. If there are insufficient funds, apart from your home, to repay the loan then the property will be sold by your lender and your mortgage will be repaid out of the proceeds of the sale. This could have a catastrophic effect upon a partner and/or dependent children living in the property.

If you are a joint borrower you will be required to take out life assurance to pay off the mortgage in the event of one or both deaths.

There are two types of life assurance, as follows.

Term assurance

Term assurance is specifically designed as a mortgage protection product. The policy is taken out for the length of the mortgage term, i.e. where the mortgage term is for 25 years, the policy would also be for 25 years. The policy guarantees to provide a lump sum to repay the mortgage if you die within the policy term. If you survive past the end of the policy term no payment is made. Term assurance is generally cheaper than life assurance. There are two types of term assurance, outlined below.

Level term assurance

You stipulate the amount you want to insure, usually the amount of your mortgage. The policy guarantees to pay out a lump sum of that amount if you die within the policy term. If you survive the policy term, no payment is made. This type of policy would usually be taken out on interest only mortgages where the amount of the capital outstanding on the mortgage never decreases.

Decreasing term assurance
This is an assurance policy that guarantees to pay a decreasing amount as each year passes. This type of policy is usually taken out to protect a repayment mortgage, where as time elapses the amount required to repay your mortgage decreases.

Whole of life insurance
With a whole of life insurance policy the insurer pays out a guaranteed lump sum when you die. Many life insurance companies now offer the option to add a provision to the policy for 'critical illness' payments. These policies are designed to pay out lump sum payments if you are medically diagnosed with one of the specified critical illnesses. It is important to disclose your full medical history to the insurer to avoid problems if you need to claim later on.

Mortgage protection insurance
This type of policy is generally known as Mortgage Payments Protection Insurance (MPPI) or Accident, Sickness and Unemployment insurance (ASU). Mortgage protection insurance is designed to protect you should you become unable to pay your mortgage due to accident, illness or unemployment. The insurer meets the cost of your mortgage payments whilst you are unable to work. There may be an initial period before the policy benefits begin and there may be a limit to the length of time the policy will pay out. You must be sure that the insurance is suitable for you and your circumstances, particularly if you are self-employed

or working on a fixed contract, which may exclude you from being covered for unemployment, or if you suffer a pre-existing medical condition which may exclude you from sickness benefits. You should also check whether you have other insurance or company benefits which protect you should you be unable to make your mortgage repayments.

There has been a considerable amount of bad press relating to this type of policy recently. This is due to the number of people who claim to have been mis-sold this type of policy or those who have tried to claim on the policy only to be turned down through some clause contained in the small print. Needless to say it is important to read the small print on all types of insurance policies and to take expert independent advice before proceeding.

HIP TIP

The Council of Mortgage Lenders has published a leaflet called *Take Cover for a Rainy Day*, outlining the pros and cons of MPPI and ASU insurance. A copy can be downloaded from their website www.cml.org.uk or contact the consumer line on 020 7440 2255.

REPAYMENT VEHICLES

In addition to the above mortgage-related insurance policies there are also policies that are designed as repayment vehicles for mortgages.

Endowment policies

An endowment policy is a combination of a savings plan and a life assurance policy. The money you pay into an endowment policy is invested by the insurance company on the Stock

Exchange. Fund managers generally aim to keep the investment risk to a minimum by investing at least 70% of the fund into real assets such as property and equity. In the early years of an endowment policy much of what you invest is spent on the high set-up costs and charges of the policy. This means that if you cash the policy in during the early years, you are penalised and may receive little or no benefit from the policy. The aim of an endowment policy is to produce a lump sum at the end of the policy term that is sufficient to repay the amount outstanding on your mortgage. If you do not survive to the end of the policy term the life assurance element pays out a guaranteed lump sum.

An endowment policy is usually taken out alongside an interest only mortgage. You pay the insurance premium each month and the premiums are then invested by the insurance company. If all goes well, the profit from the investment accrues and a sufficient sum of money is produced to repay your mortgage at the end of the term. If all does not go well and the investment does not accrue a sufficient amount to repay your mortgage, you must find the shortfall from your own resources. This type of policy is speculative and has not performed well in recent years. The policy does not guarantee to pay out a minimum or guaranteed sum and many homeowners have been left with mortgage shortfalls.

Savings plans

With an Individual Savings Account (ISA) mortgage you make payments into an individual savings account ISA in order to build up a lump sum with which to repay your mortgage at the end of the term. There is currently a tax advantage with this type of savings plan because all the income from the investment is tax free. The ISA also has the additional benefits of lower set-up charges than the endowment policy and usually no penalties are incurred if you cash the plan in before the end of the mortgage term. The efficacy of the plan relies upon sound investment by the plan provider and, as with endowments, the amount realised at the end of the term depends upon how well the plan has performed. If the plan does not perform well, and does not produce sufficient funds to repay your mortgage, you must find the shortfall from your own funds. As with the endowment plan this type of plan is speculative and does not guarantee a minimum payment. The ISA does not include any type of life cover other than the return of the value of the investment upon death. You would therefore need to take out separate life cover with an ISA mortgage.

Pension mortgages

With this type of scheme you contribute to a personal pension plan with the aim of building up a fund that is sufficient to repay your mortgage at the end of the term and to provide you with a pension. Currently, payments into the plan attract tax relief at the basic rate on payment. If you are a higher rate tax payer you can claim the higher rate tax relief of 40%. An additional tax benefit is that the lump sum payment made at the end of the plan is also tax-free. As with endowments and ISAs, the pot of money at the end of the term depends on how well the scheme has performed. If the scheme has not performed well you could find that the lump sum payout is insufficient to repay your mortgage and provide you with the level of pension you had planned. There is no life cover with this type of plan and you would need to arrange separate life cover. Another disadvantage of this scheme is that if you subsequently join a work pension plan or become unemployed, you may no longer be eligible to make contributions into a personal pension plan.

HOW TO CHOOSE THE RIGHT MORTGAGE FOR YOU

Your main mortgage options are described above, although you may find that they appear in different guises according to the lender's current promotion and marketing campaign. In order to choose the right mortgage you need to be aware of your own circumstances and personality type, as these factors will affect how much risk you are prepared to take, and the type of mortgage and insurance products you need. Use the mortgage questions below to work out your 'mortgage type'.

Mortgage questionnaire

Employment
A. I am in secure, long-term employment.
B. I work on a contract basis.
C. I am self-employed.

Earnings
A. I take home a standard basic rate of pay each month.
B. I take home a standard basic rate of pay plus overtime/ commission.
C. My earnings vary according to my contract/business profits.

Tax
A. I pay basic rate tax.
B. I pay higher rate tax.

Savings
A. I save for holidays and Christmas only.
B. I never save.
C. I save regularly and have a high level of savings.

Money

A. I live within my means and keep to a budget.

B. I am fairly disciplined with money, but inclined to splurge.

C. I am reckless with money, always overdrawn and maxed out on my credit cards.

Dependants

A. I have no plans to start a family soon.

B. I already have a dependent family.

C. I have no dependants and do not plan to start a family.

Joint borrowers

A. I am in a stable, long-term relationship.

B. I am buying with a friend/business partner whom I have known for a long time.

C. I am buying with a partner I haven't known long.

Attitude to risk

A. I would say I am fairly cautious and don't like surprises.

B. I am prepared to accept a small degree of risk if the benefits are worth it.

C. I am happy to accept a high level of risk.

Credit history

A. I have never bought anything on credit and do not own a credit card.

B. I regularly buy on credit and use a credit card, but have always met my payments on time.

C. I have had loan arrears/county court judgements.

By collating this information you will begin to understand your mortgage needs, and will be better prepared when you meet with your mortgage adviser to discuss the various mortgage and insurance options available to you.

HOW TO CHOOSE A MORTGAGE ADVISER

When searching for a mortgage it is easy to become overwhelmed with the sheer amount of information and choice available. It is important that you seek impartial, specialised advice before embarking on this major financial obligation. Check that your mortgage adviser is a member of the Financial Services Authority. Not all lenders and mortgage advisers offer advice; some will give advice only if you ask for it. Check this before making an appointment.

Different types of mortgage adviser

Mortgage advisers must, by law, be qualified to sell mortgages. The qualifications are CEMAP or less commonly MAQ. There are three main types of mortgage adviser.

Tied mortgage brokers

Most lending institutions will have an in-house mortgage adviser you can visit to discuss your circumstances. They will probably be employed by the lender. They will take details from you and prepare a KFI based on those details. You can then use this to shop around. An in-house mortgage adviser may be able to offer only their company's own products, although some do offer a limited range of other company's products.

Multi-tied mortgage brokers

These will be able to offer products from a panel of lenders. They may be self-employed or work within the insurance, mortgage or estate agency professions.

Independent mortgage brokers/IFAs

These may be self-employed or may be employed by a company. They will be able to offer products from the entire market place and most use sophisticated software to keep abreast of the current mortgage market.

PAYING FOR MORTGAGE ADVICE

Lending institutions do not tend to make a visible charge for providing mortgage advice. If you go directly to a bank or building society, in most cases, you will receive advice only on their products. Their profit will come from the mortgage itself and from commission on any insurance or investment plans that they sell you. Mortgage brokers are qualified to sell mortgages and many are self-employed, work in small partnerships or within estate agency firms. They will either charge you a fee, receive commission, or a combination of both. An Individual Financial Adviser (IFA) is qualified to give advice on any financial product. They may be self-employed, work in a partnership or be employed by a company. An IFA is obliged to offer you the choice of paying an hourly fee or of being paid by commission. Tied advisers, such as those working for banks and building societies, do not have to offer the fee option. The KFI should state how much the mortgage adviser will be paid for their services and where this payment will come from. Most lending institutions pay mortgage introducers a procurement fee for placing mortgages with them. In addition insurance/investment companies pay their introducers sales commission on products sold. These fees and commissions can be substantial and vary from organisation to organisation. The way in which mortgage advisers get paid can also vary – see below.

A. The mortgage adviser will not charge you a fee but will rely upon the commission received from the lender and any insurance/savings products they sell you. These amounts must be shown in the KFI.

B. The mortgage adviser will charge you a fee but refund any commission they receive. The amount of commission must be shown in the KFI.

C. The mortgage adviser will charge you a fee and receive commission for products sold. The amount of commission must be shown in the KFI.

Clearly, you would receive the most impartial advice from mortgage adviser B as they are not reliant upon sales commission for their income. However, if you need mortgage advice but are on a tight budget you may decide to choose mortgage adviser A or C. With some mortgages you can add the cost of mortgage advice to the mortgage – although this is an expensive way to pay for it. Whichever type of mortgage adviser you choose, provided they are FSA members, you are entitled to receive the best advice for your particular needs.

Shopping around for a mortgage

To ensure that you receive the best mortgage, shop around the various providers discussed above. Visit the high street banks and building societies, check online mortgage providers, visit or speak to a firm of independent financial advisers. Obtain lots of quotes and read the Key Facts Illustrations for each carefully.

HIP TIP

When shopping around for mortgages ask the mortgage adviser not to carry out a credit check, but to obtain a quote only check. Every time a credit check is carried out it is recorded against you. Lots of credit checks may adversely affect your credit record.

INFORMATION THE LENDER WILL REQUIRE FROM YOU

Before a lender will grant you a mortgage they are legally obliged to make sure that you are eligible for the mortgage and that you can afford the mortgage repayments. They will require you to provide the following information:

- Proof of identity. This is usually your passport and/or driving licence, plus recent utility bills or bank statements to prove your current address.

- A reference from your current employer confirming your employment status (i.e. whether you are on permanent staff, contract or temporary) and confirmation of your earnings.

- Wage slips for the past three to six months.

- If you are self-employed copies of your audited accounts – preferably for a three-year period.

- If you are employed on a contract basis they will require a copy of the contract or evidence of the length of your contract.

- A previous lender's reference if you have a mortgage, or a landlord's reference if you have been in rented accommodation.

- Details of your financial commitments – i.e. other loans and payments that you have to make every month. The lender may ask to see copies of your bank account statements for the past three to six months.

HIP TIP

If you have been making enquiries on the internet or telephone regarding mortgages and insurance you may find that you are inundated with companies 'cold calling' you. If you do not wish to receive this type of call you can prevent it by registering with the Telephone Preference service at www.tpsonline.org.uk

12

Removals, Packing and Completion Day

Relief and joy – contracts are exchanged at last, the deal is sealed and the property of your dreams is definitely yours. However, the hard work is not over yet and now is not the time to relax. By all means crack open the champagne to celebrate, but do bear in mind that the time between exchange of contracts and completion is becoming shorter and shorter and moving day will soon be upon you. There may be a month, a week or even less between the call from your conveyancer proudly announcing that they have exchanged contracts and the actual day that you must move out of or into your property.

More often than not people are pressurised into completion dates that are sooner than they would like in order to satisfy the demands of someone in the chain. To avoid a last minute panic it is important to choose a removal company and begin the process of packing before contracts are exchanged. If you leave everything to the last minute you may be forced to accept the first removal company that has a vacancy on the day, or even worse, end up having to hire a van and move yourself.

With a little organisation and careful packing you can be settled into your new home in record time and avoid spending months looking for that elusive book, CD or fish slice.

HOW TO FIND A RELIABLE REMOVAL COMPANY

◆ Get three estimates in writing. Your local paper and *Yellow Pages* should list local removal companies; or ask friends and family for a recommendation. The directory at the end of this book contains details of some companies that operate nationally.

◆ As soon as you have a tentative completion date, even before exchange of contracts, ask your chosen company to pencil it into their diary.

◆ Don't pay a deposit until you have exchanged contracts.

◆ Check that the company is adequately insured. Ask to see a copy of their insurance policy.

◆ If you have any particularly valuable items notify the removal company and ask them to confirm in writing that they are covered on the company's insurance. Will you have to pay an excess payment?

◆ Ask whether there is a cancellation fee and if so how much. Can you insure against this?

◆ Read the small print of your contents insurance to check whether it covers you for removals. If not, telephone and ask whether this is an option. One-off insurance from a removal company can be expensive and may not offer 'new for old'. Many removal insurance policies simply pay for damage to be repaired.

◆ Ask whether the removal company will charge extra if you are delayed from moving into the property and if so how much.

◆ Check whether they have overnight storage facilities – just in case.

Ask whether the quote includes the cost of packing materials. If not, you can stock up on boxes from the supermarket and buy packaging in readiness. Whatever you do don't use newspaper to wrap crockery, glasses and cutlery. You will end up having to wash it all when you unpack. The best paper to wrap cutlery, glasses and crockery is white tissue paper. It is cheaper to buy packing materials and bubble wrap by the roll from a commercial stationers than from high street stores. Contact www.helpineedboxes.co.uk if you need to buy or hire tea chests or packaging.

Ask the removal company to visit both the property you are moving from and the property you are moving into to check that there will be no access or parking problems on the day. If you have a narrow drive or overhanging trees let the removal company know. You may need permission from the police/local authority if your removal company will need to park on yellow lines or on a busy public road. Ask your removal company whether they arrange this. If not you will have to contact the local authority and police department yourself.

THE SMART WAY TO PACK

♦ When packing boxes make sure they are not too heavy for the removal men to lift. When packing heavy items such as books fill the remainder of the packing case with something lighter such as towels or cushions.

♦ If the removal company is packing for you, pack an overnight bag with clothes, toiletries, make up, etc. for the next day.

♦ Write on each box the room it is to be delivered to and its contents. Use a black marker pen as labels tend to come off. Number the boxes in the order of importance you want to unpack them.

- Draw up a sketch plan and mark on it the identity of each room to correspond with the identity you have marked on the packed boxes, i.e. kitchen, lounge, dining room, downstairs cloaks, bedroom 1, bedroom 2, bathroom, shed, garage, etc.

- Show on the plan where you want each item of furniture to be placed. Give a copy to each member of the removal team. This will save you having to lift heavy items around after the removal men have gone.

- Be available to orchestrate the move. Do not rely on the removal firm to follow your instructions.

- Consider taking anything particularly valuable or delicate such as computers, china, plants, etc. with you in the car to avoid breakages. Make sure your insurance covers you for this.

- Check the Fixtures and Fittings or Home Contents form and take down any items that you indicated would be removed. Remember, you must repair any damage you cause including filling screw holes.

- Most removal companies will provide a portable wardrobe for your clothes to avoid having to pack them into suitcases.

- Fill empty suitcases with bed linen so that you can make up the beds as soon as they are delivered.

- Arrange for the local authority to collect any unwanted items, hire a skip or take them to the local refuse tip. The sale contract provides that you must vacate the property on completion and that includes all your years of accumulated rubbish from the garage, cellar and loft. The buyer can claim the cost of clearing any items left behind.

ORGANISING THE COMPLETION DAY

The day that you finally move you will probably be exhausted from packing and cleaning, worried that all will go according to plan and a bit emotional at leaving your old home. If you have children or pets arrange for them to stay with friends or grandparents for the day. You don't need the added hassle of having to search for the cat, or having to snatch a curious toddler from under the removal man's feet.

Use the checklist below to ensure that your move goes as smoothly as possible.

Moving day checklist

Keep the following items with you.

* Your mobile phone and phone charger and a list of important numbers. BT may cut off your phone line in the morning – give your conveyancer and the estate agent your mobile number. Appoint a family member to sit by the phone and take messages from your conveyancer/estate agent if you are not going to be available. Remember to tell the conveyancer/estate agent that they have your authority to speak to that person.

* Some cash and your credit cards.

* A survival kit including: thermos of tea/coffee (in case you have to wait in the car for the keys to be released), kettle, tea and coffee, milk, sugar, biscuits, sandwiches, squash or bottled water, wine and corkscrew, medication, pet food, toilet rolls, soap and a hand towel, cups, plates, cutlery, etc. so you can have a cuppa or relieve an urgent call of nature as soon as you arrive at your destination. Do not underestimate the amount of tea removal men can drink! If you have a young baby I am sure I do not

have to remind you to have available baby formula/food, nappies and nappy changing equipment.

♦ Keep a tool box in the boot of your car together with some spare light bulbs, fuses, torch, candles, matches, etc.

♦ You may want to clean up before you start unpacking so take the vacuum, dustpan and brush, bowl and bucket, mops, cloths and cleaning products with you in the car.

♦ A box of toys to keep the children amused.

Time of completion

The contract will stipulate a cut-off time for legal completion to take place. This varies from 12 noon to 2pm and you should make a note of the actual completion cut-off time on your contract. What the cut-off time means is that the seller's conveyancer must have received the purchase money by that time and the seller must have vacated the property. However, legally the actual time of completion is the point at which the seller's conveyancer receives the purchase money. In theory the seller should give vacant possession of the property as soon as their conveyancer has the money in the bank.

The problem is that there is never a guarantee as to what time the money will actually arrive – it could be 9.30am when the banks open, or it could be late afternoon. The seller in the meanwhile has to pack up their home and arrange a time for the removal company to arrive. If the removers have been asked to come too early the seller could be left waiting around for the money to arrive. Provided that the completion money has been received by their conveyancer the seller should be ready to vacate their premises by the completion cut off time at the latest.

Some people are more disorganised than others and you may find
that the sellers are still packing and trying to move out of their
property in the late afternoon. As removal companies generally
tend to charge by the hour for any delay it makes sense to ask
them to arrive as near to the completion time as possible.

Liaising with the other parties
As soon as you have exchanged contracts you should liaise with
the seller to find out what time they have booked their removal
van for and what time they are expecting to vacate the property.
You will also need to liaise with your removal company to find
out how long they expect to take to empty the property and load
up the van; you must then allow travelling time to your new
property. If you are moving yourself allow twice the time you
think you need, and make sure you recruit plenty of help from
friends and family.

On completion day, the buyer's conveyancer will instruct their
bank to send the balance of the completion money to the seller's
conveyancer's bank. Hopefully, they will do this at 9.30am as
soon as the banking system opens. The seller's conveyancer must
then wait to receive the money. This can take minutes or hours,
depending on which banks are involved and how busy the banking
system is that day. Once the seller's conveyancer receives the
money they will telephone the seller and authorise the release of
the keys. At that point the buyer legally owns the property and the
seller should be ready to leave immediately. In theory this could
be as early as 9.45am or as late as 5.30pm. If the seller is buying
another property the seller's conveyancer then wires the money to
the next link in the chain and so on until the final sale is
completed. Consider the two examples below of a typical
completion day.

Example A

There are three people in the chain: Mr Smith, Mrs Jones and Mr Baker. Mr Smith is buying with a mortgage and his conveyancer has arranged with the lender to send the mortgage advance the day before completion.

The day before completion Mr Smith's mortgage advance arrives in his conveyancer's bank account.

Completion day at 9.30am – Mr Smith's conveyancer wires the money to Mrs Jones's conveyancer. They bank with the same bank and the money arrives at 10am.

Completion day at 10am – Mrs Jones's conveyancer immediately wires the purchase money to Mr Baker's conveyancer. He then telephones Mr Smith's conveyancer, Mrs Jones and her estate agent to confirm completion and to authorise the release of the keys. Mrs Jones's conveyancer and Mr Baker's conveyancer do not bank with the same bank and the money takes two hours to move between banks. The money arrives at 12 noon.

Completion day at 12 noon – Mr Baker's conveyancer receives the funds and telephones the estate agents to release the keys. He also telephones Mr Baker and Mrs Jones's conveyancer to confirm completion. All parties are able to move around lunch time.

Example B

There are four parties in the chain – Miss Kaun, Mr Evans, Mrs Joy and Sunnyside Developments. Miss Kaun and Mr Evans are buying with the aid of a mortgage.

Completion day at 9.30am – Miss Kaun's conveyancer has asked for her mortgage advance to arrive on the day of completion. He telephones her lender and after 20 minutes of listening to 'on hold' music he is told that the money is 'in the system'.

Completion day at 11am – Miss Kaun's mortgage advance arrives in her conveyancer's bank. He immediately instructs his bank to telegraphically transfer the funds to Mr Evans's conveyancer's bank. They do not bank with the same bank and the money takes an hour and a half to arrive.

Completion day at 12.30pm – Mr Evans's conveyancer receives the purchase money from Miss Singh's conveyancer. He has already received his client's mortgage advance and is able to wire the completion funds to Mrs Joy's conveyancer's bank. Miss Kaun has completed and is entitled to the keys, but Mr Evans cannot move out until he completes on his purchase. She is left waiting outside in her removal van fuming with rage.

Completion day at 1.30pm – Mr Evans's purchase money arrives in Mrs Joy's conveyancer's bank. However, the legal cut-off time for completion has passed. Mrs Joy refuses to complete until Mr Evans agrees to pay damages for late completion – this includes interest to both her and her seller, the developer. Mr Evans has no choice but to agree.

Completion day at 2pm – Mrs Joy's conveyancer receives a faxed undertaking from Mr Evans's conveyancer confirming they will pay the late completion damages. He then wires the completion money to the developer's conveyancer. Both Miss Kaun and Mr

Evans have now completed and are entitled to their keys. However, as Mrs Joy cannot move into her new home yet the keys are not released. They are left waiting in the removal van.

Completion day at 3.30pm – Mrs Joy's completion funds arrive in the bank of the conveyancer of Sunnyside Developments. He telephones the site office to release the keys. Each conveyancer then telephones down the chain, releasing the keys and all parties are able to move in.

Miss Singh has had to pay her removal men an extra £200 waiting time. Mr Evans has had to pay interest due to late completion in the region of £100. Everyone has been held up and all have had a frustrating and stressful day.

As you have seen, the current completion system is horribly unreliable as completion can take hours to happen and, if there are delays in the money moving through the banks, completion can be delayed altogether. As part of the general move towards e conveyancing the Land Registry is currently working on a better solution for the electronic transfer of funds.

THE FINAL CHECKS

As soon as you receive the keys to the property you should make a few cursory checks:

- The keys – check that you have been given a key to each lockable door and window and make sure they work.

- The services – test the lighting, heating, water and any gas or electrical appliances to make sure they are working.

- Appliances – if appliances have been included in the sale check that they are still in working condition.

- The meters – take a meter reading of gas, electricity and water.

- The phone – check that the phone has been connected.

- The property – have a look around the property and the grounds and check for any damage that has occurred since you visited the property. The seller is bound by the contract to hand the property over in the same condition it was in at exchange of contracts. Report any damage to your conveyancer immediately.

- Vacant possession – check the property including the loft, garage and outbuildings is cleared of people and the seller's belongings. Report any problems to your conveyancer immediately.

- The Home Contents/Fixtures and Fittings form – check the forms to make sure the seller has left behind all that they agreed to. Report any missing items to your conveyancer immediately.

- Check furniture and belongings – you won't want to open all boxes immediately, but check your main items of furniture for damage caused during the move. Report any damage to the removal company and/or your insurers immediately.

13

The Move Master Plan

Moving home or buying a property for investment should be a positive, exciting and life-enhancing experience. Sadly for many people the experience quickly deteriorates into a worrying and stressful period, filled with life-changing decisions and expense. Dealing with a battery of professionals such as solicitors, conveyancers, estate agents, surveyors and mortgage lenders can seem daunting, as can the mountains of paperwork you must wade through, and the piles of documents and direct debits you have to sign.

This chapter builds on the advice in the earlier chapters to enable you to put together your personal Move Master Plan. It will show you how to take charge and remain in control of your own destiny. It is impossible to predict every scenario in a property transaction, but with careful planning you can avoid many of the common pitfalls and problems.

HOW TO TIME YOUR MOVE CORRECTLY

It cannot be stressed strongly enough how critical it is to time your sale or purchase correctly. People buy and sell property for all sorts of reasons including job relocation, marriage, starting or growing a family, downsizing and divorce. Most people do not realise just how long it takes to buy or sell a property and consequently fail to allow sufficient time. They then attempt to force the transaction along at an unrealistic pace, causing stress to themselves, the professionals they deal with and everyone else in the chain.

If you accept from the outset that the move will take as long as it takes, and that completion dates rarely fit in perfectly with the plans you have made, you will save yourself a lot of anguish and frustration. It is impossible to predict a firm completion date at the beginning of a transaction because it is dependent upon so many people. Being in a property chain is a bit like being in a traffic jam – you can move only as fast as the slowest participant.

When to market your property

Correctly timing the marketing of your property in the run-up to the launch of the HIP in June 2007 will be doubly important.

If you place your property on the market prior to 1 June 2007 you will not be obliged to provide a HIP until after the end of the transitional period, i.e. until 1 January 2008. This transitional period means that most properties on the market prior to 1 June 2007 will avoid having to supply a HIP provided they sell the property or withdraw it from the market before 1 January 2008. Because of this it is anticipated that more sellers than usual will place their property on the market in the months leading up to the HIP. This could create a glut of property on the market, leading to saturation and reduced property prices.

Conversely, it is thought that astute buyers may wait until after the HIP launch to buy a property. They will then receive the benefit of the HIP and save hundreds of pounds on searches. If you have placed your property on the market before the HIP date and it has not sold you will be competing with sellers who come into the market post-HIP who are selling with the HIP in place. As a result you may find you are at a disadvantage to those owners selling property with the benefit of a HIP.

It is predicted that after the launch there could be a shortage of property as speculative sellers withdraw from the market. Property shortages tend to result in higher property prices.

Generally, early spring and summer are the best times to market property. During this period property sells more quickly and often achieves a higher price.

Planning the best time to move

If you are planning your move around new schools and the summer school holidays, it is best to start the process several months in advance. Families looking to complete in July or August should start to look for property in January/February.

The school holidays and the run-up to Christmas are the most popular times to move. Consequently conveyancers, lenders and removers are frantically busy. Try to avoid these periods if you want to remain stress fee.

Most people choose to move on a Friday, particularly the Friday before a bank holiday, to take advantage of the weekend to settle in. Consequently, Fridays are very busy and you may find removers are booked up. There is also more chance of problems arising as bank systems get congested and funds can be delayed. If problems crop up which delay completion you will have to wait until the following Monday (or Tuesday if it is a holiday weekend) for them to be resolved. There are contractual penalties for failure to complete. These include damages, costs and interest due to late completion, which are charged on a daily basis and will continue to run over the weekend, or until the problem is solved and completion takes place.

Avoid completing on Fridays, in the school holidays and at Christmas. These are the busiest periods when removal companies are booked up and things are more likely to go wrong.

Moving tips

♦ Don't book a holiday in the year you plan to move. If you do it is almost certain that your property chain will want to complete the week you are away. You can always book a last minute holiday after completion.

♦ Don't book a wedding in the year you plan to move. Complete your move before the wedding if you plan to move in straight afterwards.

♦ Allow enough time for the sale/purchase to happen. Follow the example time lines below.

Example one – sale time line

♦ Week 1 – using the checklist in Chapter 2 inspect the property, arrange estimates and make a list of DIY jobs.

♦ Week 2 – choose your tradesmen and arrange for any work to be done. Complete DIY jobs.

♦ Weeks 3 and 4 – finish work on the property and decorate.

♦ Week 5 – fit new flooring, spring clean and de-clutter. Research estate agents, conveyancers and HIP providers. Have the property valued and research property prices.

♦ Week 6 – appoint your conveyancer, estate agent and HIP provider. Confirm this in writing. Collate information (see below).

- Week 7 – HIP is being prepared.

- Week 8 – energy assessment or home inspection is done.

- Week 9 – HIP is ready, you can now put the property on the market.

- Weeks 10 to 14 – show viewers around the property. Hopefully negotiate and accept an offer.

- Week 15 – sale proceeding, subject to contract. Conveyancer issues a contract package.

- Week 16 – buyer's mortgage valuation is carried out.

- Week 17 – sign contract and transfer deeds.

- Week 18 – buyer's mortgage arrives. Exchange contracts. Book removals, transfer funds.

- Week 19 – conveyancer does post-exchange work and arranges completion.

- Week 20 – completion.

Example two – purchase time line

- Week 1 – assess your property needs, calculate deposit available, research mortgages, find out how much mortgage you can borrow.

- Week 2 – research conveyancers. Obtain estimates for legal costs. Research lenders, find out what costs are associated with your mortgage, e.g. mortgage application fee, mortgage valuation fee, broker's fees, etc.

- Weeks 3 and 4 – search for a property. Register with all local estate agents. Research online property websites. Check the local and national papers. Leaflet-drop preferred areas.

- Weeks 5 and 6 – view properties.

- Week 7 – make a shortlist of properties and arrange for second viewings. Take the HIP to your conveyancer for advice on any queries. Obtain estimates for defects and repairs on property you are interested in.

- Weeks 8 to 9 – make an offer on the property of your dreams. Allow time for negotiation.

- Week 10 – offer is accepted. Advise your conveyancer in writing. Apply for a formal mortgage offer. Arrange a private survey if you are having one.

- Week 11 – the legal work is proceeding.

- Week 12 – your private survey is done. The mortgage survey is done.

- Week 13 – mortgage offer is received. Legal work is completed. Sign contract and pay your deposit.

- Week 14 – exchange contracts. Book removals. Get completion funds to your conveyancer.

- Week 15 – conveyancer completes post-exchange work and finalises completion arrangements.

- Week 16 – completion.

As you will see from the examples above, even after the HIP is introduced, the period from deciding to move to the actual completion day can take four to five months. The examples shown are fairly optimistic and assume that your property is sold within the first four weeks and your conveyancing is completed in four to five weeks. In reality it can take much longer to find a property or a buyer and if you are in a chain you may be held up further.

If you want to move in the summer holidays you should start the ball rolling as soon as you have packed the Christmas decorations away. Likewise if you are planning a winter move you should get started in early summer.

One of the most common complaints and the biggest cause of stress to everyone in the moving process is timing. Everyone in a chain will have their own set of circumstances and plans. Consider this case study:

Case study
The six-month tenancy on Joe and Theresa Quick's flat runs out in a month so they have decided to put their feet on the first rung of the property ladder. The Middle family have two school-age children and are moving into the catchment area of a very good school; they need to move during the school summer holidays. Having found the perfect home to buy they accept an offer on their existing property from Mr and Mrs Quick. Millie and Frank Downsizing, an elderly couple, are moving to a brand new bungalow as they can no longer keep on top of the house and garden. When Mr and Mrs Quick agree to purchase the Middles' property they do not know that the Downsizings have to wait 12 weeks for their new home to be built. They put pressure on the Middles for an early move and, when the Middles can't meet the required date, Mr and Mrs Quick withdraw from the purchase. The Middle family eventually find another buyer, Fred Slow, a cautious first time buyer who is researching every mortgage in the market. The Downsizings are now under pressure from the developer to complete or lose their bungalow. They are not aware that Mr Slow has not even arranged a mortgage yet. The Middles are

once more under pressure to exchange, but cannot do so until Mr Slow has sorted out his mortgage. The Middles are now panicking that they won't move house in time for the new school term in September. Everyone puts pressure on Fred Slow to get a move on – he buckles under the pressure and withdraws from the purchase. Once again the chain is broken.

This case study illustrates how stresses and strains can arise when the aims and goals of a chain of people have to be shoehorned together to achieve one perfect date that fits all.

Property chains can take weeks to gel and it is only once the chain is complete, when everyone has found a property to buy, someone to sell to, and all parties have appointed conveyancers, arranged mortgages and ordered surveys that the momentum gathers and the chain can gallop towards a completion date.

HIP TIP

Plan your move at least six months ahead of your desired completion date to avoid the stress of missed deadlines – and be prepared to be flexible.

Be prepared – once you have worked out the timing of your move you can begin the process of marketing your property.

Follow the top tips below for a successful and stress-free move.

A. MOVING PLAN FOR SELLERS

Put the property into good order

Decorate *before* inviting the estate agent to value it and *before* the survey or HCR is done. You will be acting from a position of strength and confidence if you know you have a desirable property to sell. Turn to Chapters 2 and 5 for advice on how to put your house in good condition and make it ready to pass the Home Condition Report or energy survey with flying colours.

Appoint a conveyancer

Turn to Chapter 8 for advice on finding the perfect conveyancer for you. By appointing your conveyancer as soon as you decide to sell you can ask their advice on the estate agent's contract and any HIP contract you are offered. They can also get ahead with applying for the deeds and any leasehold or missing information.

Choose your estate agent

Turn to Chapter 6 for advice on how to choose the best estate agent for you. Choose an agent who specialises in your type of property. Check the estate agent contract carefully – avoid any contract that grants the agent 'sole selling' rights or demands payment for a 'ready, willing and able' buyer even if you do not proceed with the sale. If in doubt ask your conveyancer to check the contract for you.

Choose your HIP provider

If you are selling after 1 June 2007 you must have a HIP. Prior to that date you may decide to sell with a HIP voluntarily. Turn to Chapter 3 for advice on how the HIP will affect you and where to source a HIP.

Calculate sale costs

Ask your lender for a redemption statement. Don't assume the sum shown on your last mortgage statement is the total amount required to repay your mortgage. A mortgage statement does not include early redemption charges, lender completion fees, etc. which can add considerably to the amount you have to repay. If you have an early redemption clause penalty on your mortgage check with your lender when it expires. It makes sense to move after that date to avoid the charges. See the example of sale costs below.

Example of sale costs		
Mortgage repayment	£95,000.00	+
Estate agent's fee	£ 2,232.50	+
HIP fee	£ 881.25	+
Legal costs	£ 420.00	
Total cost of sale	£98,533.75	

Your sale price must exceed the total cost of your sale unless you are able to add any shortfall onto the mortgage you are taking out on a new purchase, or you can afford to make up the difference from your own funds.

Collate information

Put together an information pack for potential buyers including:

◆ Utility bills.
◆ Details of local schools, playgroups and colleges.
◆ Local bus and train timetables.
◆ Details of local gym or sports facilities.
◆ Cinema, theatre, pubs and restaurants.

- Churches and places of worship.
- Supermarkets, post office, etc.

Put a second information pack together for the HIP. This should include:

- Service agreements for central heating/hot water system.
- Certificates for gas and electricity.
- Guarantees, i.e. double glazing, timber and damp, etc.
- Planning documents.
- The Land Registry title number of the property.
- The deeds or details of where they are held. If held by your lender, bank or conveyancer their name, address, fax, email, telephone number and your mortgage account number.
- A letter of consent to the holder of the deeds authorising their release.

If the property is leasehold or commonhold:

- The name, address, telephone number and email address of the landlord and the managing agents.
- Service charge receipts for the past three years.
- Ground rent receipts.
- Any notices you have received from the landlord or commonhold association.
- Any additional regulations or requirements, etc.

Be ready for viewings

Once your home is on the market you must be ready for a viewing at any time. Keep the place clean and tidy, particularly outside. You never know when an interested viewer might be walking or driving past. Turn to Chapter 7 for advice on how to conduct successful viewings.

Negotiating the price

Expect to receive offers of less than the asking price for your property. Few buyers offer the asking price straight away. Chapter 7 outlines how to negotiate the best property price.

Sold, subject to contract

Once you have a buyer, subject to contract, it is important to get to exchange of contracts as fast as possible. At this stage your buyer is like a fish on the end of the line, one false move and they are gone. You must reel your fish in quickly to ensure that your sale will proceed. Only once contracts have been unconditionally exchanged can you be sure that the sale will proceed. Keep in touch with the estate agent, the buyer and your conveyancer to keep the sale progressing quickly. If you, or your buyer, do not want to complete quickly then consider exchanging contracts with a delayed completion date.

B. MOVING PLAN – FOR SELLERS AND BUYERS

Research tradesmen and professionals

You will be employing tradesmen and professionals to work for you, perhaps for the first time. Use the advice in Chapter 5 to source tradesmen and professionals. Always get three estimates in writing and don't necessarily choose the cheapest, consider quality and service as well as cost.

Check the small print

Read estimates and contracts carefully. Ask your conveyancer to check any wording or documents you are unsure about. It is better to pay a relatively small fee now than find out you have made a costly mistake later on.

Allow enough time
See above.

Be polite but firm
Remember that professionals in the property industry are busy people usually working to strict deadlines. Remain polite and reasonable even when things are not going to plan. If you become angry, demanding and abusive no one will want to talk to you and your calls will be avoided. On the other hand do not be overawed or fobbed off – you are paying for a service and your calls and emails should be returned within a reasonable time. If they are not call again (and again).

Be organised
Buy a selection of envelopes in different sizes and some stamps so that as soon as correspondence and documents arrive you can deal with them and send them back immediately. Store important telephone numbers and addresses, and diarise reminders on your mobile phone, or buy a Filofax or electronic equivalent. Complete and return documents promptly, a day here and there soon adds up. Urgent or important documents can be sent by special delivery or guaranteed post. Your conveyancer will send you a client care letter which you must sign and return. Nothing will happen until you do this so don't leave it behind the clock on the mantelpiece.

You will be asked to provide proof of identity. This is a legal requirement even if your conveyancer has known you for years.

If you are selling a property you will be sent either a Property Information form and Fixtures and Fittings form, or a Property

Use form and Home Contents form. Complete them accurately and return them at once. Follow your conveyancer's instructions carefully when completing and signing documents.

Arrange removals before exchange

Good removal companies get booked up weeks in advance, especially in the busy spring and summer months. See Chapter 12 for advice on removals and packing.

When to give notice

Do not give notice on tenanted property, job, or schools, and don't order carpets, curtains, furniture, cookers, etc. until you have exchanged contracts. In fact, do not believe this sale is going to happen at all until contracts are unconditionally and legally exchanged and this has been confirmed by your conveyancer. Until that happens, *nothing* is guaranteed.

Contact information – Prepare a written contact information form as shown on pages 319–20.

When you have completed your statement give a copy to your buyer/seller, your estate agent, mortgage adviser, new lender, conveyancer and HIP provider.

Private sales

If you are not using an estate agent, and have sold/bought privately, it is very important that you give details of your conveyancer to your buyer/seller and get details of their conveyancer. You must then ensure that you give the details to your conveyancer and ask them to write to the other conveyancer immediately. Inform them that there is no estate agent involved.

Example contact information form

Property: Address: Post code: Land Registry title number:	
Your full name: Address: Post code: Home telephone: Work telephone: Mobile: Fax: Email:	
Your buyer's/seller's full name: Address: Post code: Home telephone: Work telephone: Mobile: Fax: Email:	
Seller's estate agent's name: Address: Telephone number: Mobile: Fax: Email:	
Seller's existing mortgage company: Address: Telephone number: Fax: Email: Mortgage account number:	

Seller's new mortgage adviser:
Address:
Telephone number:
Mobile:
Fax:
Email:

HIP provider:
Address:
Telephone number
Email:

Buyer's estate agent:
Address:
Telephone number:
Mobile:
Fax:
Email:

Buyer's new mortgage company:
Address:
Telephone number:
Fax:
Email:
Mortgage account number:

Buyer's mortgage adviser:
Address:
Telephone number:
Mobile:
Fax:
E mail:

The name, address and telephone
number of the local authority and
water authority for the property

Progressing the sale

Telephone or email your conveyancer once a week and ask for an update on your file. Enquire whether there is anything outstanding and ask what you can do to help. If the conveyancer is waiting for information from third parties you can often chase this up. Once you have an update, telephone your estate agent and pass the information on. Ask the estate agent for an update on your seller's/buyer's progress. If the seller/buyer or their conveyancers are dragging their feet, ask the estate agent to chase them up.

C. MOVING PLAN – FOR BUYERS

Arrange your mortgage

Before you begin the process of buying a house you should ensure that you can obtain a mortgage and afford the monthly repayments. If you are self-employed or have a poor credit history you may need to employ a specialist mortgage adviser. See Chapter 11 for advice on mortgages and insurance. Find out how much you can borrow and try to get a mortgage offer in principle. This will show sellers and their estate agents that you have done your homework and are a viable buyer.

The deposit

Once you have made your mortgage arrangements you need to calculate how much deposit you can afford to add to the mortgage advance. If your deposit is in a long-term savings account, move this to an instant access account. Your deposit should be instantly available for exchange of contracts.

The cost of moving

Find out how much the purchase is going to cost you. Get estimates from conveyancers for the legal costs, find out from your lender or mortgage broker how much the mortgage costs will be and, if you are having a private survey, get estimates for the survey. Don't forget to allow for removal costs and charges for supplies such as gas, electricity, water, telephone, etc. to be connected.

Assess your property needs

Following the advice in Chapter 10 draw up a wish list of the type of property you want to buy. Keep several copies with you, to give to estate agents, and take it on viewings. It is very easy to become distracted when viewing property and your list will concentrate your mind.

Finding the perfect property

Once you have decided what type of property you are searching for and are sure you have the financial means to buy it, you can begin your search. Use the advice contained in Chapter 10 to make certain that you hear of every property in your price range that comes onto the market.

Making an offer to buy

As soon as you find your dream property move fast to ensure that you keep it. Follow the advice in Chapter 10 and let the estate agent know you are interested and, if you are sure it is the one for you, make an offer straight away. Make sure all offers are in writing and marked subject to contract.

Securing the sale

Ask the seller to take the property off the market and to cease all marketing. Push for the 'for sale' board to be removed – even a 'sold subject to contract' board advertises that a property is up for sale.

Confirm the purchase to your conveyancer

Confirm the details to your conveyancer in writing. Give them the estate agent's contact details, the address of the property you are buying and the price you have agreed to pay. If you have any queries that you would like your conveyancer to ask, put them in writing now.

Confirm the offer to the estate agent

Confirm in writing and ensure that the estate agent has contact details for your conveyancer and your lender.

The mortgage application

Make a formal mortgage application. Mortgage offers can take weeks if not months to process.

See opposite for tips to move your mortgage along more quickly.

Arrange insurances

When buying a property you may need several different types of insurance. Chapter 11 deals with the various types of insurances on offer. It is best to arrange insurance before exchange of contracts as it can take some time to research the market and obtain quotes. With life assurance and mortgage protection the insurance company may require a medical or letter from your doctor. If it is a condition of your offer that you take out insurance you must be ready to place it 'on risk' as soon as contracts are exchanged. Your lender may ask for a copy of the policy schedule and the policy number before releasing funds.

Contract and deposit

Before your conveyancer can exchange contracts for you they must be in receipt of your signed contract and cleared funds for the

How to get your mortgage moving chart

Typical mortgage application	Tips to save time
Your lender will write to your employer for confirmation of your earnings. The request often sits in an in-tray or is passed around the firm until it reaches the correct department. It may then sit in an in-tray for a few more days before being sent back. Often references get lost in the post or in the lender's offices.	Ensure your lender has the name or department in your firm that deals with mortgage references. Contact your personnel department, or the person in your company who is responsible, and ask them to respond immediately they receive the reference request. Ask them to confirm with you once they have sent the reply and then check two days later to ensure your lender has received it. If not ask your personnel officer to send it again by fax.
Your lender will apply to your existing lender (if any) for a reference. The request may be sent to the wrong department or have incorrect details. It may sit in someone's in-tray. Once the response has been sent it may become lost in the post or be lost in the lender's offices.	Give your new lender the correct contact details for your existing lender and your mortgage account number. Contact your existing lender, tell them that the request is coming and ask them to deal with it immediately and to confirm with you once they have done so. As soon as you know the response has been sent, allowing time for postage, contact your new lender to ensure it has been received. If it has gone astray ask your existing lender to fax it again.
Valuation. Lenders often wait for satisfactory references before instructing their valuer. This avoids spending the valuation fee if the references are not satisfactory. If you give the name, address and phone number of the seller, the valuer will call for an appointment. If the seller is out or away from home the valuer will wait for them to call back.	If you are certain your references will be acceptable ask your lender to instruct the valuer straight away. Give the estate agent's details as the contact for the valuer rather than the seller. The estate agent will push for an early appointment and, if the seller is away or on holiday, the estate agent can accompany the valuer to the property.
Issue of mortgage offer. Once references are received and the valuation is back the application goes into the 'underwriting' department for approval and issue of offer.	Contact the lender to ask if they have everything they need and ask them to phone you if they have any queries. Ask how long the offer will take to be issued and push for an early offer. If you are proactive and call regularly your application will be put to the top of the pile.

deposit. If you are posting the contract and enclose a cheque or bank draft with it, do send it by registered post. Remember that a cheque will take up to seven days to clear, a bank draft three days, a BACS transfer will take several days to arrive and a telegraphic transfer will arrive the same day provided it is sent early in the day. If you send money by BACS or telegraphic transfer, remember to tell your conveyancer that you have done so.

POST-EXCHANGE OF CONTRACTS CHECKLIST

Transfer the completion money to your conveyancer

To be certain that your completion proceeds according to plan, you need to make sure that your conveyancer has enough money to complete. As soon as you exchange contracts ask your conveyancer to send you a final completion statement showing how much money they need from you to complete. If you are buying, your completion statement will include the balance of the purchase price, your conveyancer's legal fees and any other outstanding disbursements. If you are selling, the completion statement will include your conveyancer's legal fees, any outstanding disbursements, the sum needed to repay your mortgage and the estate agent's fees. If time is short, which it often is between exchange of contracts and completion, ask your conveyancer to give you an approximate figure by telephone or email. Once you know the figure you should arrange to get the money to your conveyancer in time for completion.

Allowing time

To avoid delays on completion day make sure that your conveyancer has cleared funds for the completion money no later than the day prior to completion; do not leave it until completion

day to telegraph completion funds. Money transfers can and do
go wrong – always allow plenty of time. Liaise with your
conveyancer before sending funds to them. They will need cleared
funds to complete.

Ways of paying
If you intend to pay by cheque, allow seven days from when your
conveyancer will receive it for clearance. Conveyancers will often
treat a bank draft as a cash payment, although strictly speaking
they do take three working days to clear into an account. Because
of money laundering regulations there is a strict limit to the
amount of cash a conveyancer is allowed to accept.

The safest way to ensure that your money is received in time is to
arrange a BACS payment or electronic transfer directly into the
conveyancer's bank account. BACS payments take several days to
move from one account to another. Your issuing bank should be
able to tell you what date it will arrive in the receiving account.

Telegraphic transfers usually arrive the same day that you send
them provided you send them before the cut off time; this is
usually about 2pm, but check with your bank as the cut off time
varies from bank to bank.

If you intend to send a BACS or telegraphic transfer payment to
your conveyancer, ask them to confirm their bank details in
writing. Notify your conveyancer, as soon as you have transferred
the funds so that they can look out for them. There is a bank fee
for bank drafts, BACS and telegraphic transfer payments, but the
cost of these is insignificant in comparison to the costs you would
incur for late completion.

Check that you have signed all the necessary deeds and documents

If you are selling, your conveyancer must be in possession of the signed and witnessed transfer deeds before they can complete. If you are buying, your conveyancer must be in possession of your signed and witnessed mortgage deeds and the SDLT form. If you are not sure whether you have signed everything check with your conveyancer. When critical documents are sent to you, and time is short, send them back by Next Day Special Delivery through the Post Office. In dire emergency hire a courier or deliver them yourself.

Give notice

Once you have exchanged contracts it is generally safe to give formal written notice:

◆ Job – you will need to give the notice required under your contract.

◆ Schools – generally appreciate as much notice as possible before the end of term time.

◆ Landlord – check the terms of your tenancy agreement. Notice is usually one month.

Confirm removals

Now that you have exchanged you can confirm your removal date with your chosen removal company. If you are a first time buyer it is sensible to arrange to move in a day or so after legal completion. This avoids the pressure of trying to move into a house that the seller is trying to move out of.

Pack your belongings

Pack your belongings carefully to avoid breakages. Label all boxes clearly and provide the removal men with a layout plan of the property showing where each item of furniture and box should be deposited. See Chapter 12 for advice on packing.

Insurance – home and contents

Cancel home insurance on the old home and start any new insurance from completion date. If you have a single home and contents policy you must notify your insurers of the new property details and the date you are moving. Check with your conveyancer before cancelling your buildings insurance on your existing property.

Let everyone know

There seems to be a never-ending list of people you must write to and things you must do when you move house. A most useful and comprehensive website is www.iammoving.com which is a free online service in association with the Royal Mail. It enables you to tell multiple organisations that you are moving, allows you to send emoving cards to friends and family and includes loads of useful information. See the checklist below for people you may need to contact:

◆ Services – gas, electricity, oil and water. You will need to notify the properties you are moving from and to and the date. Ask for the meter to be read on completion day.

◆ Media/communications – TV licence, satellite, cable, internet, telephone and mobile. You will need to notify media providers to disconnect and reconnect at the new property. Ensure there are no restrictions on satellite dishes before proceeding to erect one.

♦ Money – bank, building society, savings, credit cards, loans, mortgage, private pension, stock broker, shareholdings.

♦ Government – council tax, Inland Revenue, national insurance and DSS, pension, DVLA, electoral roll (fill in a voter registration for your new property at www.aboutmyvote.co.uk).

♦ Health – doctor, dentist, optician, private health care, hospital or specialists, national blood bank. You may need to register with a new doctor, dentist and optician if you are moving out of the area. Check the NHS web site www.nhs.uk for a list of services in your area.

♦ Insurance – car, home, contents, life, endowment, car breakdown, pet, travel, healthcare.

♦ Other – charities, newspaper or magazine deliveries or subscriptions, library – remember to return any books – milkman, supermarket (online delivery), employer, gym, and friends and family.

HIP TIP

Use www.iammoving.com to notify everyone you are moving and send ecards to friends and family — it is free and it is safe. If you are not online prepare some change of address leaflets and put one in with every piece of correspondence you send, e.g. when you pay a bill or a credit card.

Appliances

Removal men will not disconnect or install washing machines, dishwashers, cookers, tumble dryers or gas appliances. You will need to contact a plumber, electrician and gas fitter. Remember to defrost the fridge and freezer a couple of days prior to completion.

Get your mail redirected

Do not rely on the incoming buyer or tenant to send on your mail. Having your mail redirected ensures you receive it and protects you from identity fraud. You can download a Moving Home redirection form online at www.royalmail.com of pick up one from the Post Office.

Life and mortgage related insurance

Contact your insurance companies to put life and mortgage protection insurances on risk.

Get the services connected

Arrange for services to be connected. BT will disconnect the telephone and you will need to contact them to have it reconnected. If you are buying a brand new home you must contact the electricity, gas and water authorities to order the services.

Get the meters read

Check with the seller that they have arranged for the meters to be read. If not arrange this.

Furniture delivery

Arrange for delivery of furniture, carpets, appliances, etc. to your new home. Unless there is absolutely no alternative try not to have items delivered on the actual day of completion. There will be a lot going on with furniture moving in and out of the property, meters being read, etc. Also as there is no guaranteed time for completion to take place you cannot be certain you will have access to the property when the delivery van arrives.

Mortgage conditions

Check you have complied with your lender's mortgage requirements. If you are obtaining a mortgage your conveyancer will apply to your lender for the mortgage funds. Read your mortgage offer carefully to see whether there are any conditions that you must fulfil. If there are unfulfilled conditions outstanding the lender may refuse to send the mortgage funds and completion will not be able to take place. If you are in doubt check with your conveyancer.

WHAT TO DO ON COMPLETION DAY

Arrange to inspect the property

When you are buying a property, particularly if it is a newly built home, you should arrange to inspect the property on the morning of completion. The seller is bound by contract to leave the property in the same state that it was in on exchange of contracts. This obligation includes repairing any damage caused by removing fitted furniture, mirrors, paintings, etc. You will also want to check that the items the seller has agreed to leave at the property are still there. Take the Fixtures and Fittings list or the Home Contents list with you as an aide mémoire. One of the most frequent complaints a conveyancer receives from buyers is that the seller has left the property full of rubbish or has taken items that were included in the sale.

Vacant possession is a term of the contract and that includes removing all rubbish from the loft, cellar, garage, etc. You are entitled to insist that the seller takes all rubbish away.

The keys

If you are buying check with the seller that they have keys to all the doors and windows at the property and ask them to demonstrate that they work. If you are not collecting the keys directly from the seller, ask them to confirm where they will be leaving them. This will usually be with the estate agent or the conveyancer. If you are selling, you should arrange to leave the keys with the estate agent on the day of completion. Never release keys to the buyer or allow them to move in until your conveyancer has confirmed completion. Once in the property it is very difficult to remove a buyer if completion fails to take place.

Be secure

If you do not intend to move in immediately, invest in an automatic timer to switch the lights on and off occasionally and hang some curtains to make the property look lived in. If the property you buy has previously been let out, it is worth changing the locks as you can't be sure who has retained keys.

(14)

Troubleshooting Problems

With over 25 years' experience in the property business I have completed thousands of property sales and purchases. I can honestly say that no two conveyancing transactions are alike. Every transaction is made up of a unique mix of personalities, each with their own personal goals. If you add to this mix the problems that can arise with mortgages, legal titles, planning, leaseholds, surveys, etc. it is easy to see how a property transaction can go awry.

In this chapter I have tried to list some of the more common problems and included some of the solutions that have worked for my clients.

PROBLEMS WITH MORTGAGES

Q. I am a first time buyer and have not been able to raise a deposit. Where can I get a mortgage for 100% of the purchase price?

A. The majority of high street lenders will require you to pay a deposit. Some lenders do offer 100% mortgages, but you will probably have to go to a mortgage broker or Independent Financial Adviser. Recommendation is always the best way to source a mortgage adviser – ask friends or relatives. Mortgage brokers and IFAs are listed in *Yellow Pages* under those headings. Check the FSA website www.fsa.gov.uk/consumer to ensure that the firm you choose is a registered member of the FSA.

Remember that even if you obtain a 100% mortgage you will still have to find your legal and removal costs. You could also check whether your local authority or housing association runs a 'shared ownership' or 'home buy' scheme.

Q. I started my own business a year ago. The business is doing well, but I do not have three years' accounts. Will I be able to get a mortgage?

A. Most lenders will require three years' audited accounts. Some lenders do allow you to self-certify your income without providing proof or accounts. This is called a self-certified mortgage. With this type of mortgage you usually have to find a deposit of at least 25% of the purchase price and the interest rate is often higher. Remember, you must be sure that you can afford to repay the mortgage even if the business is not doing so well. Your mortgage broker or financial adviser will be able to put you in touch with a lender that offers this type of mortgage.

Q. I have had problems with credit in the past. Will I still be able to get a mortgage?

A. This will depend upon the problems you have had and whether you have now paid off your debts. You can check your credit status with a company, such as Experian, which will provide you with a report for a small fee. Visit their website at www.experian.co.uk or freephone 0800 656 9000. If you have been bankrupt, you must wait the required period to be discharged from bankruptcy. There are mortgage brokers who specialise in repairing credit and obtaining adverse credit mortgages.

HIP TIP

To source a mortgage adviser or IFA visit www.mortgagesorter.co.uk or www.searchifa.co.uk

PROBLEMS WITH PROFESSIONALS

Q. I want to complain about my conveyancer/estate agent/ mortgage adviser. I feel that they are slow, are not acting in my best interests, do not return my calls or letters, etc.

A. If you have a complaint about one of the professionals you are working with, the first thing to do is to complain personally in writing to the professional concerned. Your letter should be polite but to the point, stating what the problem is and what you want to happen. If this does not resolve your problem, the next step is to complain to the senior partner in the organisation. Once again make your complaint in writing, state what the problem is and what you want to happen. You should state in your letter that if the problem is not resolved, you will be taking the matter up with their governing body. If this still does not resolve the problem, you must take it up with the governing body or trade association for that professional.

Listed below are details of the governing bodies for the property profession and full contact details are contained in the directory at the back of the book:

- Solicitors – The Law Society.
- Licensed conveyancers – The Council for Licensed Conveyancers.
- Estate agents – Ombudsman of Estate Agents, National Association of Estate Agents (if they are a member), or if they do not belong to a governing body the Office of Fair Trading.

- Surveyors – Royal Institute of Chartered Surveyors.
- IFAs/mortgage advisers – Financial Services Authority.

PLANNING PROBLEMS

Q. I think work may have been done to the property without the necessary consents. What should I do?

A. If you suspect that work has been done to the property that required building regulations, planning or listed building consent, and that consent has not been obtained, you will need to rectify this before you can sell the property. You should seek the advice of a qualified conveyancer. They will advise you whether the problem can be solved by an indemnity insurance policy, or whether you must apply for retrospective consent to the relevant authority. There are time limits imposed on the local authority to take action for breach of the planning or building regulations laws and your conveyancer will be able to advise you on this.

Note: there are legal indemnity insurances that cover many problems relating to lack or breach of consents for buildings and alterations. It is important that you do not attempt to contact the relevant authorities before obtaining insurance, as the insurance company will not offer cover where the potential risk has been brought to the notice of the party entitled to take action. Insurance is often a quicker and cheaper alternative to applying for retrospective consent from the local authority or original building developer.

BREACH OF RESTRICTIVE COVENANT PROBLEMS

Q. I have built an extension/conservatory/fence/erected a satellite dish, etc. and apparently, I am in breach of the restrictive covenants in my deeds. What can I do?

A. A restrictive covenant is placed on a property by the original owner of the land in order to control its future use or development. Restrictive covenants generally prevent unauthorised development or work to a property without the consent of the original land owner. They are fairly common, particularly on housing estates, where many of the restrictions are placed on the property to ensure that the estate remains uniform or protects the land owner from breach of planning consent. If work has been done to the property which has breached the consent you have two options.

First you can contact the original land owner and apply for retrospective consent. Where the original land owner is a company or local developer this may be fairly easy to do – it is a reasonably common practice. They may make a charge for providing consent. If the original land owner cannot be traced, it is more difficult – your conveyancer could try to argue that the covenant is incapable of being enforced, but the benefit of these covenants may have passed on to someone else.

The alternative is to obtain restrictive covenant indemnity insurance. Your conveyancer will be able to arrange this for you. There will be a charge for the insurance policy which will then be placed with the deeds. The policy pays out if the property owner suffers loss as a result of the breach of the restrictive covenant.

PROBLEMS WITH THE DEEDS – DEFECTIVE TITLES

Q. My conveyancer has advised me that there is a problem with my deeds and my title to the property is defective. What can I do?

A. There are many reasons why a title may be considered defective. Every title or set of deeds must provide evidence that the current seller owns the property and has an absolute title to it. Where the deeds or Land Register refer to easements or covenants then details of those easements and covenants must be available. Quite often it is simply a matter of missing documents or a failure to supply the Land Registry with sufficient information from the deeds to enable them to grant an absolute title. Your conveyancer will explain what the problem is. There are usually two solutions.

First you can track down the missing documents. They may be in your deeds bundle, with former conveyancers, or your conveyancer may be able to obtain copies from another source.

Alternatively, obtain defective title indemnity insurance. If the missing documents cannot be found, or the title cannot be rectified in another way, your conveyancer will advise that you obtain defective title indemnity insurance. Your conveyancer can arrange this for you, but you will have to pay for the policy.

LEASEHOLD PROBLEMS

Q. My landlord cannot be traced. My buyers want confirmation of ground rent and insurance payments. What can I do?

A. The landlord owns the freehold title to the property. Your conveyancer should be able to obtain a copy of the freehold official copies of the register from the Land Registry. This will show your landlord's address at the time of registration. Sometimes landlords have emigrated or are in prison and simply refuse to have anything further to do with the property. If this is the case your conveyancer may recommend that you obtain 'missing landlord' insurance. This is usually quicker and cheaper than trying to trace an unwilling landlord. A landlord is entitled to claim only six years' back ground rent from a tenant, so if ground rent is the only issue, you could offer to make an allowance to the purchaser of the six years' ground rent rather than supply a policy.

Q. My lease has only 60 years left to run and my buyer's mortgage company won't accept it – what can I do?

A. You will need to apply to your landlord to have the lease extended. Your conveyancer can arrange to do this for you. You will have to pay the landlord's costs and those of your conveyancer.

Q. I have lost my lease. What can I do?

A. You may be able to obtain a copy from the Land Registry – their details are in the directory. If not, your landlord should be able to supply you with a copy.

Q. There is a problem with my lease – what can I do?

A. Leases are often lengthy and complicated documents. Frequently they lack necessary rights of way, access for repair, adequate provisions for maintenance or insurance, etc. You have two alternatives with a defective lease.

First ask the landlord whether they would be prepared to sign a Deed of Rectification or Deed of Variation of the lease. If the landlord is willing, your conveyancer should be able to draw up the necessary deed, which will then be registered along with your lease at the Land Registry. You would have to pay the landlord's costs and those of your conveyancer.

Alternatively, obtain 'defective lease' insurance cover. Some insurance companies will offer an insurance policy for certain types of defect. Your conveyancer should be able to advise you if this is possible in your case.

DEPOSIT PROBLEMS

Q. My conveyancer has advised me that I will have to pay a deposit of 10% of the purchase price on exchange of contracts. I do not have this much as I am obtaining a mortgage of more than 90% of the purchase price/or I am selling and my capital is tied up in my property. What can I do?

A. While the sale contract traditionally calls for a 10% deposit, in practice this is often reduced and in some circumstances waived. If you are a first time buyer who is getting a mortgage of more than 90% of the purchase price, you must work out how much money you have available to use as a deposit. Advise your conveyancer of the amount and ask them to negotiate with the seller's conveyancer to accept this lower sum. If you are selling and buying, then the chain below you will be providing a deposit. Ask your conveyancer to arrange for the deposit on your sale to be passed on as the deposit on your purchase. This is common practice and is usually acceptable. In rare cases the seller may insist that you pay the full 10% deposit and you have the following two choices.

Some insurance companies offer a 'deposit guarantee scheme'. You pay for the policy and they issue a guarantee to the seller that if you withdraw from the transaction, after exchange, they will pay a full 10% deposit. Your conveyancer should be able to advise you on this.

Alternatively, arrange bridging finance. You may be able to arrange this via your bank or a specialist bridging finance company. The fees for bridging finance are often very high. Your conveyancer should be able to advise you.

Q. I have had an offer on a property accepted and the estate agent has asked me for a 'goodwill' deposit of £500. Should I pay this?

A. As your offer is on a subject to contract basis you are not required to pay any deposit at this stage. Some estate agents insist upon a goodwill deposit as they believe it shows commitment on the part of the buyer. Resist it if you can and only ever pay a deposit to a firm who is a member of a recognised body such as the NAEA, RICS or OEA – details in the directory. Insist upon a receipt and ask for evidence that the deposit will be held in a properly designated client account. Tell your conveyancer that you have paid this deposit. Deposits of this nature are usually taken into account at exchange and deducted from the amount required at that time.

PROBLEMS IN THE CHAIN

Q. Our chain has just collapsed after six months. The first time buyer has changed their mind and pulled out. What can we do?

A. It is heartbreaking and frustrating when this happens. Try to find out why the buyer has withdrawn. If it is a question of lack of finance you may be able to get together with the chain to provide the lack. Sometimes a chain breaks down just because one buyer in the chain has miscalculated and is a few hundred pounds short of the money needed to complete. The chain is usually more than happy to club together to provide the sum needed rather than face further months of uncertainty and delay. If the buyer cannot be coaxed back, consider whether anyone else in the chain would be prepared to buy the house at the beginning of the chain. Chains often end up with someone buying a new property from a developer. Developers have been known to step in and buy the first house in the chain to ensure that it does not break down. The key here is for the chain to communicate. Your estate agent should be able to negotiate with other parties in the chain via their estate agents. As a very last resort some companies do offer chain-breaking services, i.e. they will step in and buy a property, but it is usually for a much discounted price.

Q. The survey on my property is not good and my buyer has lowered their offer considerably. I can't afford to proceed with my new house if I drop my price – what can I do?

A. This is a job for your estate agent if you have one. First, you need to get the highest offer you can from your buyer. Once you have this, work out what the shortfall is and how much more money you can afford to pay towards the shortfall. If there is still a shortfall you have two options.

You can increase the amount of mortgage you are borrowing, or take out a personal loan to finance the shortfall.

Alternatively, ask your seller to reduce the price of the property you are buying. It is fairly common practice to renegotiate prices throughout the property chain so that each person in the chain contributes towards the amount needed for the deal to go ahead. Your estate agent should be able to do this for you.

Q. The person at the top of the chain is having a new home built and is refusing to complete until it is ready – it could be months and my buyers won't wait – what can I do?

A. This is a common problem when completion dates in a chain do not match up. Your estate agent should be able to help. Ideally, the seller at the top of the chain should be asked to proceed to completion and move into temporary accommodation, perhaps with family or friends, until their house is ready. If they are not prepared to do that then perhaps someone else in the chain may be prepared to move into alternative accommodation to allow the chain to proceed. If all else fails you will have to consider whether you are prepared to complete on your sale and move into temporary accommodation until your purchase is ready. If you complete on your sale without at least having exchanged contracts on your purchase there is a risk that the seller will change their mind and leave you homeless.

PROBLEMS AT EXCHANGE OF CONTRACTS

Q. I have exchanged contracts on my property transaction, but I have changed my mind and do not wish to proceed – what should I do?

A. Once contracts are exchanged you are legally bound to proceed with your sale or purchase. There are heavy financial penalties for failure to complete and you could end up having to pay damages to the whole chain. You must take immediate legal advice from your conveyancer. It is usually more cost effective to complete on a purchase and then immediately re-sell the property than to be in breach of contract. If you are selling a property, the buyer is entitled, under the terms of the contract, to sue you for specific performance of the contract. This means that a court order could be sought to make you complete the sale. If this happens you may have to pay the buyer's court costs, as well as damages, and still have to move out.

PROBLEMS AT COMPLETION

Q. We are supposed to be completing today, but my conveyancer has advised me that my mortgage advance has not arrived – what can I do?

A. The first thing your conveyancer should do is check with the mortgage company to find out why. If you and your conveyancer have complied with your lender's requirements and the money has been properly requested, your lender will usually try to rectify the problem. You and your conveyancer should put pressure on the lender to send the money by means of a telegraphic transfer, or at least arrange for a bank draft to be available for collection from a local branch. If the lender has issued the mortgage advance and it is simply stuck in the banking system, ask them to check with their bank that it has actually been sent. Once you know that the money is in the system and on its way, your conveyancer can then telephone their own bank to ensure that there are no delays there. Occasionally, if it becomes obvious that the funds are not going to arrive before the banks close for the day, the conveyancers can arrange to complete on formal undertakings. Your conveyancer will be able to advise you if this is possible.

Q. We have formally completed but the seller hasn't moved out of the house – what can I do?

A. Advise your conveyancer immediately. If it is simply the case that your seller is disorganised and still in the process of moving out, try to be patient. Arrange for your seller's conveyancer to telephone them to point out that they must now give you vacant possession. Sellers do not always understand that if they complete on a given day they must move out on that day and not when it suits them. Their conveyancer should be asked to telephone to advise them of the penalties for late completion. If, however, they appear to have no intention of moving out, your conveyancer will contact their conveyancer to have your purchase money returned with interest. You must then seek remedy under the terms of the contract. I would stress that failure to complete after exchange of contracts is, thankfully, very rare.

Q. The seller has moved out and left a broken down car on the drive, and a loft and garage full of rubbish – what can I do?

A. Under the terms of the contract the seller is obliged to give vacant possession, and that includes removing old cars and rubbish, etc. Contact your conveyancer immediately and ask them to complain to the seller's conveyancer. Advise your seller that you will give them 24 hours to remove the rubbish, failing which you will have it removed and send them the bill. If they still fail to remove the rubbish you will have no alternative but to arrange for it to be removed and then send them the bill.

Jargon Buster

Abstract of Title Abbreviated list of **title deeds**.

Advance A term for a mortgage loan.

Agreement Another word for **contract**.

Auction This is where a property is bought at an auction house. Once the gavel goes down contracts are exchanged (see **exchange of contracts**).

Bankruptcy search A search made by the **conveyancer** to check whether a **buyer** or a **borrower** has been, is or is about to be declared bankrupt.

Borrower The person taking out a loan or **mortgage** on a property, sometimes also known as the **mortgagee**.

Boundaries The boundaries define the extent of the property and are usually marked out on the ground by fencing or hedging. Boundaries are also often, although not always, shown on the deeds plans.

Bridging loan A short-term loan taken out to 'bridge' the gap whilst waiting for the sale of a property or the receipt of a **mortgage**.

Broker Generally refers to a **mortgage broker** – a third party who will arrange a **mortgage** with a **lender**.

Building insurance Insurance taken out by the owner of the property to insure the property against risks such as fire, landslip, etc.

Building survey An in-depth property survey that is carried out by a qualified **surveyor**.

Buy to let Where a **buyer** buys a property with the intention of letting it out on a commercial basis. There are usually mortgages specific to this type of purchase known as **buy to let** mortgages.

Buyer The person who is buying the property, sometimes also known as the **purchaser**.

Capital The amount of the **mortgage** or **loan** you borrow on which interest will be charged.

CAT standard mortgage A **mortgage** that complies with defined Government standards.

Caveat emptor A Latin expression meaning 'let the buyer beware'.

Certification scheme Scheme responsible for the regulation of Home Inspectors and storing of **Home Condition Reports**.

Chain The property **buyers** and **sellers** that link together to make the chain for your particular sale or purchase. The chain may consist of only two people, i.e. you as buyer and the person you are buying from as seller, or it may consist of several buyers and sellers. The beginning of the chain usually starts with a first time buyer, or a buyer with nothing to sell, and the end of the chain usually ends with a seller who is buying a brand new home or who is not buying another property.

Client The person who has asked the **conveyancer** to act for them in legal matters.

Client care letter The **conveyancer** must send the client this letter at the beginning of the transaction. The letter must give clear details of what work will be carried out, who will be doing it, at what cost and the complaints procedure of the firm. The client is usually asked to sign and return one copy. The conveyancer is not allowed to start work for a client until the client confirms in writing that they wish the conveyancer to do so.

Coal mining search If the property is in an area designated as a

Coal Mining Area the **conveyancer** will search to see whether there are any issues which currently affect the property.

Completion The day the sale or purchase is finalised and the **buyer** becomes the legal owner of the property.

Completion date The date when the purchase becomes final and the purchase price is paid by the **buyer**'s **conveyancer** and received by the **seller**'s conveyancer. The seller must move out of the property on this date. The keys are released to the buyer and they may move into the property.

Completion statement The final account that the **conveyancer** will send. It will detail their fees plus the VAT and all **searches**, etc. This is usually sent after exchange of contracts and before completion.

Conditions of sale The conditions of the sale are detailed in the **contract** that the **seller**'s **conveyancer** prepares and sends to the **buyer**'s conveyancer. There are standard Law Society conditions to which the conveyancer adds any special conditions.

Conservation area An area protected by the local authority. Properties in a conservation area may be subject to planning restrictions, particularly relating to the exterior of the property.

Contract The legal document that confirms the sale/purchase of the property. This is prepared in a draft form by the **seller**'s **conveyancer** and sent to the **buyer**'s conveyancer. Once all queries are answered it is then approved, and the seller and the buyer each sign their own copy.

Conveyance The old fashioned name for the document that transfers a property from one person to another. Conveyances are rarely used nowadays and property is usually transferred by a **transfer** document.

Conveyancer/conveyancing Conveyancing is the legal description for the work that is done to transfer ownership of a property from one person to another. Conveyancer is the job description of the person doing the legal work.

Council for Licensed Conveyancers (CLC) The organisation that governs Licensed Conveyancers in the same way that the Law Society governs solicitors.

Covenants/restrictive covenants Obligations/restrictions that are attached to the property. For instance there may be an obligation to maintain a fence or boundary, which is a positive covenant, or there may be a restriction on the type of building on the land, which is a restrictive covenant.

Credit reference agency A company or organisation that stores your details and your credit history.

Deeds/title deeds The legal documents that prove ownership of the property.

Defective title insurance A defective title means that there is a problem with the **deeds** relating to the property. They may be missing, destroyed, lost or simply inadequate. A **buyer** will not usually buy a property with a defective title unless the **seller** provides an insurance policy to protect them and their lender against any financial loss which could result from the defective title.

Deposit There are two types of deposit that a purchaser may be asked to produce. Sometimes the estate agent will ask for a **'goodwill' deposit** to secure the property. You should not pay this deposit without first consulting with your **conveyancer**. The second type of deposit is the one a purchaser will pay to the conveyancer to hand over with the **contract**. Traditionally this was 10% of the purchase price, but often less than this is accepted.

Disbursements Money that the **conveyancer** must pay to other persons on your behalf, for instance **VAT**, **Stamp Duty**, **Land Registry Fees**, **searches**, etc.

Drainage/water search A search carried out by the **conveyancer** for the **purchaser** to check whether the property is connected to mains water and drainage and whether there are any other issues relating to drainage/water affecting the property.

Early redemption fee A charge made by your **lender** when you repay your **mortgage** earlier than agreed.

Easement A right given to the property owner over adjoining property or land. Typically this could be a right of way or access, a right of drainage or a right to a water supply. By law the **seller** must disclose all latent easements but not patent easements. **Latent easements** are easements that could not be discovered by search or survey, in other words they are not easily found out. Patent easements are easements that can be discovered by **search** or **survey**.

Endowment policy A type of life assurance policy sometimes used to pay off an interest only **mortgage**.

Energy Performance Certificate (EPC) A certificate that shows how energy efficient a property is.

Environmental search A search that the **conveyancer** carries out to check whether there are any environmental issues that may affect a property. These may include matters such as flooding, coal mining and land fill.

Epitome of Title Schedule of **deeds** defining the ownership of the property.

Equity The equity in a property is the value that is left after you take the current worth of the property and deduct from that any **mortgages** outstanding on the property.

Estate agent –The estate agent acts on behalf of the **seller** to sell the property.

Exchange of contracts The point at which the sale and purchase become legally binding on the **seller** and the **buyer**.

Financial/mortgage adviser The financial adviser is usually responsible for arranging the **mortgage** or finance to purchase the property and will often arrange any life insurance, mortgage protection insurance, etc.

Financial Services Authority A Government instigated body set up to regulate the sale of **mortgages** and loans.

Fixtures and fittings list A list of items that will remain/be taken from the property. This is completed by the **seller** and a copy is attached to each part of the **contract** and is legally binding. Following the **HIP** this list will be known as the Home Contents form.

Freehold –With freehold land the owner owns the property/land outright subject only to any **mortgages**, **charges**, **easements**, **covenants**, etc. shown by the **deeds**.

Freeholder With a freehold property the property owner owns the property and the land it stands on. With a **leasehold** property the freeholder owns the property and land, but they are subject to the leaseholder's interests and rights.

Gazumping Where the seller, having agreed a sale to one **buyer**, sells to another buyer for a higher price. This can only happen before **exchange of contracts**.

Gazundering This is where the **buyer** lowers their offer on the property after agreeing a price. This can only happen before **exchange of contracts**.

Ground rent The rent paid to the landlord, usually on a **leasehold** property where there is a long **lease**. Ground rents are payable on some **freeholds**.

Home buyer's report A mid-range property survey carried out by a qualified **surveyor**. It is more detailed than a mortgage valuation, but not as detailed as a building **survey**.

Home Condition Report A mid-range survey carried out by a **Home Inspector** which may be included as an authorised document in the **Home Information Pack**.

Home Information Pack (HIP) A pack made up of the **Energy Performance Certificate**, **searches** and **title** documents.

Home Inspector A property **surveyor** qualified to prepare the **Energy Performance Certificate** and the **Energy Performance Certificate**.

Inland Revenue A government department that collects tax on behalf of the government.

Individual Savings Account (ISA) A type of savings account. It is currently tax advantageous and can be used as a repayment vehicle for an interest only **mortgage**.

Instructions Authorisation given by the client to the **conveyancer**. The client must give the conveyancer written instructions to act on their behalf in the property sale or purchase. After that the conveyancer will from time to time ask the client for instructions as to how the client wishes to proceed, for instance on what date the client wants to move.

Interest The money you are charged by a **lender** for borrowing money on a **mortgage** or loan.

Joint tenants Where two or more persons buy a property they are called joint tenants, or tenants in common, whether the property is **freehold**, commonhold or **leasehold**. Where property is held as a joint tenancy if one owner dies the property passes to the other owner automatically without a will.

Land Registry A Government department that holds the records of all property in the United Kingdom. Most property is now registered at the Land Registry.

Land Registry search/fees The **conveyancer** will make **searches** at the Land Registry to check the Land Register. The results are guaranteed by the Land Registry and the search, once made, gives the **buyer** a 'priority period' in which to register their ownership. Following completion the conveyancer will send the **deeds** to the Land Registry who will register the new owner and any new lender. The Land Registry charges a fee for searches and for registration of property.

Landlord A Landlord is the owner of the **freehold** of a **leasehold** property. Rent on a leasehold property is paid to the landlord who has the right to enforce the terms in the **lease**.

Lease A complicated document which grants to the **leaseholder** the right to occupy the property for the period of the **lease**. The lease details the matters affecting the property. Typically these will include the length of the lease, rent, service charges, rights of way, water, drainage and access and it will usually incorporate a plan.

Leasehold/leaseholder A leasehold property means that the owner of the leasehold interest does not own the property or land outright. There is a **lease** which for a term of years grants the owner the right to occupy the property/land. There may be a rent or a ground rent to pay to the landlord.

Legal charge Another name for the **mortgage deed**.

Legal executive A qualified legal professional who is governed by the Law Society.

Lender The bank or building society which lends money to property owners, sometimes also known as the **mortgagor**.

Licensed conveyancer A qualified property lawyer who holds a licence granted by the **Council for Licensed Conveyancers**.

Listed buildings Buildings protected by the local authority.

Properties that are listed are subject to planning restrictions.

Local search A search made against the property. The search covers local authority issues, such as planning, relating to the property.

Management company A company set up to deal with the day to day running of **leasehold** properties including cleaning, repairs and renewals to the common areas. The management company collects a service charge from the property owners to pay for their services, and for the upkeep and maintenance of the building.

Mortgage A loan that is secured over a property.

Mortgage application fees Fees charged by the **lender** to organise the **mortgage** for you.

Mortgage deed The document, sometimes known as a legal charge, which the **borrower** signs to agree to the terms set out in the **mortgage offer**.

Mortgage offer The formal written offer issued by the **lender** offering the **mortgage** loan. The mortgage offer will contain all the terms of the loan and the conditions upon which the money is loaned.

Mortgage term The time you are given in which to repay the **mortgage**.

Mortgage valuation fee The **borrower** generally pays a fee to the **lender** to have the property valued for **mortgage** purposes. This enables the **lender** to take a commercial view on whether the property is worth what the **borrower** says it is and whether it is suitable security for the mortgage. The mortgage valuer will not necessarily inspect the physical condition of the property.

Mortgagee The **borrower**.

Mortgagor The **lender**.

New build Where a property is being purchased for the first time from the builder or developer.

Off plan Where a property is being bought at the planning stage and is yet to be built.

Offer of advance The formal written **mortgage** offer.

Overriding interests Where a third party has an interest in the property, for instance a former spouse. Not all matters affecting property are registered or capable of being registered at the **Land Registry**. Nonetheless the property is still subject to such matters.

Preliminary or pre-contract enquiries A set of questions that is sent to the **seller**'s **conveyancer** by the **buyer**'s conveyancer relating to the property. Typically these questions will consist of enquiries relating to boundaries, **easements**, persons living at the property, etc.

Professional indemnity insurance All firms of solicitors and licensed **conveyancers** must take out insurance to the value of £1,000,000 or more to cover defective work or fraud by that firm on behalf of its client(s). Other professionals such as **surveyors**, **Home Inspectors** and **financial advisers** must also carry professional indemnity insurance to protect their clients.

Property Information form A standard form that is completed by the **seller** giving details about the property. The form is legally binding on the seller. Following the introduction of the **HIP** this form will be known as the **Property Use form**.

Property Use form After the launch of the **HIP** the Property Use form will replace the **Property Information form** (see above).

Redeeming your mortgage When a property owner pays back the **mortgage** on the property. You will first need to get a statement of what is owed, which is called a **redemption statement**.

Redemption fee A fee charged by the **lender** when you repay the

mortgage.

Redemption statement A final **mortgage** statement produced by the **lender** stating the amount required to repay the mortgage in full on a specified date.

Retention The **lender** agrees to lend you a sum of money but retains or holds part of it back until you comply with the **mortgage** conditions. Typically, mortgage money would be retained until repair work had been carried out or guarantees produced.

Searches There are many different types of **conveyancing** search, including: bankruptcy search, brine search, coal mining search, commons registration search, company search, environmental search, HM Land Registry search, HM Land Charges search, index map search, local search, tin mining search, water authority/drainage search.

Security The property is security for the **mortgage** loan. It is the **lender**'s guarantee that if you fail to make the mortgage repayments they can repay the mortgage by selling the property.

Seller The person selling the property, sometimes also known as the **vendor**.

Shared ownership property Where a property has been bought jointly with the council or a housing association.

Stamp Duty exempt Some types of purchase or transfer of land are exempt from **Stamp Duty Land Tax**. The Government has designated certain areas as exempt from Stamp Duty. Your **conveyancer** will be able to tell you whether your transaction is exempt.

Stamp Duty Land Tax The tax payable on the purchase of a property.

Stamp Duty Land Tax form This form must be completed by the

buyer and sent to Inland Revenue with any **Stamp Duty Land Tax** due within 30 days of legal completion.

Subject to contract Before **exchange of contracts** all negotiations relating to the property are subject to **contract**. This means they are not binding unless contracts are exchanged.

Surveyor The person who is responsible for surveying the property. They will usually be a member of the Royal Institute of Chartered Surveyors (RICS).

Survey A physical inspection of the property by the **surveyor** to check the physical condition of the property and to advise the **buyer** upon the value of the property.

Telegraphic transfer fee A bank charge for sending money from bank to bank.

Tenants in common Where two or more persons own a property and choose to own separate shares in the property.

Term assurance Life assurance designed to pay off a **mortgage** when the borrower dies.

Title/title deeds Evidence of the ownership of a property.

Transfer deed The legal document that transfers the ownership of the property.

Valuation See **mortgage valuation**.

VAT Value Added Tax is a Government tax charged on certain transactions.

Will The legal document that sets out what you want to happen to your property after death.

The Directory

General reference

Association of British Insurers (ABI) www.abi.org.uk Tel: 020 7600 3333.

Association of HIP Providers (AHIPP), 3 Savile Row, London, W1S 3PB. www.hipassociation.co.uk Tel: 0870 950 7739.

British Telecom www.bt.com BT Tel: 0800 800 150.

Cavity Insulation Guarantee Agency (CIGA), Ciga House, 3 Vimy Court, Vimy Road, Leighton Buzzard, Bedfordshire, LU7 1FG. www.ciga.co.uk Tel: 01525 853300.

Citizens Advice Bureau (CAB) www.citizensadvice.org.uk and www.adviceguide.org.uk Check *Yellow Pages* for local number.

Confederation for the Registration of Gas Installers (CORGI), 1 Elmwood, Chineham Park, Crockford Lane, Basingstoke, Hants. RG24 8WG. www.corgi-gas-safety.com Tel: 0871 401 2200.

Conveyancing Marketing Services (CMS), St Andrews Castle, St Andrews Street South, Bury St Edmunds, Suffolk, IP33 3PH. www.conveyancing-cms.co.uk Tel: 0845 060 33 55.

Council for Licensed Conveyancers (CLC), 16 Glebe Road, Chelmsford, Essex, CM1 1QG. www.theclc.gov.uk Tel: 01245 349599.

Council of Mortgage Lenders (CML), 3 Savile Rowe, London, W1S 3PB. www.cml.org.uk Tel: 020 7437 0075.

Dalton's Weekly www.daltons.co.uk Tel: 020 8329 0195.

Department for Communities and Local Government (CLG) www.communities.gov.uk

Department for Environment, Food and Rural Affairs (DEFRA) www.defra.gov.uk Tel: 08459 33 55 77.

Draught Proofing Advisory Association Ltd. (DPAA), PO Box 12, Haslemere, Surrey, GU27 3AH. www.dubois.vital.co.uk Tel: 01428 654011.

Driver and Vehicle Licensing Agency (DVLA), Swansea, SA99. www.dvla.gov.uk Tel: 0870 2400 009.

Energy Efficiency Advice Centre (EST) www.est.co.uk or www.saveenergy.co.uk Tel: Helpline 0800 915 7722.

Experian www.experian.co.uk Tel: 0800 656 9000.

Federation of Master Builders. www.fmb.org.uk or www.findabuilder.co.uk Tel: 020 7242 7583.

Fenestration Self Assessment Scheme (FENSA), 44–48 Borough High Street, London, SE1 1XB. www.fensa.co.uk Tel: 0870 780 2028.

Financial Ombudsman Service www.financial-ombudsman.org.uk Tel: 0845 080 1800.

Financial Services Authority (FSA), 25 The Colonnade, Canary Wharf, London, E14 5HS. www.fsa.gov.uk/consumer and www.fsa.gov.uk/tables Tel: 020 7066 1000.

Glass and Glazing Federation www.ggf.org.uk

Habitus, Kingfisher House, 21–23 Elmfield Road, Bromley, Kent, BR1 1LT. www.habitus.co.uk Tel: 08700 10 66 67.

Homecheck, Imperial House, 21–25 North Street, Bromley, BR1 1SS. www.homecheck.co.uk Tel: 0870 606 1700.

House prices www.houseprices.co.uk

iammoving.com www.iammoving.com Tel: 0845 0900 198.

Independent Financial Advisers, Unit 8, Alpha Business Park, Travellers Close, Hatfield, AL9 7NT. www.searchifa.co.uk Tel: 01707 251111.

Inland Revenue (Stamp Duty) www.hmrc.gov.uk/so/ Tel: 0845 6030135.

Institute of Plumbing and Heating Engineering (IPHE), 64 Station Lane, Hornchurch, Essex, RM12 6NB. www.iphe.org.uk Tel: 01708 472791.

Land Charges Department, Plumer House, Tailyour Road, Crownhill, Plymouth, PL6 5HY. Tel: 01752 636666.

Land Registry www.landreg.gov.uk and www.landregisteronline.gov.uk Tel: 020 7917 8888 (head office).

Law Society, 113 Chancery Lane, London, WC2A 1PL. www.lawsociety.org.uk Tel: Choosing a solicitor 0870 606 6575. Tel: Complaining about a solicitor 0845 608 6565.

Listed Buildings www.heritage.co.uk and www.culture.gov.uk

Local authorities (searches). Search for your local authority at www.direct.gov.uk

Loot, Customer Services, Loot Ltd., 1 Harrow Road, Wembley, Middlesex, HA9 6DA. www.loot.com Tel: 08700 43 4343.

National Association of Estate Agents (NAEA), Arbon House, 21 Jury Street, Warwick, CV34 4EH. www.naea.co.uk Tel: 01926 496800.

National Association of Licensed Home Inspectors (NALHI), 1 Gleneagles House, Vernon Gate, Derby, DE1 1UP. www.nalhi.org.uk Tel: 01332 225106.

National Federation of Roofing Contractors (NFRC), 24 Weymouth Street, London, W1G 7LX www.nfrc.go.uk Tel: 020 7436 0387.

National Health Service (NHS) www.nhs.uk Tel: NHS Direct 0845 4647.

National Home Energy Rating Scheme (NHER), National Energy Centre, Davy Avenue, Knowlhill, Milton Keynes, MK5 8NA. www.nesltd.co.uk Tel: 01908 672787.

National House Building Council (NHBC), Customer Services, NHBC, Buildmark House, Chiltern Avenue, Amersham, HP6 5AP. www.nhbc.co.uk Tel: 01494 735363.

National Inspection Council for Electrical Installation Contracting (NICEIC), Warwick House, Houghton Hall Park, Houghton Regis, Dunstable, Beds. LU5 5ZX. www.niceic.org.uk Tel: 0870 013 0382.

Office of Fair Trading (OFT), Fleetbank House, 2–6 Salisbury Square, London, EC4Y 8JX. www.oft.gov.uk Consumer direct Tel: 08454 04 05 06.

Oil Fired Technical Association (OFTEC), Foxwood House, Dobbs Lane, Kesgrave, Ipswich, IP5 2QQ. www.oftec.co.uk Tel: 0845 6585080.

Ombudsman for Estate Agents (OEA), Beckett House, 4 Bridge Street, Salisbury, Wilts. SP1 2LX www.oea.co.uk Tel: 01722 333306.

Royal Institute of British Architects (RIBA), 66 Portland Place, London, W1B 1AD. www.riba.org Tel: 020 7580 5533.

Royal Institute of Chartered Surveyors (RICS), RICS Contact Centre, Surveyor Court, Westwood Way, Coventry, CV4 8JE. www.rics.org Tel: 0870 333 1600.

Royal Mail www.royalmail.com Tel: 0845 60 60 406.

Sava, PO Box 5603, Milton Keynes, MK5 9XR. www.sava.org.uk Tel: 0870 837 6565.

Stamp Duty Land Tax www.hmrc.gov.uk/so/current_sdlt_rates Tel: 0845 6030135.

Telephone Preference Service www.tpsonline.org.uk Tel: 0845 070 0707.

Thatched roofs www.thatch.org

Trading Standards Central www.tradingstandards.gov.uk

Transport www.traveline.org.uk

TV Licence, TV Licensing, Bristol, BS98 1TL.
www.tvlicensing.co.uk/moving Tel: 0870 242 3349.

Up My Street www.upmystreet.com Tel: 0207 802 2992.

Vote Registration www.aboutmyvote.co.uk

Which? www.which.net Tel: 0845 307 4000.

Certification schemes
Sava, PO Box 5603, Milton Keynes, MK5 8XR. www.sava.org.uk
Tel: 0870 837 6565.

Conservation areas
Office of Public Sector Information (OPSI) www.opsi.gov.uk

Environmental searches
Groundsure www.groundsure.com Tel: 01273 819500.

Homecheck Imperial House, 21–25 North Street, Bromley, BR1
1SS. www.homecheck.co.uk Tel: 0870 606 1700. Suite 14, Level
4 New England House, New England Street, Brighton, BN1
4GH. Tel: 01273 819500.

Gas
Confederation for the Registration of Gas Installers (CORGI), 1
Elmwood, Chineham Park, Crockford Lane, Basingstoke,
Hants. RG24 8WG. www.corgi-gas-safety.com Tel: 0871 401
2200.

National Grid Gas Emergency Services. Tel: 0800 111 999.

Home Condition Report suppliers
Blue Box Partners, Westgate Chambers, 3 High Street, Chipping
Sodbury, Bristol, BS37 6BA. www.blueboxpartners.com Tel:
0845 260 3500

Habitus, Kingfisher House, 21–23 Elmfield Road, Bromley, Kent,

BR1 1LT. www.habitus.co.uk Tel: 08700 10 66 67.

Home Inspectors Assessment centres and training for Home Inspectors.

SAVA, PO Box 5603, Milton Keynes, MK5 9XR. www.sava.org.uk Tel: 0870 837 6565.

Home Information Pack suppliers

Complete HIP, Unit F1, Waterfront Studios, 1 Dock Road, London, E16 1AG. www.completehip.co.uk Tel: 020 7474 2882.

Homepack plus www.homepackplus.co.uk

Mysalepack, 11th Floor, 78 Cannon Street, London, EC4N 6HH. www.mysalepack.com Tel: 0870 285 1474.

Open Book, Green Park Offices, James Street West, Green Park, Bath, BA1 2BU. www.openthebook.co.uk Tel: 01225 320 844.

Pack provider, 10 The Point, Market Harborough, Leicestershire, LE16 7QU. www.packprovider.com Tel: 0870 737 6665.

Mortgage websites

Mortgage Sorter www.mortgagesorter.co.uk Tel: 01874 636 201.

This is money www.thisismoney.co.uk

Your Mortgage www.yourmortgage.co.uk Tel: 020 7484 9700.

Personal search companies

Council of Property Search Organisations (COPSO), 29 Harley Street, London, W1G 9QR. www.copso.org.uk Tel: 020 7927 6836.

Property Search Group, 142 Trinity Street, Huddersfield, HD1 4DT. www.psgonline.co.uk Tel: 01484 311649.

Search flow, Nepicar House, London Road, Wrotham Heath, Sevenoaks, Kent, TN15 7RS. www.searchflow.co.uk Tel: 0870 787 7625.

STL Group, Edbrooke House, St Johns Road, Woking, Surrey, GU21 7SE. www.stlgroup.co.uk Tel: 0800 318611.

Property shops
House Ladder www.houseladder.co.uk
Homes Seekers www.homes-seekers.co.uk
HouseWeb www.houseweb.co.uk

Property websites
Fish4homes www.fish4.co.uk
Prime Location www.primelocation.com
Rightmove www.rightmove.co.uk
Team www.teamprop.co.uk

Relocation agents
The Association of Relocation Professionals (ARP), PO Box 189, Diss, IP22 1PE. www.relocationagents.com Tel: 08700 73 74 75.

Removals
British Association of Removers (BAR), Tangent House, 62 Exchange Road, Watford, Hertfordshire, WD18 0TG. www.removers.org.uk Tel: 01923 699480.
Help I Need Boxes www.helpineedboxes.co.uk Tel: 0845 058 1106.

Schools
Good Schools Guide, 3 Craven Mews, London, SW11 5PW. www.goodschoolsguide.co.uk Tel: 020 7801 0191.

Search providers
Brine – Cheshire County Council www.cheshire.gov.uk Tel: 01244 602357.
Chancel repair – London Law www.londonlaw.co.uk/chancelrepair

Coal and limestone – The Coal Authority www.coal.gov.uk Tel:
01623 427 162.

Commons registration – your local County Council (see
www.Direct.gov.uk).

Tin mining Cornwall consultants www.cornwallconsultants.co.uk

Surveyors

Habitus, Kingfisher House, 21–23 Elmfield Road, Bromley, Kent,
BR1 1LT. www.habitus.co.uk Tel: 08700 1066 67.

Sava, PO Box 5603, Milton Keynes, MK5 8XR. www.sava.org.uk
Tel: 0870 837 6565.

Royal Institute of Chartered Surveyors (RICS), RICS Contact
Centre, Surveyor Court, Westwood Way, Coventry, CV4 8JE.
www.rics.org Tel: 0870 333 1600.

Timber and damp companies

Association of Accredited Wykamol Users (AAWU)
www.aawu.co.uk Tel: 01327 354857.

Peter Cox www.petercox.com Tel: 0800 789 500.

Water companies

Anglian Water Services Ltd (Geodesys), Spencer House, Spitfire
Close, Ermine Business Park, Huntingdon, Cambridgeshire,
PE29 6XY. www.geodesys.co.uk Tel: 01480 323838.

Northumbrian Water, Abbey Road, Pity Me, Durham, DH1 5FJ.
www.nwpropertysolutions.co.uk Tel: 0870 241 7408.

Severn Trent Water, PO Box 6187, Nottingham, NG5 1LE.
www.severntrentsearches.com Tel: 0115 962 7269.

Thames Water, Thames Water Property Insight, PO Box 3189,
Slough, SL1 4WW. www.twsearches.co.uk Tel: 0118 923 6656.

Water UK (for your local water company) 020 7344 1844.

Yorkshire Water www.safe-move.co.uk Tel: 0800 1 385 385.

Index